The Interı Chain (IVCⱼ anᴅ the Digital Economy

~ Digitalising Economies has Consequences: ranging from Big Tech competition risks, cybercrime, harmful online content, fake news and disinformation, to social media amplification algorithms, and much more ~

Insight and Guidance for Digital Economy Policy Makers, Regulators and Network Operators

H. Sama Nwana

Published by GIGALEN PRESS
The Internet Value Chain and the Digital Economy

H Sama Nwana

First Published in the United Kingdom in 2021 by Gigalen Press
c/o Cenerva Ltd
116 Pall Mall
London
SW1Y 5ED
United Kingdom

ISBN: 9798771346724

Version 1.0
Printed by CreateSpace, a DBA of ON-Demand Publishing Ltd

Contents

Acknowledgments i

Dedication ii

Preface iii

Table of Mini-Case Studies for Easier Reference xii

Part I — An Introduction to the Internet Value Chain (IVC): Top-level Takeaways, Externalities, Risks, Harms & Concerns of the IVC .. 1

Chapter 1: The Internet Value Chain 2

1.1 The History of the Internet Value Chains (IVC): the GSMA 2016 and Vodafone 2010 IVCs 3

1.2 A Brief Anatomy of the GSMA IVC 6

1.2.1 Content Rights Segment 6

1.2.2 Online Services Segment 9

1.2.3 Enabling Technologies and Services Segment 10

1.2.4 Connectivity Segment 11

1.2.5 User Interface Segment 11

1.3 The IVC – is it really relevant to TMT or is it orthogonal to it? 12

1.4 The TMT Sector Value Chains vs. the IVC – are they mutually exclusive? 14

1.4.1 Revisiting some traditional TMT sub-sector value chains 15

1.4.2 Much of the Traditional TMT Sector Value Chains live off the IVC, but they are not mutually exclusive 19

1.4.3 What else are not included on the IVC from the TMT value chains? 20

1.4.4 What does the non-mutual exclusivity between IVC and TMT value chains mean for Policy makers, regulators and network operators? 21

1.5 Breakdown of the Rest of the Book and How to Read the Book 22

1.5.1 Breakdown of the Book 22

1.5.2 How to read the book *24*

Chapter 2: Some Top-level Takeaways, Externalities, Risks, Harms and new Concerns of the IVC **25**

2.1 Introduction to Top-Level IVC Takeaways & Externalities *26*

2.2 A Typical PhD Thesis Study: introducing the Long Tail Theory *29*

2.2.1 The Long Tail Theory *30*

2.2.2 What is the relevance and criticism of the Long Tail Theory and the IVC? *32*

2.3 Some Positive and Negative Externalities and Concerns of the IVC by Segment *34*

2.3.1 Sources and Examples of Positive Externalities *34*

2.3.2 Case Study Illustrating New Risks and Harms of the IVC: the 5G Covid-19 Quackery – Confronting Misinformation and Fake News. *38*

2.3.3 Content Rights Segment Externalities and other New Concerns *42*

2.3.4 Online Services Segment Externalities and New Concerns *61*

2.3.5 Enabling Technologies and Services Segment Externalities *95*

2.3.6 Connectivity Segment Externalities and Concerns *107*

2.3.7 User Interface Segment Externalities and Concerns *118*

2.4 Are the Gatekeeping companies to the Internet already too big to regulate? *129*

2.4.1 Google Shopping/Google Search vs. EC *129*

2.4.2 Google AdSense vs. EC *133*

2.4.3 EC Competition Policy vs. Politics *134*

2.5 UK's Age-Appropriate Design for Apps for a "better Internet for Children" – positive externalities well beyond the UK *135*

2.5.1 The Online Age Identification Conundrum *140*

2.5.2 Tencent using Facial Recognition to Protect Children Online *142*

2.5.3 The UK's Children Code Potential Positive Externalities beyond its shores *142*

2.6 Summary *144*

Part II — Defining the New Digital Economy Policy & Regulatory Challenges Landscape *with the Internet Value Chain* 145

Chapter 3: A Definition of the New Digital Economy Policy and Regulatory Landscape 146

   3.1 Introduction to the Digital Economy Problem Definition 146

   3.2 Key Lessons from Part I of this Book 148

   3.3 A Summary set of Assumptions and Top-Level Exam Questions for Digital Economy Policy Makers & Regulators 167

   3.4 Introducing Big Tech and other Emerging Online Change Makers ... 169

   3.5 Case Study: The "Netflix Effect" on the Film and Broadcasting Industry in Thailand 172

   3.6 Online and Big Tech Regulation – how has it come to this? 177

     Case Study: Instagram and Teenage Girls 180

     Case Study: AI, Ethics, Privacy, Facebook, YouTube & Misinformation 183

     Case Study: Twitter, Fake News and Bots 190

   3.7 Case Studies: USA, EU, UK, Australia and South Korea Bills to Regulate Big Tech 192

   3.8 Digital Economy Platforms – the foundations of your Digital Economy 195

   3.9 What Outcomes do Digital Economy Policy Makers & Regulators want then? 200

     Broad Categories of Digital Economy Outcomes Sought 201

     Offline ICT/TMT Outcomes 203

     Big Tech Good Competition Outcomes and Typical Harms 205

     Online Regulation is Indispensable Now 213

   3.10 What then is the Digital Economy Problem Statement? 222

   3.11 Beware of Regulating Away your next Online Giant 224

     Section 230 of the 1996 US Federal Communications Act 224

     Articles 12-14 of the 2000 EU Commerce Directive 225

     3.11.3 Why are these two sets of laws relevant to innovation? 226

   3.12 Summary 227

Part III — Towards the Future of Data Economy Policy Making & Regulation: *some brief suggestions, recommendations and ways forward on key challenges* 228

Chapter 4: Selected Priority Digital Economy Areas 229

Selecting Thematic Areas 229

4.2 Offline TMT/ICT Policy and Regulation to achieve availability, affordability and awareness still remains top priority 230

4.3 Digital Economy Platforms Policy & Regulation 231

4.4 The Future of Content, Broadcasting & Media Policy and Regulation . 233

4.5 Online/Internet Policy & Regulation and the true cost of "free" models . 234

4.6 Big Tech Policy & Regulation 240

4.7 Cybercrime/Cyber-harms and Cybersecurity Policy & Regulation 240

4.8 Artificial Intelligence, Big Data Policy & Regulation 241

4.9 Privacy (Liberty) & Data Protection vs. Innovation Policy & Regulation 244

4.10 Electronic Commerce Laws, Policy & Regulation 246

4.11 OTT Policy & Regulation 247

4.12 Capacity Building and Training on Digital Economy 247

4.12 Summary on Thematic Areas 248

Chapter 5: Towards Future Policy & Regulations for Selected Digital Economy Areas 249

5.1 Offline TMT/ICT Policy & Regulation 250

5.2 Digital Economy Platforms Policy and Regulation 252

5.3 The Future of Content, Broadcasting and Media Policy & Regulation 255

5.4 Online/Internet Policy & Regulation 259

5.5 Big Tech Policy & Regulation 263

5.6 Cybercrime & Cybersecurity Policy & Regulation 269

5.7 Artificial Intelligence & Machine Learning Policy & Regulation 272

5.8 Privacy & Data Protection Policy & Regulation 280

5.9 Electronic Commerce Laws, Policy & Regulation 285

5.10 Over the Top (OTT) Policy and Regulation 288

5.11 Capacity Building & Training on Digital Economy Policy &
Regulation 292

5.12 Summary on Ways Forward... 293

Chapter 6: OTT Regulation 101 ....**294**

6.1 Why expound on OTT Regulation than other themes?..................... 296

6.2 What is behind the rise and rise of OTTs?..................................... 298

6.3 Briefly busting some OTT Myths 302

6.4 What is the relationship between OTTs and Net Neutrality?............ 304

6.5 What then are the typical key open OTT Regulatory issues? 306

6.6 OTT Definitions and towards a consensus definition 307

6.6.1 Two Brief Definitions of OTT..308

6.6.2 Comparing and contrasting the two definitions 309

6.7 A more fine-tuned OTT definition, Policy and Regulation.............. 310

6.8 OTTs and Taxes – Look before you leap 315

6.9 Recommendations: OTTs Emerging Framework & Checklist............ 321

6.9.1 Understand & acknowledge the new Internet value chain 322

6.9.2 Regions/Countries to take clear Position on Net Neutrality & Traffic
Management 323

6.9.3 Clear Definition of OTT Required as Basis of Regulation &
Taxation 323

6.9.4 Countries/Regions must take a view on Competition Issues, Big Tech
Regulation and Online Regulation 324

6.9.5 Continue to Employ Best Practice Regulatory & Tax Principles..325

6.9.6 Recognise and Collaborate with existing and relevant institutions to
OTTs...... 328

6.9.7 Evidenced-Based OTT Interventions including stakeholder
consultations should be mandatory 331

6.9.8 Always Carry out Economic, Social & Regulatory Impact Analyses.331

    6.9.9 Implement OTT Light Touch Controls That Foster Innovation..332

    6.9.10 Collaboration amongst IVC Oversight Institutions....................*333*

    6.10 Over and Out: Covid19 and Digitalisation....................................*334*

Selected Bibliography 336

Index 338

About the Author 362

Acknowledgments

I am sincerely indebted to all those who helped in the process of reviewing the manuscript and/or colleagues who I have deeply interacted/collaborated with, and who have educated the me over the last several years, so much so that they both inspired and shaped the ideas in this book.

They include my Cenerva Colleagues, Associates and Collaborators including James Wild, Dr Christophe Stork, Steve Esselaar, Dr Charles Jenne, Prof William Webb, Chris Taylor, Andrew Gorton, Peter Seymour, Dr Jibirila Leinyuy, Phil Dunglinson, Justin Le Patourel, Simon Perkins, Iain Williams, Dr Martin Koyabe, Johan David Michels, Prof Bob Stewart, Tom Kiedrowski, Graham Butler, Dimitra Kamarinou, Dr Sara Silva, Andin Nwana and more. They will see in this book how much I have learnt from them. I am indebted to Catherine Dawson who reviewed and improved the front and back covers of the book.

Lastly, I acknowledge my dynamic niece Nagela Nukuna – currently an MIT student – who, without her knowing that after discussions with her on some of the contents in this volume, just gave me that extra momentum to write this book with more drive.

Dedication

2021 is the year during which I lost my amazing dad Prof. Elias Muthias Nwana (1933-2021) – to whose memory this insignificant work is dedicated. I really wanted to start writing and conclude this book this in this calendar year in his honour. Papa taught his children and all the dozens he raised - by sheer example of simply living it - simplicity, humility, no complaining, strong values, striving for excellence through hard work, sharing and *professing* knowledge.

It is also dedicated to my incredible mum Mama Odilia Mantan Nwana (1942 -). Mama's contributions to the lives of all her children and her grandchildren is simply immeasurable and understated. Whilst we learnt from watching Papa living his values, Mama on the other hand *actively* did all the necessary hard grafting of *practical* daily teachings of all my siblings and I, to be the people she would be proud of – she did not and does not leave much to chance! She trained all around her to be hardworking, to be very disciplined, to be our best, to be thankful, to be efficient with our time and so much more. She is an exceptional mum and human being. There is however one more thing she taught us too through her sheer daily examples - single-mindedness. When Mama puts her mind to achieving something, she is just determined and relentless, putting in the real work to achieve it – and achieving it with excellence. No short cuts. No excuses. No prevarication. Just get on with it. All her children have unbeknownst to them 'inherited' this trait from Mama. This explains why late Papa gave *all* the credit to any successes of his children to Mama.

I am so incredibly indebted to these two – and so are dozens of others too.

H. Sama Nwana
December 2021

ii

Preface

In 2014, I published a 550-page book entitled *Telecommunications, Media & Technology (TMT) for Developing Economies – How to make TMT Improve Developing Economies in Africa and Elsewhere for the 2020s*. It was - and still is - both a brazen and unabashed manifesto for how to set up, shape and manage the TMT sectors in Developing Countries for success for the 2020s. It argues against the idea of just letting the sector creep up on us, i.e., just foreseeing it rather than shaping it. I argued that this approach [which most developing countries just allow] is fraught with so many risks that would hold back of the sector, notably having the wrong policy and regulatory frameworks in place along with no rigorous implementation. This ultimately leads to much reduced consumers and citizens benefits from the sector, severe lack of necessary investment and more. The 2014 book has scores of recommendations to shape the *offline* TMT/ICT sector of developing economies.

I was flattered the manuscript – or the H manifesto for the TMT Sector for developing countries - received good revie ws and I have been asked many a time for an *encore*. I did not relent as I had intended to play my miniscule role in the implementation of this manifesto and convincing many others on its merits. I have been attempting to do this ever since 2014 through the Atlantic Telecoms & Media Ltd (www.atlantic-tm.com) and Cenerva Ltd (www.cenerva.com) – both of which I founded and co-founded respectively.

We are still early in the 2020s meaning I/we still have much 'implementation and convincing' time, so I truly did *not* intend to write a significant follow-up manuscript on this TMT-related area anytime soon.

However just 2+ years after I published the 2014 book, I read a May 2016 truly seminal GSMA paper entitled *The Internet Value Chain – A study on the economics of the Internet*[1]. I realised at once at the time just how seminal

---

[1] GSMA | The Internet Value Chain: A study on the economics of the internet | Public Policy - https://www.gsma.com/publicpolicy/resources/internet-value-chain-study-economics-internet (last accessed August 2021)

this paper is and its far reaching implications for the TMT Sector. I had read an earlier 2010 Vodafone Internet Value Chain paper, but had frankly discounted it, hardly even mentioning it in the 2014 book. I was wrong.

So, when I read up on GSMA's 2016 Internet Value Chain (IVC) – perhaps because it was well after I had penned the 2014 book – I could see that it fundamentally adds to and/or affects the regulation of the current offline-TMT sector value chain(s) in many ways, and that it raised many more *new*, related and very non-trivial challenges to the implementation of my 2014 manifesto.

The audiences I wrote the 2014 book for are suddenly faced with new *online* IVC-inspired challenges. At the same time too, I truly believe the combined *offline* TMT/ICT sector of my 2014 book and that of the new *online* sectors should be aiming for between 7 to 15% of the GDP of big and small Developing Countries by the end of this decade, i.e. by 2030. Therefore it matters to get both of them right.

So, as a practitioner who lives, learns and practices in the TMT Sector (see www.cenerva.com), I have felt compelled to pen this follow up manuscript.

Charles Kettering famously said *a problem well stated is half solved.*

Drawing from this Kettering maxim, this manuscript unapologetically aims at realising three broad goals:

1. Introducing the Internet Value Chain (IVC) and why it is most pertinent to Digital Economy Policy makers, regulators and network operators. As a practitioner, I think the IVC is a very important tool to understand the Digital Economy, and too many professionals I meet just do not know anything about it, let alone appreciate it. I did not either. This is the subject of Chapter 1.

2. Providing some *structure* and *characterisation* of the positive and – especially - the negative externalities that come with the IVC. Why especially the negative ones you ask? This is because they form the new *risks* and *harms* that come with the IVC, and they are literally numerous. They need to be controlled or *regulated* too in the new Digital Economy through judicious new policy making and rigorous implementation. I also try to provide as many illustrations of the new risks and harms as

possible using as many min-case studies in order to explain them clearly. This is the core subject of Chapter 2.

3. Providing as best as possible a definition of the combined *offline* (as in offline TMT/ICT), Big Tech and other digital platform harms/risks and the numerous other *online* (IVC) harms. My hope is that this would accrue to defining the *problem statement* of the overall policy and regulatory challenges that face Digital Economy Policy makers, regulators and network operators going forward. Once again, as I try and define the problem statement, I have again set myself the goal of providing as many illustrations of the risks and harms as possible by using min-case studies in order to explain them clearly. I assume current ICT policy makers, regulators and network operators would have to morph into the Digital Economy ones – as they are overlaps between the two, and they are the natural ones to start addressing the combined set of challenges. This is the subject of Chapter 3, i.e. Part II of this book.

Therefore drawing from Charles Kettering maxim, I admit that this manuscript can only, at best, *half-solve* the Digital Economy problem by defining it, i.e. (i) both exploring the geography of the *online* IVC benefits, risks and harms (ii) overviewing and summarising the current *offline* TMT/ICT challenges (iii) overviewing the harms and risks of Big Tech and other key digital platforms and (iv) using these to provide a well-stated digital economy problem statement for policy makers, regulators and network operators.

It is very much work-in-progress what ICT Ministers, Digital Economy Ministers, ICT regulators, ICT policy makers and the rest of us practitioners would truly do to truly address the problem statement, i.e. goal 3 above. This is a country and country challenge, or region by region one (e.g. EU Africa or the Caribbean).

Nevertheless, I do attempt – and frankly it is only an attempt – to start realising a fourth broad goal with this manuscript, but do not hold me too strongly to this one please.

4. Taking some of the new thematic challenging areas that come with the online IVC, defining them a bit more granularly, and making some *very* brief recommendations on what, where and how Digital Economy Policy Makers can start addressing them. Challenging new IVC-related policy and regulation subjects that emerge from my analyses include (i) Digital Economy Platforms (ii) the Future of Content, Broadcasting and Media Regulation in an increasingly online world (iii) Online content harms (iv) Big Tech regulation (v) Cyber-crime (vi) Cybersecurity (vii) AI and Big Data (viii) Privacy (ix) Data Protection and (x) Electronic Commerce and (xi) Over-the-Top (OTT) regulation. In addition to current offline challenges, these new ones cannot be ignored by digital economy policy makers, regulators and network operators during the 2020s and beyond.

In other words, this manuscript also attempts to proffer some ideas about what policy makers, regulators and network operators do about some of these new online IVC-inspired challenges which come on top of the current offline ones. This is Part III of the book.

I hope this book demonstrates that controlling and regulating the *offline* TMT/ICT and the *online* Digital Economy Sectors has just become much harder – but also more exhilarating. Never a dull moment as the five key drivers for all sectors noted in my 2014 book continue to work in overdrive in the TMT/ICT and online sectors: i.e., technology changes, consumer behaviour, industry, macroeconomy and regulation.

Take the Industry driver - the reader would soon realise that the IVC revolutionises[2] some of the extant TMT/ICT Sector value chains in many ways whilst leaving others largely unperturbed as seen in the pages of this book. Consider the Technology Change driver[3] – the IVC is led by Content Rights. This means *Content* (and its benefits/harms) is as relevant to Digital Economy policy makers, regulators and network operators as *Connectivity* challenges in urban and rural areas are. Take the Consumer Behaviour driver – the Covid19 macroeconomic shock driver has exacerbated the

---

[2] Some collaborators say "evolve", which I gently disagree for reasons Part I of this book expounds on.

[3] As the Internet Protocol (IP) becomes even more entrenched within TMT/ICT

growth and growth in the use (i.e. demand) of Online Services, even in developing economies. Take the *macroeconomic* driver – coups in your country or massively high inflation would ensure the Digital Economy your country is striving for is massively delayed. As all of these drivers of work in overdrive, so should *policy making and regulation* adapt too and be agile, and adapt fast.

The respected Internet Society[4] has a famous tag line which states *The Internet Changes Everything*. This is the basis for their work on driving access to the Internet as a basic human right. Of course they are right and the tag line speaks to the *revolutionary* nature of the benefits of the Internet, not just *evolutionary*. However, digging a bit deeper, this tag line is really about the Internet Value Chain changing everything – including the poor now-old TMT/ICT Sector.

I only hope I have met the goals I set for myself with this manuscript.

As you the discerning reader would have already noticed by this paragraph, I mostly write in the *first person* and in an 'interactive' and less academic-dense fashion. I have done much 'academic dense' in the past. However, the challenges, risks and harms that this manuscript covers are too many, too interwoven, very global but yet impacting nationally with deep cultural implications, old wine but at the same time new wine because of the new online contexts – and simple to identify but yet complex to solve without metaphorically throwing the baby out with the bath water. In my humble opinion, these characteristics do not require a dense academic style.

I have read my fair share of dense policy and regulatory books/papers written by economists, political scientists and antitrust lawyers. I am neither of these anyway. I have nothing against these professions by the way. If I were to do my career all over again, I probably would be an economist like my daughter! I am just trying here to get the reader to engage with some complex stuff in a more engaging way. I should note upfront that I do ask rhetorical questions in many places to both engage and break the monotony.

---

[4] The Internet Changes Everything | Internet Society - https://www.internetsociety.org/tag/the-internet-changes-everything/ (last accessed August 2021)

I have also deliberately chosen to write the way I have in this manuscript as I am sensitive to the audience of *time-poor* and *hard-pressed* Digital economy policy makers, regulators, Ministers of ICT, digital economy students, etc. engaging many complex questions/concerns - and who all have different backgrounds ranging from economists, lawyers, engineers, political scientists and more.

Lastly, and most importantly, I hope you the reader just engage the material for the benefit of maximising benefits to consumers and citizens in your country, and more broadly for your scholarship.

List of Abbreviations

AI	Artificial Intelligence
AVOD	Advertising-based Video on Demand
BATX	Baidu, Alibaba, Tencent and Xiaomi
CERT	Computer Emergency Response/Readiness Team
CIRT	Computer Incident Response Team
CSIRT	Computer Security Incident Response Team
DOCSIS	Data Over Cable Service Interface Specification
DSO	Digital Switch Over
DTH	Direct To Home (Satellite)
EC	European Commission
FAAAM	Facebook, Amazon, Alphabet, Apple and Microsoft
FAANG	Facebook, Amazon, Apple, Netflix and Google
FANGAM	Facebook, Amazon, Netflix, Google, Apple and Microsoft
FWA	Fixed Wireless Access
GAFA	Google, Apple, Facebook and Amazon
GAFAM	Google, Apple, Facebook, Amazon and Microsoft
GDPR	General Data Protection Regulation
GEO	Geostationary Equatorial Orbit (Satellite)
GSM	Global System for Mobile Communications
HHI	Herfindahl-Hirshman Index
HTML	Hyper Text Markup Language
HTTP	Hyper Text Transfer Protocol
IANA	Internet Assigned Numbers Authority
ICANN	Internet Corporation for Assigned Names and Numbers
ICT	Information and Communications Technology
IP	Internet Protocol
ITU	International Telecommunications Union
IVC	Internet Value Chain
IoT	Internet of Things
ISP	Internet Service Provider
ITU	International Telecommunications Union

LRIC	Long Run Incremental Cost
LEO	Low Earth Orbiting (Satellite)
MEO	Medium Earth Orbiting (Satellite)
ML	Machine Learning
MNO	Mobile Network Operator
MNP	Mobile Number Portability
MTR	Mobile Termination Rate
NP	Number Portability
OECD	Organisation for Economic Cooperation and Development
PPC	Pay Per Click
NN	Neural Networks
NTE	Network Termination Element
OTT	Over The Top
QoE	Quality of Experience
QoS	Quality of Service
RIR	Regional Internet Registry
RPI	Retail Price Index
SDG	Sustainable Development Goals (of the UN)
SDH	Synchronous Digital Hierarchy
SIM	Subscriber Identification Module
SME	Small and Medium Enterprises
SMS	Short Messaging Service
SVOD	Subscription Video On Demand
TDM	Time Division Multiplex
TLD	Top Level Domain (gTLD = generic; ccTLD = country code)
TMT	Telecommunications, Media and Technology
UGC	User Generated Content
UN	United Nations
UNCTAD	United Nations Conference on Trade and Development
UNESCO	United Nations Educational Scientific and Cultural Organisation
USF	User Service Fund
USP	Universal Service Provider/Provision
USSD	Unstructured Supplementary Service Data
VFM	Value For Money

VOD	Video On Demand
VoIP	Voice over Internet Protocol
VPN	Virtual Private Network
WEF	World Economic Forum
Wi-Fi	Wireless Fidelity
WOAN	WhOlesale Access Network
WWW	World Wide Web

Table of Mini-Case Studies for Easier Reference

I use the phrase "mini-case studies" rather generously. Do not expect to read MBA-type case studies that you may be more acquainted with at Business Schools. Instead of using "case studies", I could have also used "short stories" or "short narratives". I use them across the entire manuscript in order to explain salient Digital Economy issues using real world examples and contexts.

	Name of Mini-Case Study	Chapter, Section and Context
1	A Typical PhD Thesis Study	Chapter 2, Section 2.2 Context: Introducing the long tail theory and briefly explaining the genesis of much of the positive and negative externalities of the Internet Value Chain (IVC).
2	The 5G-Covid19 Quackery	Chapter 2, Section 2.3 Context: Introducing Misinformation and Fake News
3	Social Media, News and Elections	Chapter 2, Section 2.3.4.2 Context: Social Media spreading (Mis)information and Fake News about Elections. Politicians hate this with a passion.
4	TikTok, Other Apps and National Security	Chapter 2, Section 2.3.4.3 Context: TikTok and many other apps for example were considered by India to be "prejudicial to sovereignty and integrity of India, defence of India, security of state and public order", accusing them of secretly collecting data and information from its citizens phones when they download the apps.

5	Facebook and the Role of AI, ML and Big Data Algorithms	Chapter 2, Section 2.3.4.4 Context: There are increasing and justifiable concerns about the role of algorithms within the Online Services segment of the IVC in particular (dominated by Machine Learning, AI and Big Data) that regulators must be aware of – and policy makers and regulators have the responsibility to try to mitigate their "harms" by pressuring the online media companies to address them.
6	Child on Child Sexual Abuse	Chapter 2, Section 2.3.4.5 Context: Sexual violence is now increasingly completely normalised through social media platforms and through access to online pornography leading to child on child sexual abuse. I think this is a particularly pernicious online harm that truly needs to be mitigated.
7	Regulating Content on Mega-Digital Platforms: the Facebook Conundrum	Chapter 2, Section 2.3.4.6 Context: The immeasurable public good that a platform like Facebook provides vs. negative externalities like the criminality it also "hosts". The statistical law of normal distribution tells us that a platform which hosts a third of humanity would also host extreme groups. The personal liberty vs. public good challenge is also tested to the limits on platforms of such scale. Facebook's negative externalities impact the rest of society. However, does society start interfering in the running of mega successful businesses? Do you even trust Governments not to make it worse?
8	Internet zoning, Censoring the Internet and Jurisdiction	Chapter 2, Section 2.3.4.7 Context: Where does "acceptable" zoning of the Internet stop and Internet censorship start? Also whose laws apply to websites viewable

		outside their home country? Can a foreign court in Country A assume jurisdiction over online companies who are operating from Country B?
9	Google Ads, Paid-for-Search and Competition Concerns	Chapter 2, Section 2.3.5.1 Context: There are increasing and justifiable concerns about the role of algorithms within the Enabling Technologies and services segment, particularly in the Advertising category as exemplified with Google Ads. These algorithms across Google search, Google Maps and YouTube employ much Machine Learning, AI and Big Data that regulators must be aware of too. Policy makers and regulators have typically not bothered about algorithms in the past, yet alone AI/ML algorithms. However, those days are arguably over? Do such algorithms entrench competition and concentration to the point where there is no other competitor to Google (some would argue we are there already)? Is Google now not just an essential facility?
10	The increasing concern with the power of the mega-Digital platforms	Chapter 2, Section 2.3.5.2 Context: there are clear emerging policy and regulatory concerns about the market power of the mega-digital platforms (i.e. FANGAM & BATX) enabled by the Internet value chain. Avant-garde Governments and regulatory authorities across the world have commenced regulatory inquiries into these mega-platforms.
11	Amazon vs. European Commission (Conflicts of Interest):	Chapter 2, Section 2.3.5.3 Context: Amazon has found itself being investigated by the European Commission (EC) for having breached EU antitrust rules by distorting competition in online retail markets. The EC alleges a competition conflict of

		interest since a major player like Amazon frequently effectively competes with its own customers on the platform. This has led the EC to open two cases against Amazon.
12	The Mobile/Cellular industry has literally changed the world	Chapter 2, Section 2.3.6.1 Context: The mobile/cellular industry's positive externalities are unarguable.
13	Wi-Fi positive externalities are typically underestimated	Chapter 2, Section 2.3.6.2 Context: The positive externalities of Wi-Fi are largely taken for granted and not promoted by Policy makers and regulators across the globe, particularly those in developing economies.
14	The World fixed submarine cables are invaluable	Chapter 2, Section 2.3.6.3 Context: The positive externalities of the world's submarine cables are unarguable.
15	The iPhone changed the world	Chapter 2, Section 2.3.7.1 Context: The positive externalities of the User Interface segment of the value chain are unarguable. Case in point – Apple Founder Steve Jobs arguably set in train the Internet value chain with his 2007 iPhone.
16	The Google [Android] vs. EC Case	Chapter 2, Section 2.3.7.3.1 Context: This case demonstrate the risks to competition with such high concentrations seen across the IVC. The EC found that Google was tying search (which it is clearly most dominant in) with its app store, Play Store – not good! Google was tying its web browser [Chrome] with its app store and its search app – even worse! Who knows how or whether these Google illegal actions led to the exit of the Windows Phone and Symbian devices that have fallen by the way side.

17	The Apple Music vs. EC Case	Chapter 2, Section 2.3.7.3.2 Context: It appears that Apple has obtained a "gatekeeper" role when it comes to the distribution of apps and content to users of Apple's popular devices. The EC has opened a case after a compliant from Spotify to ensure that Apple's rules do not distort competition in markets where Apple is competing with other app developers, for example with its music streaming service Apple Music or with Apple Books. The EC is having a close look at Apple's App Store rules and their compliance with EU competition rules
18	The Apple Music vs. US App Developers case	Chapter 2, Section 2.3.7.3.3 Context: Apple Music lost a class action suit in a US court that accused it of engaging in anti-competitive practices in stopping developers sharing "purchase options with users outside of their iOS app", for example. Apple Music has agreed to pay US 100 million into a Small Developers Assistance Fund in order to support independent developers with better terms on app commissions and transactions.
19	Google Apps/Apple Apps vs. South Korea	Chapter 2, Section 2.3.7.3.4 Context: Apple and Google take a commission of up to 30% on digital sales from their apps stores, and for in-app purchases such as subscriptions. South Korean lawmakers see this as anti-competitive citing the frankly irreplicable gate-keeping roles that these stores now play. South Korea has enacted a law to ban this. This new 2021 law also addresses the *harms* of (i) delaying approvals of apps into the Google and Apple Apps stores (ii) and/or removing them "inappropriately".

20	Google Shopping/Google Search vs. EC	Chapter 2, Section 2.4.1 Context: The European Commission found that Google abused its dominant position by favouring its own comparison shopping service over competing comparison shopping services.
21	Google AdSense vs. EC	Chapter 2, Section 2.4.2 Context: Google AdSense is an intermediary advertising broker between advertisers and website owners that leverage the horizon around Google search results. In 2019 the EC fined Google again €1.5bn over Google AdSense, for blocking adverts from rival search engines.
22	EC Competition Policy vs. Politics	Chapter 2, Section 2.4.3 Context: The reader sees above many EC cases against American Big Tech firms which are already arguably too big to regulate. Are Big tech gatekeeping companies much too powerful to control with traditional antitrust instruments?
23	The UK Age Appropriate Design for Apps	Chapter 2, Section 2.5 and Section 2.5.3 Context: The UK's Data regulator is creating "a better Internet for children". It's Online Children Code is likely to benefit children well beyond the UK.
23	The Online Age Identification Conundrum	Chapter 2, Sections 2.5.1 and 2.5.2 Context: How do you ensure children do not lie about their age online and bypass age-appropriate controls?
24	The NetFlix Effect in Thailand	Chapter 3, Section 3.5 Context: Netflix brands itself as "the global Internet TV network". This case study shows

		how the traditional Thai film and broadcasting industry is being disrupted by an OTT in Thailand. It portends key lessons for other top content-producing markets like Nigeria (Nollywood) and India (Bollywood).
25	Instagram and Teenage Girls	Chapter 3, Section 3.6.1 Context: In September 2021, the *Wall Street Journal* (WSJ) laid its hands on some Facebook internal research on Instagram and went on to report that 'Facebook Knows Instagram is Toxic for Teen Girls, Company Documents Show'[1]. The sub-title to the article also damningly reads "its own in-depth research shows a significant teen mental-health issue that Facebook plays down in public". This is a clear public policy concern to Digital Economy policy makers and regulators.
25	AI, Ethics, Privacy, Facebook, YouTube & Misinformation	Chapter 3, Section 3.6.2 Context: The AI, misinformation and hate speech problem is non-trivial. Its harms or negative externality to society when got wrong is deadly as demonstrated in this case study with real offline violence as part of Myanmar Rohingya Muslim story [allegedly] resulting from online hate speech and misinformation instigated by the Military junta who rule Myanmar as of November 2021. Worse, in my humble view from a policy and regulatory perspective, the problem is too replete with conflicts of interest on the part of Facebook.

---

[1] Facebook Knows Instagram Is Toxic for Teen Girls, Company Documents Show - WSJ

26	Twitter, Fake News and Bots	Chapter 3, Section 3.6.3 Context: According to a 2018 MIT study published in the journal *Science*[2], *f*actual news takes 6x longer than fake news to be seen by 1500 people on Twitter. This finding raises significant ethical concerns, and the role of bots present even added policy and regulatory concerns particularly with their potential impact on elections.
27	USA, EU, UK, Australia and South Korea Bills to Regulate Big Tech	Chapter 3, Section 3.7 Context: What are the emerging Big Tech Bills, Laws, Acts and/or Codes emerging from these leading Digital Economy jurisdictions?
28	The Pillar Digital Economy Platforms	Chapter 3, Section 3.8 Context: What are they? How developed are they in your country?
29	Offline ICT/TMT areas of Regulation	Chapter 3, Section 3.9.2 Context: What *offline* ICT/TMT areas that typically are regulated today. This book notes that the offline policy and regulatory challenges are still top priority despite the new online challenges.
30	Big Tech Competition Harms	Chapter 3, Section 3.9.3 Context: What are the typical Big Tech *competition* harms? Big Tech markets concentrations and shares in most countries are very significant in their relevant markets. It is important to be aware of how they may abuse their dominant positions.

---

[2] *Science*, DOI: 10.1126/science.aao4960 & Fake news travels six times faster than the truth on Twitter | New Scientist

31	Online Regulation is Indispensable now	Chapter 3, Section 3.9.4 Chapter 5, Section 5.4 Context: How has it come about that Online regulation is now much needed? What does it entail?
31	Beware of regulating away your next online giant	Chapter 3, Section 3.11 Context: If Section 230 in the USA and Articles 12-14 of the e-Commerce Directive in the EU did not exist, I would easily venture that that the mega-digital platforms (Facebook, Twitter, Instagram, TikTok, YouTube, etc.) would be nowhere near the sizes they have attained. Therefore outside Europe and USA, e.g. in South East Asia, Africa, Caribbean and Latin America – if laws are introduced that stifle such innovation – do not be surprised at the consequences either of a still-birth Digital Economy. Do not say you have not been warned. A word to the wise is enough!
32	OTT Regulation	Chapter 6 – a deep dive into details of any OTT regulation.

Part I — An Introduction to the Internet Value Chain (IVC): Top-level Takeaways, Externalities, Risks, Harms & Concerns of the IVC

Chapter 1 Punchline: Digital Economy Policy makers, regulators and network operators need the input of the tool of the Internet Value Chain (IVC) in order to think about the digital ecosystem, the Digital Economy and its policy and regulatory implications.

Chapter 2 Punchline: The expansive Digital Economy that all countries crave in order to power their economies comes with significant consequences.

Chapter 1

The Internet Value Chain

"The GSMA commissioned this research to construct a high-level view of the internet economy—the players, economic analysis of different segments and the competitive landscape. We sought a factual assessment, based on available data, of all of the links in the internet value chain to better understand the trends and dynamics 1".

Foreward of paper, by John Giusti, Chief Regulatory Officer, GSMA, May 2016

There are not that many times one reads a truly seminal paper which makes one look at his professional world/industry very differently. The GSMA-commissioned *Internet Value Chain – a study on the economics of the Internet*[2] is in my humble opinion one of such seminal papers. In the above quote, the GSMA explains why they commissioned the paper from AT Kearney.

The foreward of this GSMA paper by Giusti goes on to state:

We hope this study will be an interesting and useful input at a time when policymakers around the world are thinking about the digital ecosystem and its policy implications. Capturing a macro view of the entire internet value chain is no small feat, and we are grateful to A.T. Kearney for this thorough and highly readable report.

I wholeheartedly agree. Giusti notes the paper should be an input as policymakers think "about the digital ecosystem and its policy implications"

---

[1] Foreword of the paper, GSMA | The Internet Value Chain: A study on the economics of the internet | Public Policy - https://www.gsma.com/publicpolicy/resources/internet-value-chain-study-economics-internet (last accessed August 2021)

[2] *Ibid*

– hence the genesis of this feeble manuscript: *the Internet Value Chain and the Digital Economy.* The paper does an excellent job in capturing a macro view of the entire Internet value chain, and TMT Consultants A.T. Kearney are indeed to be commended on such a quality report on such a complex area.

1.1 The History of the Internet Value Chains (IVC): the GSMA 2016 and Vodafone 2010 IVCs

I note in my preface of this book that this 2016 Internet value chain articulation was not the first attempt to carry out such a study; there was indeed a 2010 one too which had been commissioned by Vodafone entitled *Internet Value Chain Economics*[3]. Vodafone had similarly commissioned A. T. Kearney back in 2009 to do this latter paper. I note in my preface to this manuscript that I had read and discounted the Vodafone-commissioned paper circa 2012/13, the proof being I did not even mention it in my 2014 555-pages book. How wrong I was.

Figure 1 presents GSMA's 2016 IVC.

---

[3]Internet value chain economics - article - Kearney - https://www.kearney.com/communications-media-technology/article?/a/internet-value-chain-economics (last accessed August 2021)

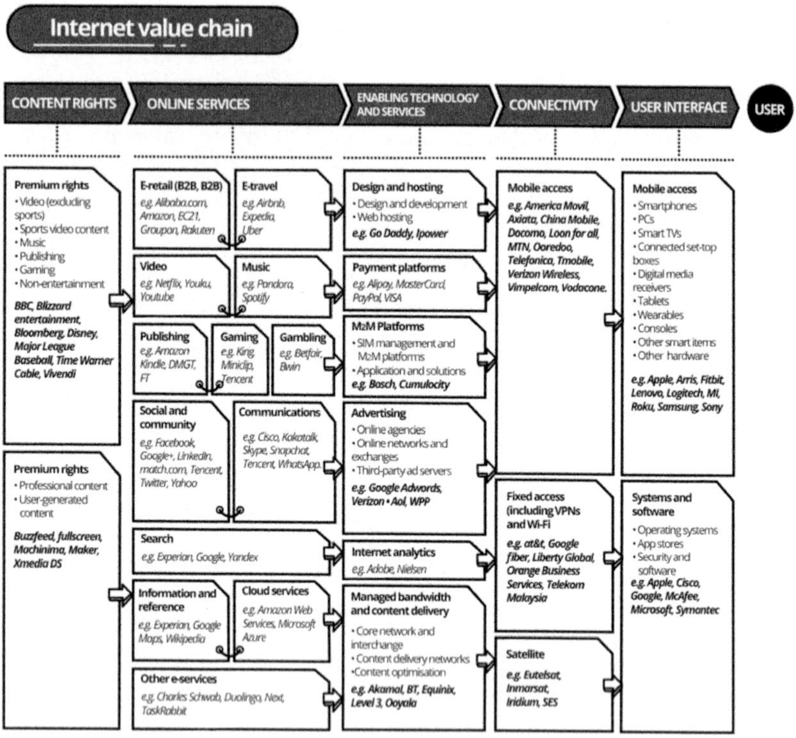

Figure 1—The GSMA/A.T. Kearney Internet 2016 Value Chain[4]

Figure 1 clearly depicts an IVC with five distinct segments: Content Rights, Online Services, Enabling Technologies, Connectivity and User Interface. As can be seen in Figure 2, A.T. Kearney retained the same five main segments from their 2010 IVC. The later 2016 one (i.e. Figure 1) is subdivided into 37 categories.

The areas and categories are also largely retained from the 2010 IVC (cf. Figure 2) albeit with some redefinitions and additions. For examples:

- the category 'media rights owners' in 2010 is redefined as 'premium rights' in 2016;

- 'user generated content' in 2010 becomes a subcategory of 'made for digital' in 2016;

---

[4] *Ibid as footnote 6*

- the Connectivity segment in 2010 had subcategories 'core network', 'interchange' and 'retail internet access' – in 2016 IVC, Connectivity consists of 'mobile access', 'fixed access (including VPNs and Wi-Fi)' and 'satellite';

- the User Interface segment in the 2010 IVC had the subcategories of 'applications' and 'devices' vs. the 2016's subcategories of 'hardware devices' and 'systems and software'; etc.

I do not cover all the changes between the 2010 and 2016 IVCs above as I do not judge it that necessary since there is still much consistency between 2010 and 2016 IVCs.

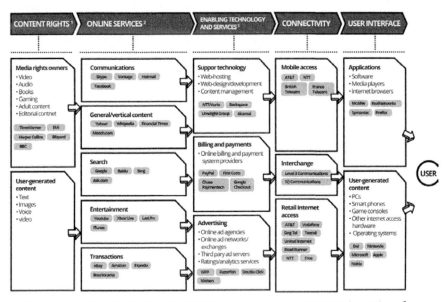

Figure 2—The Vodafone /A.T. Kearney Internet 2010 Value Chain[5]

The 2016 GSMA-commissioned IVC paper proceeded to value each of the 5 market segments by category as shown in Figure 3 whilst comparing each segment's growth from the earlier 2010 Vodafone-commissioned IVC paper.

---

[5] *Ibid as footnote 6*

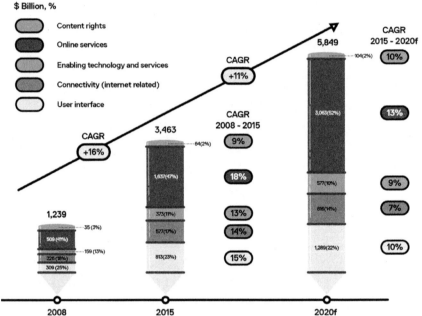

$ Billion, %

- Content rights
- Online services
- Enabling technology and services
- Connectivity (internet related)
- User interface

CAGR +16%

CAGR 2008 - 2015

CAGR +11%

CAGR 2015 - 2020f

2008 — 1,239
- 35 (3%)
- 509 (41%)
- 159 (13%)
- 226 (18%)
- 309 (25%)

2015 — 3,463
- 64 (2%)
- 1,637 (47%)
- 373 (11%)
- 577 (17%)
- 813 (23%)

CAGR 2008 - 2015:
- 9%
- 18%
- 13%
- 14%
- 15%

2020f — 5,849
- 104 (2%)
- 3,063 (52%)
- 577 (10%)
- 816 (14%)
- 1,289 (22%)

CAGR 2015 - 2020f:
- 10%
- 13%
- 9%
- 7%
- 10%

Figure 3 — Internet value chain size and growth by segment[6]

1.2 A Brief Anatomy of the GSMA IVC

As noted earlier, the GMSA IVC consists of five distinct segments: Content Rights, Online Services, Enabling Technologies, Connectivity and User Interface. I review each of the segments briefly following.

1.2.1 Content Rights Segment

Much Internet or Online Content today - just think about the BBC, Netflix, YouTube, Facebook (now part of Meta[7]), Instagram, Twitter, etc. - is either

---

[6] *Ibid as footnote 8*

[7] On the 28th October 2021, Fakebook's Founder and CEO Mark Zuckerberg announced that Facebook had changed its name to *Meta* which he said would better "encompass" what it does as the company broadens its reach beyond social media into other areas like virtual reality (VR). Individual *platforms* that new parent company Meta owns such as Facebook, WhatsApp, Messenger, Oculus and Instagram maintain their names. https://www.bbc.co.uk/news/technology-59083601

'Premium Rights Content' in the case for the former two (i.e. BBC and Netflix) or 'Made for Digital' as per the latter four. Content Rights owners who possess premium rights to their content include media companies like the BBC, Time Warner Cable, Bloomberg, etc. They own and sell their rights to their various genres on content (video, sports, music, publishing, games, etc.) for distribution via the Internet. The GSMA IVC paper argues that content creation and production of content such as sports, music and cinema would happen anyway – and that what is truly related to the Internet is the sale of the 'Internet Rights'. This is why the IVC segment is called "Content Rights" segment.

So for example, the most popular cricket league in the world is the Indian Premier League (IPL) because of the hundreds of millions of cricket-mad Indians follow cricket in India. Disney+Hotstar purchased (via Hotstar's parent Star India[8]) the 5-year set of IPL rights for a record US$2.5 billion in 2017, and these premium rights will expire at the end of the 2022 season.

Whilst much of this $2.5 billion was predicated on broadcast TV rights on terrestrial/cable in India and the rest of the world, a minority of the sum paid was for 'digital' rights. The IPL by itself generates 50% of the video streaming platform's ad revenues in India, presumed to be circa US$100 million from IPL ad sales. Such digital rights video streaming sales would be counted on the IVC whilst those sold to terrestrial and cable broadcasters would *not*. In 2022, there is likely to be fierce competition when the rights come back for auction from giants like Facebook, Amazon, and possibly even Reliance Industries, India's largest conglomerate. Facebook and Amazon participation would ensure that such digital rights sales would be valued highly.

Some important points about the Content and Content Rights Segment of the IVC include:

1. The Internet and digital age changes the nature of content and truly *democratises* it, from a historical limited pool of proven content 'talent' from top media houses like the BBC, CNN or Time

---

[8] Star India takes global IPL cricket rights for five years - SportsPro Media

Warner Cable to a scenario where every individual has the opportunity to generate their own content and monetise it, e.g. on Instagram or Twitter.

2. The Internet's global nature supports *long tail* economics, i.e. relatively small numbers of geographically dispersed readers, viewers, or listeners with a common interest can now be aggregated to form a sizeable audience. We observe this long tail economics daily today on digital platforms such as Twitter, Facebook, YouTube and more. I explain "long tail" more later.

3. As I note earlier, the IVC distinguishes between two categories within its Content Rights segment: premium rights and made-for-digital. *Premium rights* category covers professionally curated content distributed via the Internet and for non-Internet channels (e.g. payTV), and paid-for through user subscriptions and/or advertising funding. *Made-for-digital* covers content primary curated for distribution through the Internet – spanning User-Generated Content (UGC) and professionally produced content.

4. As Figure 3 shows, the total IVC market size worldwide was estimated by GSMA/A.T. Kearney in 2016 at $3,463 Billion, of which the Content Rights segment was estimated at circa $US 64 Billion or 2% of the value chain (see Figure 3). Much of this $64 Billion is attributed to Premium rights category whilst the made-for-digital category is still nascent.

5. It is important to highlight that much Internet content is user-generated content (UGC) including individuals' pages on Facebook, or a "tweet" message on Twitter, posts on LinkedIn or similar pictures/videos on Instagram. The content creators here are not paid, and these creators typically retain copyright and/or privacy protection on how their content is used by 3rd parties. The content rights quantified in the 2% of the IVC (see Figure 3) above does *not* include such UGC 'rights'; rather it quantifies the rights to the provisioning of content to Online Service Providers (OSPs) such as music, games, news, digital books, short videos, etc. Content rights owners like the BBC or Netflix license their content for a share of revenues and/or license fees, typically retaining between 40 – 70 percent of the revenues generated by the OSP as in the case with what iTunes would pay music majors for any album downloaded.

1.2.2 Online Services Segment

This segment covers the wide and diverse range of services accessed by Internet users. As Figure 3 shows, the Online Services segment was valued in 2016 at $1,637 Billion of the total $3,463 Billion, i.e. 47% of the IVC. The size of this segment was expected to have almost doubled by 2020 as forecasted from 2015 as can be seen in Figure 3, growing to 52% of the IVC, with the biggest driver being E-retail which is relatively fragmented.

The 2016 IVC paper groups them into five bigger clusters:

i. *E-Commerce* inclusive of (i) E-retail including major B2C brands like EBay, Alibaba and Amazon and other dedicated B2B exchanges (ii) E-travel including Expedia, Uber, Airbnb, etc. The cluster captures the shift from offline to online retail.

ii. *Entertainment* inclusive of (i) Publishing including ft.com, eBooks (ii) Gaming including platform-based video gaming (iii) Gambling including Online gambling platforms with an Internet connection (iv) Video including YouTube, Netflix content operating in more than 200 countries, TikTok, etc. (v) Music including both streaming services and 'buy and download.

iii. *Search, Information and Reference Services* inclusive of (i) search services such as Google, Bing, Baidu (ii) information and reference services such as Wikipedia and Google Maps.

iv. *Social, Community and Communications* inclusive of Social and community services like Facebook, Tencent, Twitter and LinkedIn (ii) Internet-based communication services such as WhatsApp and Skype.

v. *Cloud and other E-Services* including (i) Cloud services spanning data storage, fully hosted software services, online data processing (ii) other e-services including user-paid services such as e-learning, paid apps, advertising-based web services, Internet of Things front ends, etc.

1.2.3 Enabling Technologies and Services Segment

This segment is one that is generally invisible to the end users, but is quintessential to the technical delivery of web content as well as the generation of revenues for much of the value chain.

Analytics services that gather data by tracking usage patterns on particular retail sites fall into this segment, as do the data that can be sold to other retailers too. As Figure 3 shows, this segment was valued at $373 Billion i.e. 11% of the IVC in 2016. The size of this segment was expected to grow significantly by 2020 as forecasted from 2015 as can be seen in Figure 3, growing to USD 577 Billion.

The Enabling Technologies and Services segments has three main clusters:

i.   *Enabling Platforms* inclusive of (i) Design and hosting covers from basic to more advanced complex sites that distribute content (ii) Payment platforms covers services like PayPal, Online Banking, Mobile Payments platforms like MPESA in Kenya, billing platforms, etc. (iii) Machine-to-machine (M2M) platforms includes companies that provide M2M services like smart meters or smart asset tracking services.

ii. *Advertising Services* – these cover companies that act as agents to place online ads, who would do media campaigns, inventory acquisition for such online campaigns and who would charge commissions based on ad spend volumes. This category also includes online advertising exchanges such as Google's Google Ads (formerly Google AdWords) where advertisers bid to display brief advertisements, service offerings, videos and products to web users. Third-party ad service providers that host and distribute online ads also fall under this category as well as ratings analytics service providers.

iii. *Managed Bandwidth and Content Delivery* covers service platforms such as content delivery platforms and content management platforms. For example, Akamai using both its core and edge network servers, provides content delivery services that help improve the speed and reliability of the connection to end users.

Cloud computing services clearly fall under this segment too, dominated by the big two online giants - Amazon and Microsoft (Azure).

1.2.4 Connectivity Segment

The connectivity segment of the IVC was valued at $577 Billion in 2015 (i.e. 17% of the total IVC), forecasted back then to grow to $816 Billion in 2020 as per Figure 3. The Connectivity segment covers the Internet access services provided by telecommunications network operators, whether fixed, satellite or wireless. These are the three core subcategories.

i. *Mobile access* covers service providers such as Vodafone, Airtel, Verizon, China Mobile etc. particularly in their provision of voice and data services. This segment excludes SMS revenues as well as traditional circuit-switched voice revenues – concentrating mainly on data sources of revenues.

ii. *Fixed access* covers connectivity of Internet service providers over fixed networks such as DSL, cable (DOCSIS), fibre and public Wi-Fi. Fixed networks would cover both core, last mile and interchange/transit operators that operators such as BT and Verizon typically possess.

iii. *Satellite access* covers satellite connectivity whether by LEOs, MEOs or GEOs. There has been so much advancements in the satellite sector through players like SpaceX[9] whose activities have brought launch costs down 75%.

1.2.5 User Interface Segment

The User Interface segment of the IVC was valued at $813 Billion in 2015 (i.e. 23% of the total IVC), forecasted back then to grow to $1289 Billion in 2020 as per Figure 3.

The User Interface segment is an invaluable part of the Internet value chain, comprising two core clusters:

---

[9] SpaceX, a Tesla for the skies | The Economist

i. *Devices* such as smartphones (from the likes of Apple and Samsung), PCs, tablets, connected TV set-top boxes game consoles and mobile phones; and

ii. *Systems and Software* that includes app stores, operating systems (such Play Store/Android vs. Apple Appstore/iOS vs. Windows 10), web browsers (Google, Bing, etc.), media players and games used to render services to end-users. This cluster also includes security and software market like McAfee and Office 360.

The financial profits truly stem from the User Interface segment too.

1.3 The IVC – is it really relevant to TMT or is it orthogonal to it?

We have now covered in the previous section the five segments of the IVC.

However, I have been asked this question (i.e., the title of this section) by many clever policy and regulator trainees/professionals when I introduce the Internet value chain to them – is the IVC really relevant to TMT/ICT? They would ask if the IVC is not orthogonal – or in this context, not relevant and/or unrelated to their TMT policy making and regulating? The answer is more complicated as much of the rest of this chapter expounds upon.

To answer this relevance question of the IVC to TMT, I would typically respond by asking them to bring out their phone. In all cases, it has always been an expensive Iphone or Android smartphone.

Image 1 – The Classic Nokia 3310 Phone (Source – Wikipedia[10])

I then ask them – if they are old enough – to recall the old iconic Year 2000 Nokia 3310 classic phone shown as Image 1. Then I ask how many apps they bought and downloaded to the Nokia classic 3310 from its User Interface? Does this user interface drive any revenue buying decisions bar calling and texting?

I do this to make them realise that the *User Interface* segment of the IVC is just so obvious today with our usage of smartphones, Ipads and other devices. Then I ask, what rich audio/visual content (sports, video, music, games, etc) could the Nokia 3310 phone render? How much user generated content (USG) did it engender? How much professional content was developed for this phone?

---

[10] Nokia 3310 - Wikipedia - https://en.wikipedia.org/wiki/Nokia_3310 (last accessed August 2021)

By this stage the trainees typically quickly realise that the Late Steve Jobs, Founder of Apple Inc, truly changed the digital world with the Iphone in 2007.

The *Content Rights* segment follows seamlessly from the rich user interface segment. Then I would ask – rhetorically - if pre the Iphone launch in 2007 they could access thousands of *Online Services*? Pre 2007, we had 2G "apps" – if we could even call them that. We had 3G apps. However, we had applications (or apps) intimately linked to their underlying technology as in 2G or 3G or Wi-Fi, etc. Steve Job's Iphone changed all these with the help of the IP protocol, leading to the delineated *Connectivity Segment* of the IVC (fixed, mobile, Wi-Fi or satellite), i.e. well delinked from the Online services segment, partly because of the *Enabling Technology and Services* segment.

I point out to them that most of what they regulate *offline* is now part of the Connectivity segment, and that OTT players now sit in a completely different segment of the IVC - the Online Services segment.

The IVC just makes sense - completely. I did not get it pre the publication of my previous 2014 book (Nwana, 2014). How silly was I? I make amends for that with this book.

1.4 The TMT Sector Value Chains vs. the IVC – are they mutually exclusive?

Then the smart policy/regulatory professionals would ask how much overlap is there between the GSMA 2016 Internet Value Chain and the traditional TMT Sector value chains? I already briefly note earlier that much of what they regulate today is now part of the Connectivity segment of the IVC.

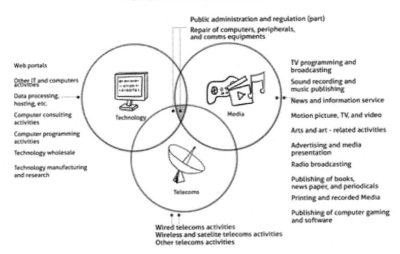

THE TMT SECTORS AND SOME OF
THEIR KEY AREAS (SOURCE: DELOITTE)

Public administration and regulation (part)
Repair of computers, peripherals,
and comms equipments

Web portals

Other IT and computers
activities

Data processing,
hosting, etc.

Computer consulting
activities

Computer programming
activities

Technology wholesale

Technology manufacturing
and research

Technology

Media

Telecoms

TV programming and
broadcasting

Sound recording and
music publishing

News and information service

Motion picture, TV, and video

Arts and art - related activities

Advertising and media
presentation

Radio broadcasting

Publishing of books,
news paper, and periodicals

Printing and recorded Media

Publishing of computer gaming
and software

Wired telecoms activities
Wireless and satellite telecoms activities
Other telecoms activities

Figure 4: The TMT Sectors and Some of their Key Areas (Source: adapted from Deloitte)[11]

However, to answer this question more fully, it is important to start with a reminder of the what the traditional Telecoms, Media and Technology (TMT) sectors are like, and their individual value chains.

1.4.1 Revisiting some traditional TMT sub-sector value chains

Nwana (2014) describes the TMT Sector in detail using Figure 4, taking each TMT subsector in turn, dissecting and describing its key activities. So this sections draws much from Nwana (2014).

Each of these TMT subsectors have their own value chains and sub-value chains. For example, Figure 5 shows the typical pre-4G mobile value chain – part of wireless telecoms of Figure 4. It consists of equipment suppliers like

---

[11] *London—Enabling a World Leading Digital Hub*, Deloitte, July 2013, www.deloitte.com, Appendix C.

Huawei/Ericsson who provide equipment to mobile/cellular operators to build their networks, who in turn provide services like voice calls/SMS to their customers. The wired telecoms activity subsector value chain has a similar equivalent to Figure 5.

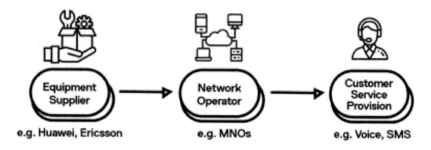

Figure 5: Pre-4G/Data Age (i.e. 2G/3G) Typical Mobile Value Chain

Turning to the Media subsector, Figure 6a[12] shows the typical terrestrial broadcast value chain. Most of TV content distribution has been digital for more than a decade and a half now, and it is the transmission across the airwaves that has been digitised or is being digitised too across some parts world still, e.g. in South East Asia or Africa as of October 2021. This is through the digital 'switchover' [analogue to digital TV DSO] projects in order to release 600MHz, 700MHz and 800MHz frequencies for 4G/5G mobile broadband.

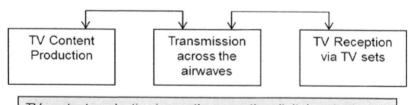

Figure 6a – Broadcast Value Chain

---

[12] Borrowed from Nwana (2014), page 341

Figure 6b[13] depicts the depicts the links in the chain from an old analogue video tape to reception of motion TV/video picture (c.f. Figure 4) using direct-to-home satellite telecoms.

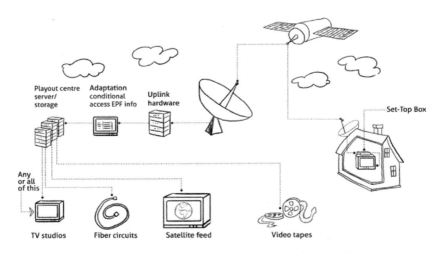

AN EXAMPLE OF THE LINKS IN THE CHAIN FROM VIDEO
TO VIEWER USING SATELLITE DIRECT TO HOME (DTH)

Figure 6b—An Example of the Links in the Chain from Video to Viewer,
Using Satellite Direct to Home (DTH)

As shown with Figure 6b with satellite TV, digital video and audio (delivered live from TV studios, fibre circuits, satellite feeds, or tapes) first go through a content protection system (called conditional access) to ensure only those who are allowed to will receive and view the content at the receiving end. The content is uplinked from a large satellite dish to a satellite, where it is broadcast to all consumers' satellite dishes throughout the satellite's footprint or area of coverage. At the receiver end, satellite TV requires a satellite receiving dish and a receiver set-top box at the customer end. Direct-to-home (DTH) satellites typically operate in the Ku-band with uplink of frequencies in 14.0 to 14.6 GHz and downlink frequencies of 11.7 to 12.2 GHz. Three equally spaced satellites 35,700 km above the

[13] *Ibid.* p. 392

equator can cover almost the entire surface of the earth. Therefore the biggest advantage of satellite is its widespread footprint.

One further example - let us turn to fixed network links from a home office, say in Lagos (Nigeria) accessing a server on the west coast of the USA as shown in Figure 7[14].

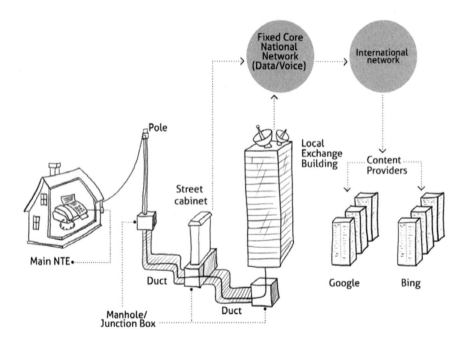

Figure 7: Fixed Network Link from a Home or Office in Africa Accessing a Bing or Google Server[15] in California or Someone calling California

Figure 7 shows what the access network covers, *inter alia*, access to network elements within the end user's house or office and other associated facilities

---

[14] Borrowed from Nwana (2014), page 56

[15] A server is a computer that holds digital information shared between many users who can connect to it across the Internet or other networks.

(which may involve the connection of equipment) by fixed access to physical infrastructure, including buildings, poles, ducts, and masts Everything in Figure 7, from the home/office all the way to the exchange, is part of the *access network*. The main network termination element (NTE), the end socket in the home/office, the poles that the fixed telephone and broadband router are plugged into, the ducts, the street cabinet, manholes, and junction boxes up to the exchange building *are all part* of the access network.

The voice or data of the person who is calling California (or accessing the Internet there) has to travel, firstly, over this access network via the copper, coaxial, or fibre lines which run in the ducts and poles via the street cabinet into a local exchange building. In some cases, the data goes directly into the fixed core data network via the street cabinet without going via the local exchange, as is shown in Figure 7.

1.4.2 Much of the Traditional TMT Sector Value Chains live off the IVC, but they are not mutually exclusive

The Internet value chain is clearly becoming more pervasive as alluded to in Section 1.3, but as can be seen from Figures 5, 6a and 6b, much of the traditional TMT sector value chains *live off* the GSMA Internet value chain.

Practically all of 2G/3G-only value chains (Figure 5) do *not* live on the Internet or the IVC, i.e. much of the traditional 2G/3G voice/SMS revenues are not captured within the IVC of Figure 1. Much of the terrestrial TV broadcasting value chain (Figure 6a) is off the IVC for the simple reason that it is both linear, terrestrial and *not* online. Similarly, much of the Direct-to-home (DTH) value chain (Figure 6b) live off the IVC for a DTH satellite service to a satellite service subscriber. Therefore rightly, most (if not all) of both the linear terrestrial broadcast and the satellite DTH revenues are not included in the IVC of Figure 1. The new trends towards Video on Demand (VoD) services like Netflix and Amazon Prime are clearly online services, and are therefore on the IVC.

However, the case for fixed access, fixed national core networks and fixed international networks as depicted in Figure 7 is much different than from satellite DTH networks with respect to the IVC. This is because the connectivity segment of the IVC includes the elements of the access, core and international network elements that contribute to providing Internet services to the home office user in Lagos, Nigeria. The access network in Lagos, Nigeria may include Wi-Fi – in which case it sits on the IVC. It may be 4G, in which case the 4G data package subscription revenues would be included in the IVC. Much of the fixed core national network (in Nigeria say) is going Internet Protocol (IP) - if not all already. Indeed many national core networks are migrating online onto the IVC as they are built on national IP fibre backbones. The international networks are practically all IP networks built on international submarine fibre cables and numerous super-exchanges which both peer and route the Internet traffic. All this peering/routing use a core Internet technical standard defined by the Internet Corporation for Assigned Names and Numbers (ICANN). In short, all international network connectivity is IP-transit Internet traffic. My point? Much of the revenues of fixed national and fixed international transit traffic are included on the Internet value chain.

In summary, the traditional TMT value chains and the IVC are *not* mutually exclusive, but whilst some of the subsector TMT value chains are moving rapidly onto the IVC (e.g. fixed networks as in Figure 7), others like DTH services (Figure 6) are not necessarily.

1.4.3 What else are *not* included on the IVC from the TMT value chains?

Recall the IVC (Figure 1) has five segments: Content Rights, Online Services, Enabling Technologies, Connectivity and User Interface. Let us review briefly some key aspects *not* included in the IVC. The following non-exhaustive areas by IVC segment illustrate what are *excluded:*

- Content Rights: Traditional TV and Radio programming and broadcasting rights (see Figure 4) - only the content rights market corresponding to the provisioning of content to Online Service Providers on a commercial basis are included.

20

- Content Rights: Publishing of offline books, newspapers and periodicals.

- Content Rights: Nollywood (Nigeria) and Bollywood (India) CDs and other offline content rights.

- Online Services: all offline advertising services like TV and newspaper advertising.

- Online Services: offline advertising billboards and offline advertising campaigns.

- Online Services: Offline computer gaming/software, Offline gambling, etc.

- Online Services: Offline B2B and B2C retail as in shopping malls and those on the high street.

- Enabling Technology & Services: Payment platforms such as M-PESA in Kenya based on 2G/USSD technology are excluded – though clearly the MPESA platform enables millions of dollars of Online transactions in Kenya. PayPal as "pure play" online payment service provider is clearly and fully on the IVC.

- Connectivity: 2G/3G revenues are excluded apart from the revenues that are data packages revenues.

- User Interface: analogue and/or non-IP devices such that they cannot connect to the Internet, e.g. old analogue TV sets, etc.

1.4.4 What does the non-mutual exclusivity between IVC and TMT value chains mean for Policy makers, regulators and network operators?

Simply, the answer to this question is that ICT policy makers, regulators and network operators have to contend – not only with the *offline* TMT sectors – but also with the rapidly burgeoning Internet-inspired online segments of the IVC.

I hope Sections 1.4.1 to 1.4.3 clearly establish the point that whilst the Internet Value Chain is all pervasive, "absorbing" and/or substituting some

TMT value chains, there are still are large swathes of TMT activities in Figure 4 "offline", i.e. not on the IVC.

Nevertheless, TMT policy making and regulation can no longer ignore the "online" – and the tidal wave of externalities it brings need the attention of the same policy maker and regulators. The Digital Economy that all countries crave has consequences.

1.5 Breakdown of the Rest of the Book and How to Read the Book

1.5.1 Breakdown of the Book

Following is a breakdown of the rest of the book. It consists of three broad Parts only:

I. *Introduction to the Internet Value Chain for Policy Makers & Regulators: Top-Level Takeaways, Externalities, Risks, Harms & Concerns* - **Part I** includes this introductory **Chapter 1** on the Internet Value Chain (IVC) and a further one, Chapter 2.

Chapter 2 describes the top-level takeaways, risks, harms, new concerns and externalities of the IVC - and the implications for ICT Policy making and regulation. It introduces and critiques the long tail theory and its relevance to the IVC, and proceeds to (non-exhaustively) list the externalities (largely the negative ones) that come with the five segments of the IVC - by segment. It also notes the source of the IVC's positive externalities too. It is important to overview these because Policy and Regulation is in the business of minimising risks and harms[16] whilst promotive the positive benefits. The chapter covers many of the new IVC-inspired harms and new areas for policy and regulatory consideration, and why this follow-up book was necessary to the Nwana (2014) TMT for Developing Economies book.

---

[16] Read 'negative externalities', i.e. harms that consumers and citizens may/should have to be prevented from. For example, children having access to content online that is not age-appropriate.

II. *Defining the New Digital Economy Policy & Regulatory Landscape with the IVC:* **Part II** consists of just a *single* chapter (**Chapter 3**) which attempts to draw from the two chapters of Part I in order to help articulate what the new ICT Regulatory landscape is like in a world of the exponential growing influence of the Internet value chain. Part II is really core too to this entire book and its core mission: to help Digital Economy Policy makers, regulators and network operators understand and *define* the new emerging 'combined' challenges of the Digital Economy, i.e. those of the *offline* TMT/ICT regulatory landscape and the new *online* IVC-inspired ones.

III. *Towards the Future of Digital Economy Policy Making & Regulation: some brief suggestions, recommendations and ways forward on key challenges* - **Part III** consists of three chapters. **Chapter 4** identifies eleven new Digital Economy priority areas and elaborates on them further. It then proceeds to explain why they are prioritised. The priority areas include (i) Digital Economy Platforms (ii) the Future of Content, Broadcasting and Media Regulation in an increasingly online world (iii) Online content harms (iv) Big Tech regulation (v) Cyber-crime (vi) Cybersecurity (vii) AI and Big Data (viii) Privacy (ix) Data Protection and (x) Electronic Commerce (xi) Over-the-Top (OTT) regulation. The chapter argues that in addition to current *offline* TMT/ICT regulatory challenges, these new *online* IVC-inspired ones cannot be ignored by digital economy policy makers, regulators and network operators during the 2020s. **Chapter 5** takes each of these chosen Digital Economy thematic areas, defines them a bit more and proceeds to make some suggestions on how policy makers, regulators and network operators can start addressing them in their countries. **Chapter 6** is the last chapter of this book which takes one of the themes in particular – Over The Top (OTT) Services Policy & Regulation – and provides a more expansive way forward for policy makers, regulators and network operators than I do in Chapter 5. I justify doing this because all the content, applications and services of the Online Services segment of the IVC are OTT services. Yet many policy makers, regulators and network operators in many countries are attempting to regulate just one of the categories of this Online Services segment, i.e. Social Media. I explain why this is shortsighted and how OTT should be looked at in the round from a policy and regulatory perspective. This chapter attempts to provide the level of detail and more that each of the other themes should be further developed as Digital Economy policy makers are pressed "to do something about OTTs". I demonstrate in this chapter how this request covers a "multitude of sins" or harms that clearly need to be teased out. A key contribution of me adding this chapter is that of making this simple but fundamental point, in addition to providing some – hopefully – more evidenced approach and recommendations on "what you do" about OTTs.

This sort of critical and detailed approach applies to all the other nine thematic areas that I do not expound upon beyond Chapter 5.

1.5.2 How to read the book

Regarding how you may choose to read the book, I recommend you read my Preface first and thereafter you can read the chapters in any order you like – though sequentially would be better.

Frankly what matters more is for you to be inspired enough to read all the chapters in the book in whatever order you choose.

Chapter 2

Some Top-level Takeaways, Externalities[17], Risks, Harms and new Concerns of the IVC

There was a period pre the Iphone (2007) when the telecommunications [mobile] value chain was just the simple classic vertically integrated 3-layer one of the TDM services layer (voice/SMS services), the network layer and the equipment layer. Then the IP-based Internet and its content-led value chain came along with its attractive devices, numerous online services, thousands of apps and unlimited content that wows subscribers – completely "over-running" the erstwhile mobile telecoms 3-layer value chain. These positive benefits for consumers and citizens also include social media apps like Whatsapp, Facebook, Viber, etc. Indeed, all the "Online Services" in the Internet value chain of Figure 1 are all OTT services, and perhaps blowing away the first myth: OTT is not equal to social media apps! E-Retail, streaming, gaming, search and cloud services apps (and more) all also run over-the-top. Rich interactive apps and great devices along with fantastic content which telcos can never produce are being lapped up by subscribers, driving more network demand, but also driving the need for enhanced networks. Mobile operators have suddenly found themselves delineated to the connectivity layer/segment of the Internet value chain whilst other players dominate other layers. The Internet value chain has "supplanted" parts of the erstwhile telecoms one with OTTs sitting in a totally different segment (Online Services) whilst operators sit in the connectivity segment. There goes another myth: the different segments should be looked at by regulators differently.

Nwana (2019)[18]

---

[17] An externality [of the IVC] refers to a benefit or cost that just comes intrinsically with the new Internet value chain, whose true costs to society are not reflected in the price of the service (e.g. "free at the point of use" because of advertising comes with much later costs such as disinformation).

[18] Internet Security Primer-research-190701 (itu.int) - https://www.itu.int/dms_pub/itu-d/oth/07/1a/D071A0000070001PDFE.pdf (last accessed August 2021)

2.1 Introduction to Top-Level IVC Takeaways & Externalities

This is one of the key chapters of this manuscript as I hope in it to explore the Internet Value chain (IVC) in some level of detail, pointing out its positive and in particular its negative externalities or harms. It is meant to be an excursion of the literally numerous challenges that that come with the IVC in some sort of a *structured* manner, with no real intention to fully specify their respective policy and regulatory responses. However, I do cover many [potential] harms and risks in places in reasonably lengthy detail in order to elucidate and illuminate the cultural, policy and regulatory devils that lie in some of the details. I try and provide as many illustrations of the new risks and harms as possible using min-case studies in order to explain them clearly. I also allude to some solutions (and perhaps do even more) in many places in this chapter mainly to provide further contexts in order to make the concepts, risks and harms 'come alive' more to the reader.

I hope this excursion, providing some sort of structure and categorisation of the challenges that come with the IVC, is a one of the core contributions of this book. I warn the challenges are not exhaustive but I hope they are far more than illustrative.

It is uncomfortable that I start a chapter with a 2-year old quote from myself, but I felt it was prescient to introducing this chapter, and you the reader can see if you agree or disagree. I wrote the above in 2019 when I was invited to speak on regulating OTTs by the ITU in October 2019 in Geneva. I hope it provides another type of summary to the introduction to the IVC [of Chapter 1] whilst proceeding to link to the goal of this Chapter, which is to look at the top-level takeaways, concerns and externalities of the IVC and the implications on Digital Economy Policy making and regulation.

I also prefer to use the term 'externality' much in this chapter (and in the entire book) because Digital Economy policy makers, regulators and network operators typically worry too about it. We regulate externalities because the price of the product or service does not always reflect the true cost to society of producing and/or consuming that product or service.

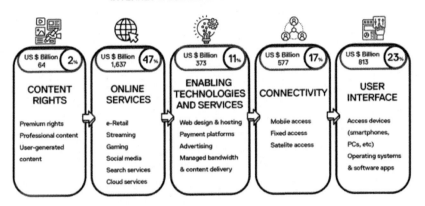

INTERNET VALUE CHAIN BY MARKET SIZE

CONTENT RIGHTS	ONLINE SERVICES	ENABLING TECHNOLOGIES AND SERVICES	CONNECTIVITY	USER INTERFACE
US $ Billion 64 — 2%	US $ Billion 1,637 — 47%	US $ Billion 373 — 11%	US $ Billion 577 — 17%	US $ Billion 813 — 23%
Premium rights	e-Retail	Web design & hosting	Mobile access	Access devices
Professional content	Streaming	Payment platforms	Fixed access	(smartphones,
User-generated	Gaming	Advertising	Satelite access	PCs, etc)
content	Social media	Managed bandwidth		Operating systems
	Search services	& content delivery		& software apps
	Cloud services			

Figure 8 – A Simplified Version of the GSMA 2015 IVC in Figure 1

For example, many online services are 'free' [at the point of use] because they are paid through advertising, but if consumers/citizens excessively consume it (e.g. spending inordinate amounts of time online to the detriment of their health, on gambling or pornography sites say), there is a clear cost to society in that service being free, e.g. with increasing unhealthy and 'zombie' children, some who end up being seen by scarce health and social services professionals. This free service generates externalities that may need regulating despite its clear benefits. Regulating negative externalities compels the producer (e.g. Facebook or Ebay) and/or the consumers to bear the full costs of production, rather than passing them on to other players like taxpayers.

If consumers or citizens suffer from data breaches, or lose monies from their online wallets, the companies should be held responsible for these first, before the State may consider stepping in.

Returning to my quote above that opens the chapter, I use it to start to tease out *just* some of the top-level [non-exhaustive] takeaways and implications. As the reader reads some of the following top-level takeaways/implications, it may be worth revisiting the simplified 2015 GSMA IVC of Figure 8). Drawing aspects and briefly elaborating from the quote:

- "Then the IP-based Internet and its content-led value chain [see Figure 1/or Figure 8] came along with its attractive devices, numerous online services, thousands of apps and unlimited content that wows subscribers...", *Takeaway:* content, content and more content. Attractive devices, numerous online services and apps that just trounce anything the traditional mobile value chain, broadcast value chain, etc. has to offer.

- "OTT is not equal to social media apps! E-Retail, streaming, gaming, search and cloud services apps (and more) all also run over-the-top", i.e. *Takeaway:* all of the Online Services [segment] are OTT services, not just the social media subcategory (see Figure 8).

- "Rich interactive apps and great devices along with fantastic content which telcos can never produce are being lapped up by subscribers...", *Takeaway:* rich content and hundreds of thousands of apps are not the core competences of mobile operators.

- "Mobile operators have suddenly found themselves delineated to the Connectivity layer/segment of the Internet value chain whilst other players dominate other layers ... with OTTs sitting in a totally different segment (Online Services) ... there goes another myth: the different segments should be looked at by regulators differently", *Takeaway:* different segments of the IVC have different players, risks, opportunities and would have different policies and regulations to address any issues they face. Digital Economy policy makers and regulators have to contend with this new reality and fact.

Such takeaways and implications as above are not exhaustive, but clearly they are already profound enough. The last I mention above is the most profound, i.e. the IVC dictates that Digital Economy Policy makers, regulators and network operators need to understand the reality of different players in the different segments of the IVC having different risks/opportunities, and presenting different policy and regulatory challenges to them. This is at the core of the title to this book, *the Internet Value Chain – Insight and Guidance on Digital Economy Policy and Regulation.*

Let me return to my narrative. There is more, particularly with regard to externalities. In my Nwana (2019)[19] ITU contribution, I proceeded the above quote [that starts this Chapter] with the following:

> The reality is that consumers and citizens love the positive externalities of this new value chain. However, it must be acknowledged that it comes with many negative externalities too: increased cyberfrauds, the breakdown of the interconnection regime through bypasses enabled by IP, increased revenue/tax "leakages" (which irk Governments), content harms, fake news, data breaches, loss/lack of control by regulators of players in their markets and more. All of these are true. So regulators are not only still needed, but they have to regulate differently. The need to rethink telecoms/ICT regulation in our new world of the IP-based Internet value chain is clear, and it is already getting acute: OTTs are just one symptom of such much needed rethinking. Along with the positive externalities of the new value chain comes numerous negative ones too.

As with most things in life, the positive externalities of new innovations also come with many – if not more - negative ones too. The Digital Economy we all crave to power our economies has consequences.

2.2 A Typical PhD Thesis Study: introducing the Long Tail Theory

How do I introduce this esoteric concept called the long tail? Let me try. In the late 1980s I did doctorate in a *niche* and obscure topic in Artificial Intelligence (AI), and AI was already niche enough. To be fair most PhDs are by definition similarly niche and obscure. It was very hard in the 1980s and expensive to physically gather researchers, may be from twenty to thirty universities, across the entire world's geography interested in this same niche topic for a conference. This means *matching supply and demand* (i.e. the right researchers [demand] to the niche conference [i.e. supplier]) was both costly and vert inefficient. All the research journals and publications were practically in paper form only, and hence offline.

---

[19] *Ibid*

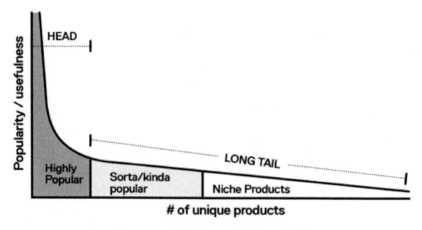

Figure 9 – The Long Tail Model[20]

We the researchers knew of each other's research interests only through people-based recommendations (no Google or Bing existed then). Writing (or *production costs*) of papers took much longer because your university library would typically *not* hold the niche journals which had published the papers you needed. The local university library would have to procure them from the few other super-libraries that did, like from the British Library in the case of the UK[21]. The papers we received submitted for reviews to our niche conferences and journals were all by snail mail post. When the reviews were done and journal issue finally produced, the *distribution costs* of copies of the journal issue to the few libraries that subscribed to them were very high in terms of postage and time. Subscription costs for the journals too were high.

2.2.1 The Long Tail Theory

Why do I bore you the reader with this sad 1980s pre-Internet story? One obvious reason is to show how the world has been changed with the Internet, because many of these challenges I highlight in italics in my story above are addressed with the Internet and the IVC. However, the more specific reason

---

[20] Source: <u>How will long tail affect the leisure branch? | by Jasper Dik | Medium</u> (last accessed August 2021)

[21] <u>The British Library - The British Library (bl.uk)</u>

is because I want to use this story to introduce (briefly) the Long Tail theory (see Figure 9) and its links to the IVC.

The essence of the long tail theory according to Wikipedia is "the retailing strategy of selling many unique items with relatively small quantities sold of each (the "long tail") - usually in addition to selling fewer popular items in large quantities (the "head")[22]". The long tail is depicted in Figure 9. Niche products or services like in my preceding story clearly fall in the long tail, whilst blockbuster mainstream products fall in the head. The rest fall in the "sorta/kinda popular" category.

The long tail theory in relation to marketing was popularised by Chris Anderson in his bestseller book The Long Tail (Anderson, 2006)[23]. In it, Anderson explains the drivers that lead to such long tails developing. I believe they are both very relevant and pertinent to the IVC (and to why the Internet has changed massively the costs in my earlier 1980s story).

So why do long tails develop? Anderson (2006) provides the following three drivers (he uses music and movies to exemplify the drivers):

i. *Democratisation of the means of production*: clearly, obscure movies and niche music would occupy the long tail of Figure 9 on platforms like YouTube. Such movies/music emerge because amateur producers today have access to cheap digital video cameras and editing software to home-produce their own music and movies, i.e. the *production* of such music and video content has been completely democratised.

ii. *Democratisation of distribution:* once the niche music/movies or books are produced, they can distributed to reach people on the Internet cheaply through platforms like Ebay, Itunes, Spotify, Amazon, Ebay, etc., i.e. *distribution* is democratised online too.

iii. *Bringing together & matching supply and demand:* the final driver is that of bringing together the demand and supply, and better still, even matching them via (i) search tools like (Google, Baidu, Bing)

---

[22] Long tail - Wikipedia - https://en.wikipedia.org/wiki/Long_tail (last accessed August 2021).

[23] Anderson, C. (2006), The Long Tail: the Future of Business is Selling Less of More, New York: Hyperion.

and/or (ii) through recommendation/advertising services like blogs, Craigslist, and others employing AI techniques.

I hope you the reader can realise how these three drivers have addressed the challenges of my 1980s PhD thesis story: (i) 1980s production costs of curating journal papers are so much lower with all or (at least) most reference papers/journals/books literally a few clicks away online (ii) distribution costs are even lower of any equivalent 1980s journals as many journals are now distributed online (iii) lastly, bringing together niche researchers (demand) to an organised niche conference (supply) are now so easy online using applications like Zoom and Microsoft Teams.

In summary, the long tail theory explains the genesis of much of the positive externalities of the Internet Value Chain (IVC), and as you would note soon the negative ones too.

2.2.2 What is the relevance and criticism of the Long Tail Theory and the IVC?

Anderson's three drivers above appear to be exactly at the core of key segments of the IVC and its positive externalities, and the negative ones too.

The democratisation of (i) digital production (ii) digital distribution and (iii) and the bringing together/matching of supply and demand – are core drivers to the *Online Services* segment of the IVC (see again Figure 1):

- Indeed, so much so that social and community sub-segments (of Online Services) have emerged along with their own specific 'marketplaces' such as Facebook marketplace, LinkedIn marketing solutions, etc. that *match supply and demand,* and more

- The Publishing sub-category of the IVC's Online Services segment provides the core democratisation of digital publishing services, i.e. both digital *production* and *distribution.*

- Whilst the E-retail (B2B/B2C), E-Travel. Video, Music, Gaming and Gambling subcategories *democratises distribution* of miscellaneous digital and physical products.

However, the IVC even offers more value-add services, even to niche businesses, due to the other segments. For example, *Enabling Technology and Services* offer payment platforms, advertising platforms, data analytics and more. *Connectivity* provides the connection of geographically dispersed users to millions of Internet backend servers boxes, whilst the *User Interface* provides the buying device and buying window via millions of apps.

Therefore, the IVC has enabled millions of businesses including long tail ones wherein, as noted in the last chapter - relatively small numbers of "geographically dispersed readers, viewers, or listeners with a common interest can now be aggregated to form a sizeable audience".

Both the *online and offline* world support hundreds of thousands of highly popular/middle popular products and services (see Figure 9), but only the *online* world (aided by the IVC) truly houses millions of long tail services/products.

The IVC's enabling of long tail Online Segment services/products is at the core of its numerous positive and negative externalities. As an example, User Generated Content (UGC) niche content on the Internet clearly occupies the long tail. However, whilst such UGC provides massive positive externalities as part of the *Social and Community* sub-category (of Online Services), e.g. through the benefits of WhatsApp groups/Facebook groups for example - many negative externalities like Misinformation, Fake News, Illegal Content or Harmful Content also permeate much UGC content too.

There are criticisms of the long tail theory from a marketing economics perspective when one tries to use the theory to base the digital marketing strategies of corporations. For example, whether more monies would be earned from the long tail products/services because of the IVC or whether the "head" highly popular products/services would continue to dominate. Frankly I am not qualified to enter such debates. I only want to limit myself to the obvious drivers of the benefits (or positive externalities) of the IVC and the concomitant negative externalities too, though I also mention some market failures and/or new concerns where relevant, e.g. new competition concerns that come with the new IVC.

2.3 Some Positive and Negative Externalities and Concerns of the IVC by Segment

This section would mostly concentrate on the negative externalities because this manuscript is unapologetically about Digital Economy policy making and regulation to address the *harms* and *risks* (e.g. fake news, misinformation, illegal content, etc.) and new *market failures* that come with the IVC over and above the traditional TMT ones. Such new harms, risks and market failures need to be *controlled,* or regulated.

About market failures, a very learned textbook on understanding regulation states "regulation's purpose is to achieve certain publicly desired results in circumstances where, for instance, the market would fail to yield these" (Baldwin *et al.*, 2012, p. 41).

However, also note that most regulation is ultimately all about *control:* controlling to pre-empt market failures, address markets when they fail and/or controlling to minimise/eliminate harms to consumers and citizens. As Baldwin *et al.* (2012) state in the first sentence of Chapter 6 of their text,

> regulation can be seen as being inherently about the control of risks, whether these relate to illnesses caused by exposure to carcinogens, inadequate utility services, or losses due to incompetent financial advice.

Numerous harms and risks come with the IVC.

2.3.1 Sources and Examples of Positive Externalities

I hope it is becoming clearer so far from the preceding sections of this chapter that most of the core benefits/externalities of the IVC [arguably more so for the Content Rights and Online Services segments mainly than for Connectivity and User Interfaces] derive from Anderson's long tail drivers of the democratisation of both digital production and distribution, and efficient matching suppliers to producers.

In the *offline* world, we were and still are

(i)   limited by geography in everything to producing only what those local to you would consume.

(ii)   limited by geography, by scarce shelf spaces that we have locally to store the inventory in local warehouses and limited by store shelves. For example, it is estimated that less than 10% of books published annually in English make it into a bookstore. I know this book you are reading will *not* get into a book store because it is niche.

(iii)   limited typically to only producing and stocking the highly popular "head" products (see Figure 9 again), ignoring the long tail ones.

(iv)   limited to physical products that you can touch and feel like books and CDs/vinyl records which go digital to e-books/audiobooks and digital music, and so on.

CHARACTERISTIC	INSTAGRAM	FACEBOOK	SNAPCHAT	PINTEREST	TWITTER
Viewing photos	77%	65%	64%	59%	42%
Watching videos	51%	46%	50%	21%	32%
Sharing content with everyone	45%	57%	46%	21%	32%
Sharing content one to one	31%	43%	45%	12%	20%
Networking	23%	33%	21%	10%	26%
News	18%	38%	17%	9%	56%
Finding/shopping for products	11%	15%	5%	47%	7%
Promoting my business	9%	7%	6%	5%	7%

Table 1 – Illustrating Positive Externalities: Social Media Activities by Social Media Users in the USA for February 2019

Source - Statista[24]

---

[24] U.S. social media activities by platform | Statista

In the *online* world of the IVC, most of these preceding geographical and physical (as in goods) limitations fall away. Digital bits of music, books and videos replace pre-1980s vinyl records, physical books and video tapes respectively. With reduced production, distribution and matching [demand and supply] costs, the Internet and the IVC is so much more efficient than anything offline can offer for numerous products and services (though not all). Hence Ebay, Amazon, ITunes, Netflix, YouTube etc. can now offer millions of products and services to millions or billions of consumers all the way from the "head" highly popular products to long tail niches ones.

Table 1 is from Statista's February 2019 report on what social media users do on five platforms: Instagram, Facebook, Snapchat, Pinterest and Twitter. I include this table to briefly illustrate the enormous positive externalities that these platforms provide that this book acknowledges but would take for granted to a large extent. Just reflect on the following:

- Photos that would (otherwise in the offline world) have been in physical book albums and perhaps seen only by those who physically visit your homes, or just lost in cupboards. Online [on these platforms], it is available for all your geographically dispersed friends and families to view. These platforms provide this incalculable positive benefits.

- Sharing content with everyone on these platforms provides daily, weekly, monthly, etc. updates on yourself/business to your friends/families and businesses. How do you even put a value on this?

- Watching videos online (absent traditional terrestrial and cable TV) has definitely exponentially increased the amount of audio-visual content watched/consumed by the average person globally - from a pitiful offline base to that of Facebook's active users of 2.85 Billion (as of July 2021). How does one put a value on this too? There is so much 'unpaid for' entertainment that citizens enjoy online.

- Sharing content one to one has now virtually replaced written letters. When is the last time you wrote one by hand? We can now communicate daily, monthly, weekly, hourly and more with practically anyone whether on email or any of these platforms. How much more value has been created to consumers and citizens with such unlimited person to person communications, anytime and from anywhere including from on your toilet seat?

- On news, I am personally perturbed that so many US citizens get their news from these platforms (as Table 1 suggests). However, they do. Yet again – how do you place a value on informing your citizens?

- Networking using these platforms is just invaluable. There are tens of millions[25] of Facebook groups used by individuals, businesses and brands up to end of July 2020. 1.8 Billion people use Facebook groups. There are more than 1 Billion Whatsapp Groups[26] being used networking families, businesses, Boards of companies, alumni students, church groups, etc. It is totally incalculable the *citizen value* that these platforms provide as networking platforms.

- Finding/shopping for products online is so much valuable to millions on citizens, and so is promoting their businesses.

I have pedantically gone through the above list to illustrate – just using social media apps – why the value that online platforms provide are truly incalculable. People truly value such services as *citizens* too beyond the value they accrue as consumers. It could be an educational health programme on Facebook or Twitter. How do I place a value on you using such health tips to your advantage? There is value to this *access* [on WhatsApp and Facebook groups], and how these their members feel *included*. What about these platforms helping provide more educated citizenry?

What is my point? Simply – the positive externalities of these platforms are truly immeasurable.

---

[25] 47 Facebook Stats That Matter to Marketers in 2021 (hootsuite.com)
[26] WhatsApp Statistics & Facts for 2021 | Usage, Revenue, History (fortunly.com)

2.3.2 Case Study Illustrating New Risks and Harms of the IVC: the 5G Covid-19 Quackery[27] – Confronting Misinformation and Fake News

Before we start looking at the negative externalities (in particular) that come with the IVC, please indulge me to attach this 5G-Covid19 quackery piece that I published on LinkedIn[28] just at the start of the covid pandemic's first lockdown in March/April 2020. It is included to show a real example of dangerous long tail user generated content (UGC) *misinform*ation (cf. Content Rights segment) that goes viral very quickly on social and community media platforms like Facebook, Twitter, Instagram, etc. (cf. Online Services segment).

The sheer scale, i.e. numbers of individuals online [which could be in the hundreds of thousands] user-generating similar misinformation and/or amplifying it in their millions within Social & Community media groups, is simply overwhelming.

It is said, a lie gets halfway round the world before the truth can put its boots on. Confronting it is so much harder when the truth [like my article below] takes 6x longer than fake news to be seen by 1500 people on Twitter. This is according to according to an MIT study published in the journal *Science*[29].

---

[27] (25) The 5G Covid-19 Quackery | LinkedIn - https://www.linkedin.com/pulse/5g-covid-19-quackery-h-sama-nwana/

[28] A Social and Community platform, part of the Online Services segment of the Internet value chain

[29] *Science*, DOI: 10.1126/science.aao4960 & Fake news travels six times faster than the truth on Twitter | New Scientist

The 5G Covid-19 Quackery

Published on April 5, 2020   ✏ Edit article | ⌁ View stats

H Sama Nwana
Managing Partner at Cenerva Ltd & Director at Atlantic Telecoms & Media   2 articles

I have been hearing this Covid-19 - 5G misinformation all week now. I wrote this as it appears to be "spreading" exponentially. It was a "rant" at one of my WhatsApp fora with some "Pastors" in it. Here was the essence of my rant ....

This 5G-corona virus is beyond conspiratorial nonsense which is typically benign, arguably like birds start falling from the skies because of mobile/cellular masts. This sort of 5G-corona nonsense is positively dangerous. I say this as I have heard on social media fora and elsewhere so-called Pastors and "experts" stand up and assert a proven biological virus a "hoax" and blame it on 5G airwaves radiation. And tell their congregations to act as business as normal and not to use modern phones. What quackery!!! Then the congregation infect one another and some - typically the older or sicker ones die. The key epicentre of the corona virus in South Korea is a church. The pastor has since apologised on his knees in South Korea.

These pastors, "experts" and others do not even know that we are reusing some of the same old frequencies we have been using for mobile communications for the past 20 years for the new 5G technologies - without their complaining. That is the frequencies that radio techniques use today like 2G voice, 3G and 4G LTE for data, that Verizon, AT&T, MTN, Vodafone, etc. use, are being reused too for newer 5G technologies.

5G is just newer and more efficient set of radio techniques, just like 4G was newer/more efficient than 3G, etc.

Like newer more efficient airplanes such as Airbus 350-900 or the Boeing 787-9 are more efficient than the old DC-10s now all phased out.

Guess what - these new efficient planes all use (or land on) the same runways - my equivalent of new radio technologies like 4G and 5G reusing the same old frequencies like 1800MHz, 3500MHz, etc, i.e. the same old runways. Yes some other frequencies are envisaged for 5G too like 26GHz, 40GHz, etc. - but these are hardly being used today.

Why would newer planes using the same old reliable runways be a problem? Just like why would new radio techniques using the same old frequencies then be a problem today? The runways are the same. The new planes are more efficient. The frequencies are the same. The new radio techniques are more efficient.

There is nothing unique about 5G to be dangerous to humans any more than 4G or 3G. And ICNIRP levels are always well regulated. Forget I wrote this.

Anybody linking a proven biological virus to radio frequency communications - should be completely ignored.

What bothers me more are the Pastors who stand in front of thousands of congregants and hundreds of thousands of live TV viewers and spew this. Or via their allegedly heavily listened too or watched "God-ordained" broadcasts and/or podcasts.

Churches have been liberalised in most countries - and many quack churches and pastors have emerged over the past 20 years. They need to be regulated and most shut down.

My own brother recently reminded me that he has been working with 5G equipment and devices for the past 5 years and more - well before covid-19. [Covid-19 denotes a class of corona virus discovered in 2019]. He also notes correctly that 5G is sometimes just a software upgrade on extant 4G equipment. Same equipment - software upgrade, and then it becomes an issue? Birds start falling from the skies? Mobile masts with the same equipment as before the software upgrade suddenly start creating biological human pandemic? So your laptop computer suddenly becomes a biological virus danger to you (and flies dropping from the ceilings) because its software is upgraded? My brother and his dozens of fellow engineers also never caught covid-19 in 2015, nor in 2016, nor in 2017, nor in 2018, nor in 2019 when covid-19 broke out. Then quacks believe it is a problem in 2020. I am also equally perturbed by so called experts (who claim to have worked for mobile companies) and or engineers peddling much nonsense too about 5G!

If there is one silver lining I am seeing so far - experts and expertise are on their way back to being respected.

President Trump had to back down recently to expertise of Drs Tony Fauci and Deborah Birx and agree to effectively closing down the USA for the full month of April 2020. Not trust his "instincts" or "guts".

Boris Johnson succeeded in taking the UK out of the EU 28 based on similar quackery - his key minister Michael Gove MP said "people in this country have had enough of experts" during the Brexit debates.

Now they have both succumbed to experts on the covid-19 virus following their advice at every turn (since U.K. citizens are dying alarmingly) with Boris Johnson himself literally falling sick to the virus.

Let's hear less from quacks for a change. Ignore quackery! Embrace expertise.

Jeff Rich is credited with this brainy quote: "if you think education is expensive, try ignorance". I never fully appreciated it. In this case, these "experts" and/or pastors' ignorance kill - literally - when they congregate innocent people with covid-19 sick or asymptomatics amongst them.

I hope there is a world-wide legacy after the covid-19 crisis is over in a post 2020 covid-19 era: that of re-embracing experts and expertise.

2.3.3 Content Rights Segment Externalities and other New Concerns

The key positive externalities of this segment [beyond the key sources of positive externality of Section 2.3.1] is in the sheer unlimited content that come with the Content rights segment, i.e. premium rights content, even more professional content and the incredibly voluminous user-generated content available online. Consumers and citizens truly have virtually unlimited choice of miscellaneous content.

However, there is arguably much more categories of harms/risks that come with this Content Rights segment too. We have seen one example of a Content Rights negative externality in the previous section - *misinformation* on covid19 and 5G. What are the others? The simple answer is that there are numerous, and many are much worse. I penned this sub-section on content rights externalities on Friday 13th August 2021, the day ex-USA President Donald J Trump was allegedly going to be reinstated to the US Presidency.

3 In 10 Republicans Believe Wacky Conspiracy Theory Trump Will Be 'Reinstated' As President This Year, Poll Shows

Jemima McEvoy Forbes Staff
Business
I'm a British-born reporter covering breaking news for Forbes.

Follow

Image 2 – The Trump Reinstation Disinformation (Source – Forbes[1])

Well this reinstatement of Trump of President Biden obviously did not happen - it was not only *misinformation*, it was *disinformation*. As Wikipedia notes, misinformation is false, inaccurate or misleading information communicated regardless of an *intention* to deceive, including false rumours. Disinformation – on the other hand – is a subset of misinformation that is *deliberately* designed to be deceptive.

Image 2 (the Trump reinstatement misinformation) was obvious disinformation from many well-placed senior Republicans close to former President Trump, and the latter himself did or said nothing to disavow and correct this.

Recall the Content Rights segment of the IVC covers premium rights, professional content and USG. Misinformation such at the 5G-Covid quackery and disinformation such as the Trump reinstatement typically start online as long tail user-generated misinformation or disinformation content – indeed a *conspiracy theory* - which gets propagated exponentially within the Online Services segment of the value chain to the extent. Such a large

---

[1] 3 In 10 Republicans Believe Wacky Conspiracy Theory Trump Will Be 'Reinstated' As President This Year, Poll Shows (forbes.com) (last accessed August 2021)

43

percentage of Republicans (30%) believing this conspiracy theory has already proven very dangerous leading to the infamous 6th January 2021 insurrection against the US Capitol to "stop the steal" (alleging President Trump won the 2020 US elections) – yet another massive disinformation incredulously promoted by former President Trump himself and other senior Republicans including top senators and congressmen.

It gets even worse than just disinformation, with even deadlier outcomes from conspiracy theories leading not only to deaths at the Capitol on January 6th 2021, but even to a parent killing his kids over QAnon[2] conspiratorial thinking. This illustrates some of the true scale of the risks of disinformation online – a parent murdering his own children!

I tabulate some of such emerging harms/risks. Table 2 depicts a non-exhaustive list of negative externalities of the Content Rights segment of the IVC.

Content Rights Externality	Brief Definition	Example(s)/Commentary
Misinformation	Wikipedia notes misinformation is false, inaccurate or misleading information communicated regardless of an intention to deceive, including false rumours. Misinformation is usually "factually false"	• The 5G-Covid19 Quackery - see previous subsection)

---

[2] Wikipedia describes QAnon as a disproven far-right conspiracy theory that alleges a cabal of Satanic, cannibalistic paedophiles operating a global child sex trafficking ring that conspired against former President Trump during his time in office. QAnon motos were used at Trump rallies and the FBI later published a report calling QAnon a potential source of domestic terrorism. QAnon - Wikipedia

Disinformation	Disinformation – on the other hand – is a subset of misinformation that is *deliberately* designed to be deceptive (Wikipedia).	• Trump Reinstatement (see Image 2 above) • "Stop the Steal": the deep roots of Trump's 'voter fraud' strategy (BBC)[3]
Political Misinformation	Kuklinski *et al.* (2000) defines this as incorrect, but confidently held, political beliefs (p. 792) which sometimes leads to large segments of the public being misinformed in the same direction through shared misperceptions that can systematically bias collective opinion. Bode & Vraga (2015, p. 621) notes that the American political system currently "abounds" with such misinformation.	As we saw in the USA on 6th January 2021, such misinformed people can take political action based on the political misinformation – leading to the 'Stop the Steal' insurrection[4].

---

[3] 'Stop the steal': The deep roots of Trump's 'voter fraud' strategy - BBC News - https://www.bbc.co.uk/news/blogs-trending-55009950 (last accessed August 2021)

[4] *Ibid.*

| Conspiratorial thinking/theories and Rumours | Wikipedia defines a conspiracy theory as an explanation for a situation or event that involves a conspiracy by sinister and powerful groups, often political in motivation, when other explanations are more probable. The consequences of conspiracy theories have proven and continue to prove deadly.

As quoted in Jerit & Zhao (2020), "Berinsky (2017, pp. 242–43) defines rumors as "statements that lack specific standards of evidence" but that gain credibility "through widespread social transmission" ... | • "California dad killed his kids over QAnon and 'serpent DNA' conspiracy theories, Feds claim[6]". Clearly, this is just desperately sad.

• The 'Birther' conspiracy theory that former US President Barack Obama was born in Kenya when he was indeed born in Hawaii, USA. Clearly political in motivation questioning Obama's citizenship to undermine him as not qualified to be President of the USA by falsely claiming he was not born in the USA. Former President Trump peddled this conspiracy theory for years, which arguably contributed to his success to ascend to the Presidency of the most powerful nation on earth. How is this counteracted in democracies?

• QAnon conspiracy theory that alleges Trump is fighting against a cabal of child sex- |

---

[6] California dad killed his kids over QAnon and 'serpent DNA' conspiracy theories, feds claim (nbcnews.com) - https://www.nbcnews.com/news/us-news/california-dad-killed-his-kids-over-qanon-serpent-dna-conspiracy-n1276611 (last accessed August 2021)

	Rumors are not "warranted beliefs" in the sense of being supported by scientific or expert opinion, but as Flynn et al. (2017, p. 129) point out, they occasionally turn out to be true. This characteristic distinguishes rumors from misinformation"[5]	abusing and Satan-worshipping Democrats[7] • See Disinformation examples earlier
Fake News	Misleading information presented as "news". This term "fake news" is also been lazily used to refer to 'misinformation', 'disinformation', parody, "unfavourable coverage", etc. All news that Former President Trump	• Pope Francis endorses Donald Trump[8]. This was clear false from the start.

[5] Political Misinformation | Annual Review of Political Science (annualreviews.org) - https://www.annualreviews.org/doi/10.1146/annurev-polisci-050718-032814#abstractSection (last accessed August 2021)

[7] Roose, Kevin (4 March 2021). "What Is QAnon, the Viral Pro-Trump Conspiracy Theory?". *The New York Times - https://www.nytimes.com/article/what-is-qanon.html (last accessed August 2021)*

[8] Pope Francis Archives - FactCheck.org (last accessed August 2021)

	saw as "unfavourable" was branded "fake news" by him.	
"Breaking News" Risks	Publishing news increasing seems to be valuing *speed* of news over the underlying *content* of the news. The risks may be low on trusted/branded channels like the BBC or CNN. However, should we trust breaking news on social media?	According to an American Press Association 2016 study, half of Americans get news on social media, but most have a high degree of scepticism[9].
Hate Speech/Inciting violence	Whilst Free speech is much desired and protected in many countries, hate speech online is now rife. Hate speech refers to any communication which is abusive or threatening, is intended to harass,	Examples include Speeches or expressions "that denigrates a person or persons on the basis of (alleged) membership in a social group identified by attributes such as race, ethnicity, gender, sexual orientation, religion, age, physical or mental disability, and others"[10].

---

[9] What makes people trust and rely on news (americanpressinstitute.org) - https://www.americanpressinstitute.org/publications/reports/survey-research/trust-news/single-page/ (last accessed August 2021)

[10] Hate speech | Britannica - https://www.britannica.com/topic/hate-speech (last accessed August 2021)

	alarm or distress someone (Wikipedia) – and this is typically outlawed offline and increasingly online too. Hate speech sometimes sadly results in violence against some demographics of the population.	
Deepfakes	Synthetic media in which a person in an existing video is replaced with someone's likeness (Wikipedia).	Fake Obama created using AI tools to make phoney President Obama speeches[11]. Even videos now need to be fact-checked.
Illegal Content	Unlawful content as in explicitly prohibited by law. By definition, illegal content will vary from country to country.	In most countries, child sexual abuse content would be illegal, and it abounds as USG content online.
Harmful (and sometimes Legal) Content & other	This refers to any content online that is causes a person	UK Teenager Molly Russell, 14, killed herself in 2017 after seeing graphic images of

---

[11] Fake Obama created using AI tool to make phoney speeches - BBC News - https://www.bbc.co.uk/news/av/technology-40598465 (last accessed August 2021)

Social Ills	distress and/or harm. A huge amount of content online would fall under this category, and is almost certainly both subjective and culturally-sensitive.	self-harm and suicide on Instagram (source BBC)[12] According to the UK Safer Internet Centre operated by SWGfL[13], harmful content and social ills include (i) online abuse (ii) bullying or harassment (iii) threats (iv) impersonation (v) unwanted sexual advances (not image based) (vi) violent content (vii) self-harm or suicide content and (viii) pornographic content.
Pornography	Pornography is the undisputed lead harmful content class on the Internet. According to Webroot Smarter Cybersecurity - "Pornography hurts adults, children, couples, families, and society. Among adolescents, pornography hinders the development of a	Similarly, according to Webroot Smarter Cybersecurity[15], 35% of all internet downloads are related to pornography. 34% of internet users have experienced unwanted exposure to pornographic content through ads, pop up ads, misdirected links or emails. One-third of porn viewers are women.

---

[12] Molly Russell: Social media users 'at risk' over self-harm inquest delay - BBC News - https://www.bbc.co.uk/news/uk-england-london-55986728 (last accessed August 2021)

[13] Report Harmful Content | SWGfL - https://swgfl.org.uk/services/report-harmful-content/ (last accessed August 2021)

[15] Ibid.

	healthy sexuality, and among adults, it distorts sexual attitudes and social realities. In families, pornography use leads to marital dissatisfaction, infidelity, separation, and divorce"[14]	
Cyber-bullying [Cyberthreaths]	Cyber-bullying is another pernicious form of online bullying involving the use of electronic communications to bully a person by sending messages of an intimidating or threatening nature.	According to the UK National bullying Helpline, cyberbullying can include: • Emailing or texting you with threatening or intimidating remarks • Mobbing (a group or gang that target you) • Harassing you repeatedly • Intimidation and blackmail • Stalking you on-line and continually harassing you • Posting embarrassing or humiliating images or video's without your consent • Posting your private details on-line without consent

---

[14] Internet Pornography by the Numbers: A Significant Threat to Society | Webroot - https://www.webroot.com/gb/en/resources/tips-articles/internet-pornography-by-the-numbers#:~:text=35%25%20of%20all%20internet%20downloads,of%20porn%20viewers%20are%20women.

		• General Bullying or Stalking
		• Grooming (enticing or goading you on-line to self-harm or commit a crime)
		• Setting up a false profile, Identity fraud or identity theft
		• Using gaming sites to attack or bully you
		• Theft, Fraud or deception over the internet
Decreased trust in media sources and Government	This refers to the general trend of the scepticism of online information – due to all the misinformation and disinformation – also leading the decreased trust in formerly trusted sources like the BBC, Bloomberg and even Government. There is an increasing trend with the younger audiences getting their news online	Governments are struggling to fight off disinformation and misinformation about Covid19 vaccines across many countries in the world. E.g. see the EU's fight against corona virus disinformation[16] Part of the challenge here is that is captured in the following conclusion from the reputable UK media regulator Ofcom's detailed review of BBC news and current affairs: "Although the BBC's online news services currently reach a broad audience, our work suggests that its heavier online users

[16] Tackling coronavirus disinformation | European Commission (europa.eu) - https://ec.europa.eu/info/live-work-travel-eu/coronavirus-response/fighting-disinformation/tackling-coronavirus-disinformation_en (last accessed August 2021)

	which is arguably less trustworthy.	are generally those in older age groups who are already well served by BBC television and radio, rather than the younger audiences who are turning away from those platforms. As more people rely on social media and aggregator platforms for news, the BBC's online content needs to do more to stand out – or risk losing its reputation and status as a trusted voice"[17]
Election Risks/Rules and Botnets & Democracy	This covers issues including how political adverts are handled and the integrity of election processes, e.g. the role of bots (or automated accounts) 'creating' content online.	US intelligence authorities have concluded in the Muller Report that Russia mounted an assault on the 2016 US election campaign across several fronts including social media, with the intention of helping Donald Trump and harming Hilary Clinton, his Democratic opponent. Twitter told the US Congress in October 2018 that it had discovered 36,746 Russian accounts that posted *automated* material about the US election, and that Russian state operatives were behind at least 2,752. Twitter later revised the latter number to

---

[17] Review of BBC news and current affairs (ofcom.org.uk) - https://www.ofcom.org.uk/__data/assets/pdf_file/0025/173734/bbc-news-review.pdf (last accessed August 2021)

		more than 3,800 accounts that had been traced back to Russian state operatives attacking Hillary Clinton and her performances in the presidential debates[18]. The harm to democratic elections could be huge.
Bad Social Norms/Offensive Language	Offline social bads, norms and etiquettes are being eroded online, which in turn erodes offline social bads or ills, norms/etiquettes, particularly amongst the younger generations.	Examples includes sexting, offensive language, terrorism online going offline, child sex abusers grooming children online and harming them offline and so much more not worth elaborating on here.
Amplified conspiracy, rumours and misinformation theories	It is said, a lie gets halfway round the world before the truth can put its boots on. This is definitely true on many social and communication platforms online	The earlier example from Twitter is very apposite here. Factual news on Twitter takes 6x longer than fake news to be seen by 1500 people on Twitter. This is according to according to an MIT study published in the journal *Science*[19].
Offense harms	Defining Offensive online boundaries is	

[18] Twitter admits far more Russian bots posted on election than it had disclosed | Twitter | The Guardian

[19] *Science*, DOI: 10.1126/science.aao4960 & Fake news travels six times faster than the truth on Twitter | New Scientist

	non-trivial – what content is deemed appropriate and not appropriate online?	
Copyright Content Infringements	It is so easy to infringe copyright in the online world compared to the offline world. According to Investopedia "Copyright infringement is the use or production of copyright-protected material without the permission of copyright holder. Copyright infringement means that the rights afforded to the copyright holder, such as the exclusive use of a work for a set period of time, are being breached by a third party. Music and movies are two of the most well-known forms of entertainment	• Recording a film in a movie theatre • Using someone else's content on YouTube without permission • Using copyrighted Images (e.g. from Google Images on your website without purchasing the rights • Using a Music major's copyrighted songs • Streaming a football match live using technologies like Periscope and Meerkat[21] or equivalents • Piracy • Neighbouring rights – or 'related rights' closely related to copyright.

---

[21] What do Periscope and Meerkat mean for broadcasting copyright? | Twitter | The Guardian - https://www.theguardian.com/technology/2015/may/11/periscope-meerkat-broadcast-copyright-premier-league

	that suffer from significant amounts of copyright infringement"[20]	
Intellectual Property Rights (IPR) Infringements	As with Copyright, the way intellectual property rights (IPR) are used, accessed and exploited has evolved online has created severe challenges for rights-holders seeking to protect their rights online.	• E.g. patents – it is unlawful to make, use, sell, resell, rent out or supply patented objects or processes without licence from patent holder. However, soft patents are easily infringed online. • Trademarks used by entrepreneurs to distinguish their products or services • Design rights, e.g. wallpaper patterns, design of household items like clocks – however, these designs must first be registered. • Database rights, e.g. UK Statistic Agency Database
Violent/Disturbing or Graphic Content	This refers depictions of especially brutal, vivid and realistic acts of violence in visual media such as film, TV and video games. It may be	• Horror/action films • Graphic music videos • Violent video games • Graphic pornography • Etc.

---

[20] Copyright Infringement (investopedia.com) -
https://www.investopedia.com/terms/c/copyright-infringement.asp (last accessed August 2021).

	real, simulated live action or animated (Wikipedia). "Graphic" usually means explicit.	

Table 2 —Non-Exhaustive List of Negative Externalities of the Content Rights Segment of the IVC

The above table (Table 2) is not meant to be exhaustive, but hopefully captures a good representative list of the many evolving Content Rights segment harms/risks.

2.3.3.1 Content Rights: Brief View on Consolidation, Competition and Cultural Concerns

Recall again the Content Rights segment covers (i) premium rights content, (ii) professional content and the (iii) incredibly voluminous user-generated content (USG) available online.

Arguably most of the harms of Table 2 relate to the USG category, though admittedly harms around IPR and copyright may be more applicable to premium rights and professional content categories in a more profound way.

Returning to traditional media for a moment, whilst linear television is at a crossroads with the rise and rise of non-linear SVOD services, there are some key trends that very respected media researchers like Augusto Pretta of IT Media Consulting see [even within traditional offline media] that derive from the Internet value chain (IVC) going forward[22]:

1. Some clear consolidations are happening involving significant Content Rights segment actors and Connectivity sector players which evidently derive from the new IVC as seen in Figure 10: AT&T (Connectivity segment) and Time Warner Cable (Premium

---

[22] Augusto Pretta - PowerPoint Presentation (iicom.org) - https://www.iicom.org/wp-content/uploads/Day-1-Augusto-Preta-IT-Media-Consulting.pdf

Content Rights segment) transaction with Connectivity player in the lead; Walt Disney and 21ˢᵗ Century Fox transaction (both of Content Rights segment); and Comcast (Content Rights segment) and Sky (Content Rights/Connectivity) transaction. This is really key.

2. Linear television is at a crossroads

3. Non-linear services (VOD) are growing and becoming popular with Subscription VOD (SVOD) revenues growing very fast a compound annual growth rate of 15% over the last several years.

4. OTT is the new arena for global Content Rights competition (see Figure 11).

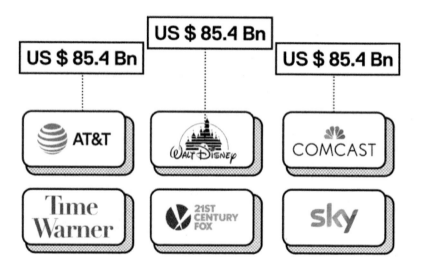

Figure 10 – Consolidations taking place *across* of the IVC *because* of the IVC

Source (Augusto Pretta, 2019, IT Media Consulting[23])

These trends that Augusto Pretta highlights are very clear to me at least. The growing and increasingly popular SVOD segment in Europe is already very

---

[23] *Ibid.*

concentrated as can be seen in Figure 11b dominated by Netflix and Amazon. This potentially is a *competition concern.*

Figure 11a shows mostly American companies leading on Content rights production and acquisition. From a *cultural and competition* perspective, this is hardly healthy even from the European Content Rights segment vantage point, yet alone from the vantage points of African countries, Asian countries, India, Caribbean and elsewhere. Augusto Pretta points out the need for three things for Europe: (i) more concentrated investments in original and local content (ii) partnerships between EU broadcasters and pay-TV operators and (iii) regulations on European content quota and non-linear services (VOD) obligations. It may be the case that other regions and other major content rights producing countries such India (Bollywood) and Nigeria (Nollywood) may have to adopt similar Content Rights strategies. *Cultural concerns* are looming even larger than ever with the Content Rights segment of the IVC.

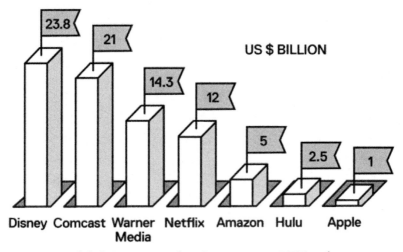

Figure 11a – Global Content Rights Competition: OTT is the new arena
Content production/acquisition by major SVOD companies
Source (Augusto Pretta, 2019, IT Media Consulting[24])

---

[24] *Ibid.*

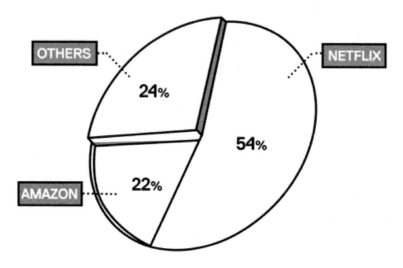

EUROPEAN SVOD MARKET SHARE (SUBSCRIBERS)

OTHERS · · · · · · 24%

NETFLIX

54%

AMAZON · · · · · · 22%

Figure 11b – Global Content Rights Competition: OTT is the new arena
Source (Augusto Pretta, 2019, IT Media Consulting[25])

2.3.3.2 The Emerging Roles of Big Data and AI by other Players in order to compete with Emerging Future Content Behemoths

Augusto Pretta clearly highlights in his presentation[26] from which I borrowed Figure 10 how the consolidations in the picture create data and content packages (via quad plays across voice, data, fixed, mobile Internet access and video/TV). However, he also highlights the greater role of Big Data and Artificial Intelligence in the identification and servicing of subscribers. This means shifting from a B2B strategy to a direct to consumer offering in order to compete with emerging future content behemoths like Netflix and Amazon (see Figure 11b).

Here is a context where Big Data and AI would arguably play very positive roles for competition, thereby generating consumer and citizen positive

---

[25] *Ibid.*

[26] *Ibid.*

externalities. We will see contexts later where Big Data and AI present concerns negative and/or ethical concerns.

2.3.4 Online Services Segment Externalities and New Concerns

Online Services is clearly the biggest segment of the IVC by segment market size, and would undoubtedly host the biggest harms too by impact size. The benefits of this segment are obvious from the IVC itself of Figure 1: numerous e-Retail services that users have access too, numerous e-travel services, numerous video and music services, numerous streaming services, numerous gaming/gambling services, numerous publishing services, numerous social & community/social media services, numerous Information and reference services (e.g. Wikipedia, Google Maps, etc.), key search services and numerous cloud services.

Online users are truly spoiled for choice online thanks to the services offered by the Online Services segment. Practically all of these Online services are OTT services too, not just the Social and Community services category of Figure 1.

The positive benefits that emanate from the sub-categories of IVC's Online Services segment are truly humongous. Just consider the contributions of E-retail from Ebay, Alibaba, Amazon, etc. The latter (Amazon) has innovated Online services for decades leading to its founder Jeff Bezos ascending to the richest billionaire in the world. Amazon has created so many efficiencies across the value chains of so many other sectors: books, B2B retail, B2C retail, logistics and more. The travel procurement sector is now mostly online, i.e. E-travel. Video and music are similarly mostly online on YouTube, Netflix, Spotify and more. Later, Figure 14 shows the absolute scale of active users on platforms like Facebook, YouTube, WhatsApp, Facebook Messenger and WeChat. Like noted earlier with all segments of the IVC, this book largely takes their positive externalities for granted and not dwell on them much.

Therefore, Table 3 depicts a non-exhaustive list of *negative* externalities of the Online Services segment of the IVC commencing with the dark/deep web – the part of the online web not indexed by web search engines. I have grouped some of the harms 'logically' for brevity.

Online Services Externality	Brief Definition	Example(s)/Commentary
Dark and Deep web vs. Open Web	Most people would not realise there is significant part of the online web not indexed at all (and hence not searchable) by web search engines like Google, Baidu and Bing. Wikipedia defines the *dark web*[27] as the WWW content that exists on 'overlay networks' that use the Internet but require specific software, configurations and authorisations to access, i.e. it is *not* the open web most know. Through the dark web, private computer networks communicate and transact without divulging identifying information such as the users location or identity. The dark web itself is part of	• Users of the dark web regularly refer to regular web as Clearnet because it is unencrypted. • Dark web networks include Tor[28], Invisible Internet Project (I2P)[29] and numerous more. • Numerous negative externalities of the online world emanate from the dark and deep webs including (i) ransomware attacks (ii) Botnets (iii) Hacking groups and services (iv) Illegal and child pornography (v) Terrorism and violence (vi) illicit arms sales (vii) illicit drugs (viii) all sorts of frauds, violence and criminal transactions/black markets (ix) illicit crypto-markets using cryptocurrencies like Bitcoin for money laundering. • From the just preceding rap sheet, Governments are rightly concerned about the dark web being a haven of criminality, but interestingly others like Ghappour (2017) argue that the dark web promotes civil liberties including "free speech, privacy and anonymity". It may at first glance read as bizarre, but it is a powerful argument and illustrates clearly the non-triviality of "regulating" Online harms – do we want them to move to the dark web? It seems there is a 'macabre' balance to be struck here.

---

[27] Dark web - Wikipedia

[28] Tor (network) - Wikipedia

[29] I2P - Wikipedia

	the *deep web*, the part of the WWW not indexed by web search engines.	
Cybercrime	This simply refers to criminal activities carried out online, i.e. thanks to the Online services segment of the Internet (and not necessarily inside the dark/deep web either). These criminal activities use computers or the Internet.	• There are dozens of types of cybercrimes covering (i) frauds (ii) identity theft (iii) Phishing scams (iv) viruses (v) Revenge porn (vi) Online hate crime (vii) Grooming (viii) Stalking (ix) Holiday fraud (x) Dating fraud (xi) Bullying (xii) Online fanaticism and extremism (xiii) Child sexual exploitation (xiv) terrorism (xv) data breaches for sale – this list just goes on and on and on.
Online Terrorism streamed live, Cyberterrorism & Alt-right Extremism	"Cyberterrorism is the use of the Internet to conduct violent acts that result in, or threaten, the loss of life or significant bodily harm, in order to achieve political or ideological gains through threat and intimidation. It is also sometimes considered an act of Internet terrorism where terrorist activities, including acts of deliberate, large-scale disruption of computer networks,	• Christchurch (New Zealand) mosque shootings live-streamed on Facebook[31]: An alleged white supremacist, Australian Harrison Tarrant, orchestrated two consecutive mass shootings at mosques in a terrorist attack wherein he live streamed the first shooting on Facebook on 15th March 2019. In March 2020, he pleaded guilty to 51 murders and 40 attempted murders. Facebook announced curbs on its streaming feature for some time after the shootings and had to remove 1.5 million copies of the massacre video[32] from the platform running weeks after the event. • The FBI Chief has actually referred to the riots at the US Capitol as "domestic terrorism"[33]. He also noted much of this was fomented online. • Online-inspired terrorism is obviously a major concern for Intelligence agencies the

---

[31] Christchurch mosque shootings - Wikipedia

[32] Christchurch attacks: Facebook curbs Live feature - BBC News (last accessed August 2021)

[33] Capitol riot 'inspiration for extremism', FBI boss warns - BBC News

	especially of personal computers attached to the Internet by means of tools such as computer viruses, computer worms, phishing, and other malicious software and hardware methods and programming scripts[30]" (Wikipedia).	world over. From Al-Qaeda using the Internet to communicate with supporters and recruiting new members (Worth, 2016); to financial frauds like "*600 million gone: the biggest crypto theft in history*[34]"; to dark web originated attacks; to sabotaging Critical National Infrastructures (CNI) like electricity grids which the UK *House of Commons warns is a matter of 'when, not it*[35]'; etc
Privacy Harms, Data Protection, Fraud and Identity Theft, Private information made public & People pretending to other people	I really like this Wikipedia definition of Privacy: "the ability of an individual or group to seclude themselves or information about themselves, and thereby express themselves selectively[36]". Hence, it is a massive invasion of an individual's privacy when their information is stolen. Privacy is a fundamental human	• Identity Theft: Even major celebrities like Tiger Woods, Oprah Winfrey, Steven Spielberg, Will Smith and more have fallen prey to identity theft[37]. • Data Breaches: U. S. approve $5B Facebook settlement over privacy issues[38] - Facebook fined for violating consumers' privacy rights. Facebook was forced by US regulator FTC to expand its privacy protections across Facebook itself, Instagram and WhatsApp – which includes protections of information such as individual user's phone numbers. • Exposing Personal Information: In September 2017, Equifax announced a data breach which had exposed the personal information of 147 million people and was

---

[30] Cyberterrorism - Wikipedia

[34] Poly Network hack: Some $600 million stolen in biggest crypto theft in history - CNN - https://edition.cnn.com/2021/08/11/tech/crypto-hack/index.html (last accessed August 2021)

[35] A major cyber attack on the UK is a matter of 'when, not if' (shorthandstories.com) (last accessed August 2021)

[36] Privacy - Wikipedia

[37] 5 Famous People Who've Had Their Identities Stolen - CardRates.com - https://www.cardrates.com/news/famous-people-whove-had-their-identities-stolen/ (last accessed August 2021)

[38] Facebook fine: FTC fines company $5 billion for privacy violations (usatoday.com)

	right – and a *quid pro quo* to this maxim is that organisations who hold individuals' private information must not only guard their privacies, but also only use the data ethically.	fined at least US $425M to help people affected by the breach[39]. • Jennifer Lawrence denounces nude photos hack as 'sex crime'[40]
Online Child Sexual Exploitation, Cyber-Grooming, Cyber-Paedophilia, Child sexual abuse images & Cyberstalking	This for me is arguably one of the most insidious - if not the most insidious - criminal activities facilitated by the Online Services segment of the IVC. It is also known as cyber-molestation due to its virtual, distanced and anonymous nature according to Wikipedia. It can both result in face to face consequences in the form of statutory rape, forcible sexual assaults, harassment, etc. or online cyber-bullying, grooming and sexual abuse. The child sexual abuse images online are particularly some of the most gruesome images	• Andrew Puddephatt – Chair of the Internet Watch Foundation (IWF) in the UK wrote of this issue about the UK alone "It was sobering for me to hear from the specialist police unit that deals with child sexual exploitation that, in their estimate, something in the region of 100,000 men in the UK try to access images of children being sexually abused. We all need to recognise the scale of this problem and the unpleasant fact that where there is demand there will always be supply … last year our analysts found over 100,000 URLs of children being sexually abused. We should remember that each URL can contain hundreds, if not thousands of images"[41]. I have had to read many reports, books and papers in my time – this one ranks as one of the most sobering. • In the UK, sex abuse between children has doubled in two years[42]. I personally truly regret this negative externality which involves children.

---

[39] Equifax Data Breach Settlement | Federal Trade Commission (ftc.gov) (last accessed August 2021)

[40] Jennifer Lawrence denounces nude photos hack as 'sex crime' | Jennifer Lawrence | The Guardian

[41] Once upon a year - IWF Annual Report 2018.pdf (last accessed August 2021).

[42] Reports of sex abuse between children double in two years - BBC News

	which many Police forces (who investigate cybercrimes) claim to have ever seen.	
Extremism and radicalisation	"Extremism is possible in any ideology, including (but not limited to) politics and religion. Extremism can affect mental well-being, amplify hostility, and threaten democratic debate"[43] (UK Parliament). Extremism and radicalization just seem to go with the online segment of the value chain. Having a handful of extremists in your town may not be much of an issue. However, aggregating geographically dispersed creators, readers, viewers, or listeners with a common interest in some extremist or fanatical belief/view to form a sizeable audience online – easily leads to dangerous scenarios, even offline on the	"Extremist content may be found on mainstream sites and 'alt-tech' platforms that have been created or co-opted for the unconventional needs of specific users. The Internet may facilitate extremism in multiple ways, including recruitment, socialisation and mobilisation. Countering online extremism requires a coordinated approach. Methods include content removal and social interventions."[44]

[43] POST-PN-0622.pdf (parliament.uk) - https://researchbriefings.files.parliament.uk/documents/POST-PN-0622/POST-PN-0622.pdf

[44] Ibid.

	streets. The long tail effect easily drives such online extremism and radicalisation.	
Spam emails	Email spam or junk mail is just rife in all our e-mail boxes, completely unsolicited messages sent in bulk by e-mail.	• According to the respected Statista, an incredible 28.5% of total e-mail worldwide traffic in 2019 was spam traffic, down from 59.8% in 2016[45]. Both these numbers are eyewatering. • "About 14.5 billion spam emails are sent every day… 3.36% of all spam is some form of advertising … Spammers receive 1 reply for every 12,500,000 emails sent… Spam earns around $7,000 per day" (Source: [46])
Unwelcome Friend Requests, Trolling & Cyberbullying	Most of us on online social media would have received requests from people that we do not want to be online friends with. The problem is that it is often difficult to reject their friend requests without them knowing. An online troll is an individual who posts insulting, insincere, threatening or off-topic contributions to an online community, typically on social media, to provoke other readers to weigh in with similar posts	• "Trolling is a phenomenon that has swept across websites in recent years. Online forums, Facebook pages and newspaper comment forms are bombarded with insults, provocations or threats. Supporters argue it is about humour, mischief and freedom of speech. But for many, the ferocity and personal nature of the abuse verges on hate speech." (Source BBC News[47])

---

[45] • Spam e-mail traffic share 2019 | Statista

[46] 15 Outrageous Email Spam Statistics that Still Ring True in 2018 | Propeller CRM Blog

[47] Trolling: Who does it and why? - BBC News - https://www.bbc.co.uk/news/magazine-14898564 (last accessed August 2021)

	and manipulate others' perceptions of the trolled individual. Some may argue trolling is humour and freedom of speech, but it is very close many-a-time to hate speech and/or cyberbullying.	
Social and Community Media Harms	There are many, and I like this recent May 2021 post on "20 Reasons Not to Use Social Media"[48] by UK citizen Paul Goodman who lives in Florida. It aptly covers most of the potential social media harms.	Paul Goodman lists his 20 reasons not to use social media[49] as (alleged social and community media harms) including: a) Scams and Deception b) Privacy Issues c) Over-promotion and Spam d) Incorrect Information e) Echo Chamber f) Information Overload g) Time-Waster h) Bullying, Stalking, and Harassment i) Terrorism and Hate Groups j) Social Disconnect and Depression k) Low Self-Esteem l) Superficial Friends m) Unwelcome Friend Requests n) Data Safety o) Political Manipulation p) Cheating Tool q) Copyright Issues r) Permanent Problems s) Sexual Issues t) Disproportionate Power

---

[48] 20 Reasons Not to Use Social Media - Soapboxie - https://soapboxie.com/social-issues/Reasons-Not-to-Use-Social-Media (last accessed August 2021).

[49] *Ibid.*

		He examines each of the above social media downsides in his article.
Internet Addiction (spending too much time online)	Internet addiction is an umbrella term that refers to the compulsive need to spend a great deal of time on the online. And this is usually to the point where relationships, family work and health are allowed to suffer which may lead to medical issues including mental disorders. Looking at the Pew Research data on the right tells us that there is a real Internet Addiction problem that needs to be addressed too – with both Policy and Regulation.	According to a 2010 Kaiser Foundation report I read a while back United States "kids aged 8 to 18 now spend an *average* of 10 hours and 45 minutes a day, seven days a week with media. That translates into 75 hours and 15 minutes per week, nearly twice as many hours as their parents put into full-time jobs according to research published by the Kaiser Family Foundation in January 2010[50].". I remember being stunned at the time when I read this, so I really wanted to revisit this issue as I wrote this section on Internet addiction. I had more concerns requiring more recent evidence. The following Pew Research 2020 statistics[51] answered my concerns: • "61% of internet users are addicted across the world • Internet addiction is common among all age groups and its prevalence is as follows: 13-17 (73%), 18-24 (71%), 25-34 (59%), 35-44 (54%), 45-54 (40%), 55-64 (39%), and 64+ (44%). • According to Pew Research, 48% of people aged 18 to 29 go online almost constantly. Also, 36% of adults aged 30 to 49, 19% of those 50 to 64, and 7% of those 65+, use the internet almost constantly. • Generation X [born circa 1965-1980] users are more addicted to the Internet, particularly to social media than Millennials [born circa 1981 to 1996]. • Both genders, male and female, are

---

[50] Generation M2: Media in the Lives of 8- to 18-Year-Olds - Report (kff.org)

[51] 46 Internet Addiction Statistics: 2020/2021 Data, Facts & Predictions | CompareCamp.com

		caught in Internet addiction. Actually, 64% of female and 55% of male internet users are internet addicts.
		• Another study revealed that, in the US, 29% of men and 27% of women use the internet almost constantly.
		• A 2019 study revealed that 3.4% of high school students had severe internet addiction. On the other hand, 39% had low-level addiction, and 32% had moderate-level internet addiction.
		• In another study, it was revealed that 65.5% of junior high school students belong to the internet addiction-risk group. Also, the study found that 6.5% of the students were in the severe internet addiction group"
Piracy, IPR and Copyright Infringements	Similar as covered in Content Rights segment of the previous section. Such infringements pervade many of the Online Services segment's sub-categories including video, music,, publishing, gaming, social and community, communications, e-retail and information and reference.	Similar as covered in Content Rights segment's harms of the previous section
'Immoral and indecent' Entertainment Concerns	This refers to concerns of 'taste and decency' of some of the content published as	• Pakistan banned short video-sharing platform TikTok after users complained about the immoral and indecent content shared on the platform, asserting it offends

	'entertainment'	the culture and living of Pakistan. However, the band was lifted in July 2021[52].
		• Pakistan has also banned Tinder, Grindr and three other dating apps for "immoral content"[53] Pakistan's Telecom and media regulator – the PTA - asked video-sharing platform YouTube "to immediately block vulgar, indecent, immoral, nude and hate speech content for viewing in Pakistan"[54]
Competition Concerns	See later	See later
AI and Big Data Algorithms Concerns	See later	See later
'National security' Concerns	See later	See later
Internet Censorship and Surveillance	Wikipedia notes that this provides information on the types and levels of Internet censorship and surveillance that is occurring in countries around the world. As Figure 10 depicts, surveillance is classified as 'pervasive', 'substantial', 'selective' or 'little/none'. Pervasive censorship	• As Figure 12 depicts, Internet censorship and surveillance is *pervasive* not only in China, but Bahrain, Iran, Kuwait, North Korea, Oman, Pakistan, Qatar, Saudi Arabia, Syria, Turkmenistan, UAE, Uzbekistan and Vietnam. This makes fifteen countries under pervasive censorship and surveillance. • Indeed, some argue China is arguably creating a different kind of Internet: monitoring millions via the Internet using close to 200m million surveillance cameras across the country[56] using advanced AI facial recognition technology, online systems allegedly collecting voice recognition samples to boost surveillance[57],

---

[52] TikTok resumes operation in Pakistan after third ban in nine months lifted - JURIST - News - Legal News & Commentary

[53] Pakistan blocks Tinder and Grindr for 'immoral content' - BBC News

[54] PTA on Twitter: "Press Release: PTA has asked video-sharing platform YouTube to immediately block vulgar, indecent, immoral, nude and hate speech content for viewing in Pakistan. https://t.co/luZWrrsOnM" / Twitter

[56] Mass surveillance in China - Wikipedia

[57] China: Voice Biometric Collection Threatens Privacy | Human Rights Watch (hrw.org)

(or surveillance) countries refer to those "classified as engaged in pervasive censorship or surveillance when it often censors political, social, and other content, is engaged in mass surveillance of the Internet, and retaliates against citizens who circumvent censorship or surveillance with imprisonment or other sanctions[55]".	connected to a DNA database of millions of people "to help solve crimes"[58], moderators deciding on what people post/not post, etc. Even if some of this AI software is currently brittle, this is truly Frankenstein in approach. • Perhaps more concerning are the allegations that China is currently export its surveillance Internet to other countries. As the Atlantic notes: "In the early aughts, the Chinese telecom titan ZTE sold Ethiopia a wireless network with built-in backdoor access for the government. In a later crackdown, dissidents were rounded up for brutal interrogations, during which they were played audio from recent phone calls they'd made. Today, Kenya, Uganda, and Mauritius are outfitting major cities with Chinese-made surveillance networks" (Source – The Atlantic[59]).

Table 3 – Online Services Segment Negative Externalities

---

[55] Internet censorship and surveillance in Asia - Wikipedia

[58] China's massive effort to collect its people's DNA concerns scientists (nature.com)

[59] China's Artificial Intelligence Surveillance State Goes Global - The Atlantic - https://www.theatlantic.com/magazine/archive/2020/09/china-ai-surveillance/614197/

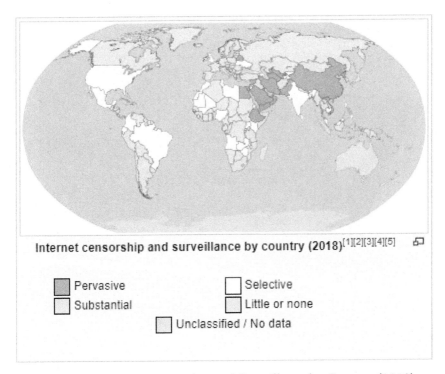

Internet censorship and surveillance by country (2018)[1][2][3][4][5]

Pervasive
Substantial
Selective
Little or none
Unclassified / No data

Figure 12 – Internet Censorship and Surveillance by Country (2018)
Source (Wikipedia[60])

It is apposite to end this Online Services segment with the evolution of the Internet Censorship and surveillance. This is a very worrying trend indeed with immense implications on free speech and privacy.

2.3.4.1 Online Services: Some New Competition Concerns

It is undoubtedly true that new bottlenecks have emerged along the Internet Value Chain (IVC) which many national and transnational regulators are grappling with, without much help and with much difficulty.

---

[60] Internet censorship and surveillance by country - Wikipedia

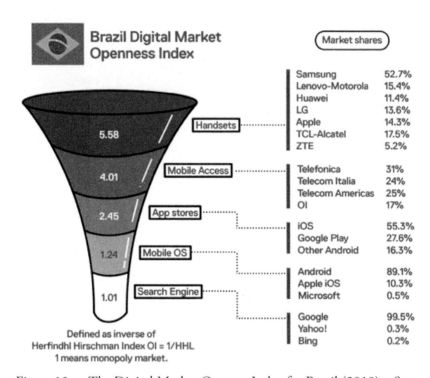

Brazil Digital Market Openness Index

Market shares

Samsung	52.7%
Lenovo-Motorola	15.4%
Huawei	11.4%
LG	13.6%
Apple	14.3%
TCL-Alcatel	17.5%
ZTE	5.2%

Telefonica	31%
Telecom Italia	24%
Telecom Americas	25%
OI	17%

iOS	55.3%
Google Play	27.6%
Other Android	16.3%

Android	89.1%
Apple iOS	10.3%
Microsoft	0.5%

Google	99.5%
Yahoo!	0.3%
Bing	0.2%

Handsets — 5.58
Mobile Access — 4.01
App stores — 2.45
Mobile OS — 1.24
Search Engine — 1.01

Defined as inverse of
Herfindhl Hirschman Index OI = 1/HHL
1 means monopoly market.

Figure 13a – The Digital Market Openess Index for Brazil (2018) – Source (Illustrated fromTelefonica[61])

Figure 13a clearly depicts that in the Online Services segment's category of Search services in Brazil in 2018, Internet users there truly only have a choice of *one* search engine – and that is Google at 99.5%! For the UK in 2017 (see Figure 13b), it is still Google for search services with a bit of smattering of Bing and Yahoo!. Such *concentrations* are monopolistically high.

Market concentration is a way to measure and quantify the structure of a market. It is a useful tool for both for considering the likely effects of a merger for example. It is also useful to consider the effectiveness of competition as a whole in protecting and promoting competition across the economy.

---

[61] https://www.telefonica.com/digital-manifesto/assets/a_manifesto_for_a_new_digital_deal.pdf (last accessed August 2021)

The Herfindahl-Hirschman Index (HHI) is typically used by economists to measure concentration. HHI is calculated by squaring the market share of each firm in the market, and summing the resulting numbers. This gives a score of that can range from close to zero to 10,000. 10,000 is clearly a monopoly because you have one firm with 100% of the market, and the square of 100 is 10,000. From Figure 13a, the Search concentration in Brazil as measured by the HHI $(99.5)^2 + (0.3)^2 + (0.2)^2 = 9900.38$. This is so close to 10,000 that it shows clearly that Google is a virtual monopoly in Brazil as elsewhere in the Search market.

In Figure 13a. we get the concentration number for Brazil for search by doing a calculation of 10,000/9900.38, which equals 1.01. This basically says there is only 1 Search player in Brazil. There is closer to only one mobile operating system (OS) in Brazil with a concentration of 1.24 whilst there is effectively two choices on mobile OS in the UK (see Figure 13b) with a concentration number of 1.96. I hope this explains the concentration numbers in Figures 13a and 13b.

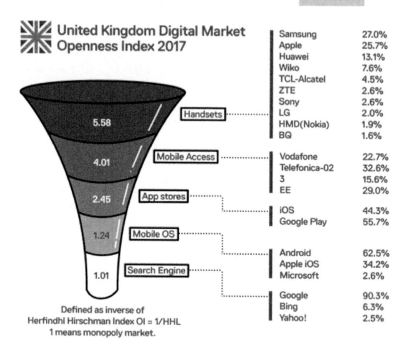

Figure 13b – UK Digital Market Openness Index for the United Kingdom (Source – Telefonica[62])

Such concentration as seen in the Search subcategory would be considered by offline TMT/ICT sector policy makers and regulators extremely unhealthy for competition in most of most areas they regulate – but how do you regulate a global behemoth like Google? It is a software/technology business, not a telecoms business who require obvious bottleneck assets like spectrum, numbers, access to physical infrastructure and more.

As Figure 14 also shows, other categories of the Online Services segment beyond Search including Video, Social & Community and Communications categories also exhibit significant concentration concerns too (revisit Figure 1 please). YouTube is the undisputed behemoth in the

---

[62] https://www.telefonica.com/digital-manifesto/assets/a_manifiesto_for_a_new_digital_deal.pdf (last accessed August 2021)

Video category; Facebook for the Social and Community category; WhatsApp and Facebook Messenger for the Communications category outside China; WeChat for the Communications category/Social Media in China.

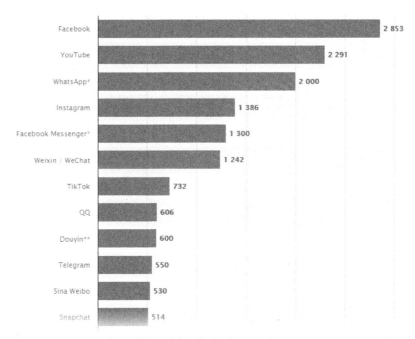

Figure 14 – Number of Worldwide (July 2021) Active Users (in millions) across (i) Video, (ii) Social and Community and (iii) Communications sub-categorires of the Online Services segment of the IVC (Source – Statista[63])

Indeed as Figure 14 shows, Facebook has three of the top five apps by number of active users (Facebook, WhatsApp and Facebook Messenger). Even in China, Chinese conglomerate Tencent owns both WeChat, or Weixin in China (1.24 billion active users) and QQ (606 million active users). WeChat's incredible array of offerings range from sending text messages, playing games, processing digital payments to making video calls. QQ provides an instant messaging platform which effectively killed email in

---

[63] Most used social media 2021 | Statista

China[64]. It was frankly an eye opener for me to learn that WeChat has close to 1.5 million monthly active users in the USA, and that 23% of US Internet users in the 18-24 age group use WeChat[65].

It needs to be mentioned that China actively blocks many external cloud-based apps like Facebook, WhatsApp, Facebook Messenger and more – helping contribute to the dominance of Tencent in China with both WeChat and QQ.

There are clear competition concerns galore with such concentrations.

2.3.4.2 Social Media, News and Elections

In addition to the competition challenges briefly overviewed just above, this polemic of social media platforms and the spread of misinformation influencing elections is a major elephant in the room with politicians across the globe. This is why I highlight it in a somewhat unique way here.

Whether in Africa in countries like Uganda, Kenya, Zambia or Cameroon - or whether in Asia/Central Asia in countries like Indonesia, Myanmar, Pakistan, Kazakhstan, Kyrgyzstan, Tajikistan, Turkmenistan, Uzbekistan and China - or most Middle East countries and their neighbours like UAE, Iran, Turkey, Saudi Arabia, Syria, etc. – the fact is most of their Presidents and senior politicians are arguably rightly concerned about this issue of social media and the spread of (mis)information – particularly having observed closely the happenings in the US's 2016 Presidential elections.

Policy maker and independent regulators do *not* live and operate in a vacuum devoid of the political class who enact the statutes which create the very regulators and agencies in the first place. Many politicians in the countries listed in the previous paragraph are not only worried about social

---

[64] How chat app giant Tencent won big by correctly predicting that email was totally wrong for China — Quartz (qz.com)

[65] 55+ WeChat Statistics - 2021 Update | 99firms (last accessed August 2021)

media platforms, they are positively paranoid about them. The fact that the serious and informed opinions are clearly divided on role of social media in the Arab Spring[66] which commenced in Tunisia in 2011 would not reduce these paranoid thoughts amongst the political class.

I believe this topic leaves policy makers/regulators in a slightly perilous position with their political classes, particularly in countries with fragile and immature legislative, executive and judicial institutions that can be easily usurped by the executive branches – which frankly is the case more member countries of the United Nations than not.

I believe there is a minimum of a major perception problem amongst the political class – if not a real one indeed – between social media and the *magnitude of the spread* of information they perceive as *unfavourable to them*. Already, a well-cited Gallup 2020 study led by Megan Brenan[67] has shown Americans remain distrustful of mass media with only four in ten U.S. adults saying they have a "a great deal"/"a fair amount" of trust and confidence in their media to report the news "fully, accurately, and fairly". This leaves six in ten (i.e. 60%) having "not very much"/"none at all".

Another well-cited and peer-reviewed 2020 Harvard paper's title could not have been clearer on this issue: *Misinformation in action: Fake news exposure is linked to lower trust in media, higher trust in Government when you side is in power*[68]. This peer-reviewed Harvard paper and the Gallup 2020 study appears to reinforce my point that the political class have reason to be concerned about the magnitude of the spread of information they perceive as unfavourable to them on social media.

---

[66] Social media and the Arab Spring - Wikipedia

[67] Americans Remain Distrustful of Mass Media (gallup.com) - https://news.gallup.com/poll/321116/americans-remain-distrustful-mass-media.aspx (last accessed August 2021)

[68] Misinformation in action: Fake news exposure is linked to lower trust in media, higher trust in government when your side is in power | HKS Misinformation Review (harvard.edu) (last accessed August 2021)

I do not propose to venture a policy and regulatory solution at this juncture, not least because it would vary country by country with their different current laws and regulations on Media regulation. I only clearly highlight this major elephant in the room that regulators and policy makers in most countries would have to grapple with.

2.3.4.3 TikTok Case Study: Illustrating National Security Concerns across some Online Services Categories

Any country can typically cite 'national security[69]' concerns with respect to online services. National security (or national defence) is a very broad term that countries assert. Wikipedia defines it as the security and defence of a nation state, including its economy, citizens and institutions – which is rightly regarded as one of the most primary duties of Governments.

In yesteryear, national security was mostly about *physical* military attack concerns against a nation state. In the digital age, non-military dimensions are more concerning including cyberterrorism, minimization of cybercrime against citizens, minimization of other cyber-risks by both state and non-State actors, minimization of state secrets thefts, minimization of personal information collection/transfer of citizen data to foreign enemy states and more.

It is exactly in the vein of the last perceived risk (i.e. information collection/transfer of citizen data to an enemy state) that in June 2020 India banned TikTok – the short video-sharing app – and 59 other Chinese phone apps[70]. Indeed amongst the banned Chinese apps is the popular messaging app WeChat too. TikTok and WeChat are clearly examples of the Online Services Segment *Video* and *Communications* categories respectively. Many of the other apps banned cover other Online Segment categories including Gaming, Gambling, Music and more.

---

[69] National security - Wikipedia
[70] India bans TikTok, WeChat and dozens more Chinese apps - BBC News

What reason did India cite for these bans? The Indian Government issued a statement saying the apps were "prejudicial to sovereignty and integrity of India, defence of India, security of state and public order"[71].

India's Government alleged that these apps are illegally and secretly collecting data and information from its citizens phones when they download the apps. The Indian Government asserts that letting its citizens use these apps is a threat to India's national security. Essentially, that TikTok and these other apps allegedly collect and misuse Indian citizens' data by passing it on to the Chinese Government. TikTok India protested to no avail stating it does not even operate in China, and that it stores all data outside China, and that it does not operate under Chinese law. TikTok India argued further:

> TikTok has democratised the internet by making it available in 14 Indian languages, with hundreds of millions of users, artists, story-tellers, educators and performers depending on it for their livelihood, many of whom are first time internet users[72].

Clearly an app that made itself available in fourteen languages in India was clearly providing significant positive externalities in India. However, TikTok is owned by China's short video-sharing platform ByteDance, and perhaps this is a core reason the Government of India ignored the protestations from TikTok India, and banned TikTok from India.

Since TikTok was banned, Instagram's short-video platform, Reels has hugely benefitted. Instagram reels was launched India in July 2020 just after the TikTok ban. Since then Reels has become the clear short video-sharing platform in India. According to the-Ken[73], Indian Instagram Reels Indian users are uploading nearly six million short-form videos on average every day, compared to 2.5 million per day for its nearest competitor in September 2021, Moj, which was also launched in July 2020. Reels – they claim –

---

[71] *Ibid.*

[72] We don't share data with Chinese govt, says TikTok after India bans 59 mobile apps | Latest News India - Hindustan Times (last accessed August 2021)

[73] Instagram Reels' growth hacks for India's creator era - The Ken (the-ken.com)

benefitted from Instagram and Facebook's estimated 210 million and 340 million Indian users, respectively. This is network effects in action.

However, is the TikTok India and 59 other Chinese apps ban a case of

(i) protectionism of the large 1.3 Billion people strong Indian market to allow for Indian apps to emerge? Afterall China has "protected" its 1.4 Billion people market from digital mega-platforms like Google Search, Google Ads, WhatsApp, etc?

(ii) a real national security concern as the Indian Government states?

(iii) clearly trusting more the data and privacy protections of Western apps providers like Instagram, and equally clearly not trusting Chinese apps?

I think it is likely a case of all three reasons above and more.

It is important to note that it is not only India who has 'national security' concerns against TikTok and other apps. Former US President Donald Trump had also sought to ban both TikTok and WeChat in the USA citing threats to "the national security, foreign policy and economy of the United States". President Joe Biden has since 'paused' the TikTok and WeChat bans[74]. Pakistan banned TikTok but later rescinded the ban as noted earlier. Other countries that have attempted TikTok bans include Indonesia and Bangladesh.

2.3.4.4 Facebook Case Study: The Role of AI, ML and Big Data Algorithms

We mentioned AI and Big Data earlier in the context of their likely importance in the creation of quad play type services by current players to compete vigorously against some emerging future *Content Rights* and streaming behemoths like Amazon and Netflix.

---

[74] US President Joe Biden 'pauses' TikTok and WeChat bans - BBC News

82

Here in this section, I am briefly highlighting the equivalent legitimate concerns against AI, Machine Learning and Big Data across some of the categories on the Online Services segment's categories. Specifically Machine Learning (ML) and AI techniques pervade the algorithms behind

i. Twitter and Facebook (Social and Community category of Online Services)

ii. YouTube (Video category)

iii. Amazon (E-Retail, Publishing and cloud Services categories)

iv. Google, Baidu, etc (Search category)

v. Etc.

Consider the controversial issue of *organic reach* with Facebook as an example[75]. Organic reach refers to percentage of the number of people that a specific post would reach without paid-for distribution. Manson (2014) reports that in 2012, Facebook famously restricted organic reach of content published from brand pages[76] to about 16%. Fans' News Feeds, e.g. a brand page for a B2B or a B2C business, was a critical aspect of Facebook's appeal to marketers because it allowed the business to build its community of fans who would be contacted and engaged regularly by content published to the business brand page. Organic reach was at its highest in the late noughties during the early years of today's social media giants, and then these platforms typically displayed content in News Feeds in a reverse chronological fashion, i.e. the newest content was topmost. This quickly became impractical to view all the content with increases by hundreds of millions in annual active users, and social media companies' algorithms now prioritised content that would enrich users' online experiences. Manson (2014) writes:

---

[75] Microsoft Word - Facebook Zero Paper.docx (techenet.com) - http://www.techenet.com/wp-content/uploads/2014/03/Facebook-Zero-a-Social@Ogilvy-White-Paper.pdf (last accessed August 2021)

[76] "A brand page (also known as a page or fan page), in online social networking parlance, is a profile on a social networking website which is considered distinct from an actual user profile in that it is created and managed by at least one other registered user as a representation of a non-personal online identity. This feature is most used to represent the brands of organizations associated with, properties owned by, or general interests favored by a user of the hosting network" (Wikipedia).

In December 2013, another round of changes reduced it [organic reach] even more. By February 2014, according to a Social@Ogilvy analysis, organic reach hovered at 6 percent, a decline of 49 percent from peak levels in October [2013]. For large pages with more than 500,000 Likes, organic reach hit 2 percent in February. (Manson, 2014).

Why did I detail the above quote? I have specifically highlighted this quote (and what preceded it) to emphasise how changes in the algorithms impact the likelihood of the information reaching other users on the platform. The reader can imagine the implications of this for current News (e.g. news about Presidents Trump and Biden) on online platforms. Most of these changes to the algorithms are today driven by Machine Learning analyses of big data (collected from users' usage patterns) and/or other AI techniques.

Facebook obviously generates a huge amount of data every day: data on its users posting content, daily logs on the various Facebook APIs, reports from users, etc. all getting to more than 4 petabytes a day, i.e. 4 million gigabytes!! This is data goldmine for Facebook to mine using its AI/ML-enabled algorithms.

For example, Facebook has been iterating its algorithms, with the most significant set of changes being those announced by Founder Mark Zuckerberg in January 2018[77]. This was after it came under much scrutiny post the 2016 US Presidential elections on its [Facebook's] role with the online propagation of 'political misinformation and hate speech'. In the 2018 changes, Facebook prioritised posts from friends and family over posts from brands and publishers. Zuckerberg explained:

I'm changing the goal I give our product teams from focusing on helping you find relevant content to helping you have more meaningful social interactions... The first changes you'll see will be in News Feed, where you can expect to see more from your friends, family and groups. As we roll this out, you'll see less public content like posts from businesses, brand and media... For example, there are many tight-knit communities around TV shows and sports teams. We've seen people interact way more around live videos than regular ones. ... Now I want to be clear: by making these

---

[77] Facebook Is Making Big Changes To Your News Feed (buzzfeednews.com)

changes, I expect the time people spend on Facebook and some measures of engagement will go down. But I also expect the time you do spend on Facebook will be more valuable. And if we do the right thing, I believe that will be good for our community and our business[78] (12th January 2018).

[Facebook's greatly employs AI and Machine Learning (ML) techniques in its News Feed algorithm which does the core rankings called EdgeRank[79], though it uses other non-ML algorithms too].

We can debate the issue of responsibility resting on one person (CEO Mark Zuckerberg) on a platform with 2.85 Billion active users as of July 2021. We can debate the merits of this significant Facebook algorithm changes of early 2018, though (as an ex-regulator) I personally believe they are in one way better because the changes allegedly prioritised consumers/citizens welfare over those of businesses and brands.

What is my core point of this sub section? It is this. There are increasing and justifiable concerns about the role of algorithms within the Online Services segment of the IVC in particular (dominated by Machine Learning, AI and Big Data) that regulators must be aware of – and policy makers and regulators have the responsibility to try to mitigate their "harms" by pressuring the online media companies to address them.

2.3.4.5 Child on Child Sexual Abuse – a true concern regulators must regulate to mitigate

One particular negative externality of online Social Media/community (e.g. Facebook, Instagram), communications (e.g. WeChat) and Video (e.g.

---

[78] Mark Zuckerberg - One of our big focus areas for 2018 is... | Facebook - https://m.facebook.com/zuck/posts/one-of-our-big-focus-areas-for-2018-is-making-sure-the-time-we-all-spend-on-face/10104413015393571/#:~:text=I%27m%20changing%20the%20goal,have%20more%20meaningful%20social%20interactions.&text=And%20the%20public%20content%20you,encourage%20meaningful%20interactions%20between%20people. (last accessed August 2021)

[79] EdgeRank - http://edgerank.net/ (last accessed August 2021)

Tiktok) categories of the IVC that really concerns me immeasurably is child-on-child sexual abuse. I mentioned it Table 3 above. The BBC in the UK aired a programme called *Who's Protecting Our Kids*[80]?

The BBC found that reports of UK children sexually abusing other children doubled in the two years to 2019[81], and this is rape and other sexual assaults I am writing about here. Numbers in the UK doubled from 8,000 reports per year amongst under-18s in 2017-18 to 16,000 in 2019-20. I truly want Digital Economy policy makers, regulators and network operators to read and digest the following carefully from the UK's experience of child on child sex abuse, and pre-empt them.

- The majority involved boys abusing girls.

- What is even more depressing is that 10% of the alleged abusers were aged 10 years or under.

- Consensual and non-consensual sharing of private sexual images appears rife amongst the UK young.

- Girls are asked for nude pictures of themselves by up to 11 boys a night according to the UK Inspector of schools – Ofsted[82]

- Young girls feel unsafe at schools[83].

Dr Rebekah Eglinton[84], the chief psychologist for the Independent Inquiry into Child Sexual Abuse told the BBC Panorama programme that unwanted touching, as well as being pressured into sharing nude photos, had become a part of everyday life for children

> to the point where they wouldn't bother reporting it... What children have said to us is that sexual violence is now completely normalised through social media platforms [and] through access to online pornography[85].

---

[80] BBC One - Panorama, Who's Protecting Our Kids?

[81] Reports of sex abuse between children double in two years - BBC News - https://www.bbc.co.uk/news/uk-58332341

[82] Girls asked for nudes by up to 11 boys a night, Ofsted finds - BBC News

[83] Sexual assault at school: 'I still feel unsafe, something needs to change' - BBC Three

[84] Speaking the unspeakable | The Psychologist (bps.org.uk)

[85] *Ibid.* Reports of sex abuse between children double in two years - BBC News

I think we must protect our young children. Is it okay the type of "normalisation" Dr Eglinton is referring to above? I cover later in this chapter what the UK Government and regulators are doing to protect children – the UK's Children code. I urge other countries to look at this particular harm most closely. Any society totally loses the innocence of youth at its peril!

2.3.4.6 Regulating Content on Mega-Digital Platforms: the Facebook Conundrum

> There is no power or authority without responsibility, and he who accepts the one cannot escape or evade the other.
>
> The Late Ethiopian Emperor Haile Selassie

Yes quoting Late Emperor Haile Selassie may be controversial, but hey I am African and others who one typically quotes from also have controversial histories. For example, USA founding President George Washington inherited, bought and sold slaves - and ordered Indians to be killed.

When a digital platform exists with 2.85 Billion active human users (as of July 2021), there would be millions [if not hundreds of millions] of really "bad actors" amongst them too. This is not only an a feature of an online platform like Facebook - it is also inherent in any normal distribution[86], not least across a sample size of a third of humanity. As we now know, the long tail theory explains how geographically dispersed "bad actors" and criminals can easily be aggregated on such an online platform like Facebook.

Consider the following:
- There are an estimated 200 million Facebook Groups [business and brands create Facebook groups] on the platform, and an

---

[86] A normal distribution explains how a large data set (e.g. of peoples' heights) is arranged in which most values cluster in the middle of the range, and the rest taper off toward either extremes, symmetrically.

incredible 1.8 billion people using the Facebook groups monthly[87]. Does the long tail theory suggest to you that all of these groups are all well-meaning? Does the normal distribution of 200 million Facebook groups not tell you there would be extremes too? I believe you the reader knows the answers to these questions are self-evident.

- BBC: Who would forget the infamous Christchurch (New Zealand) mosque shootings live-streamed on Facebook[88]? A convicted white supremacist, Australian Harrison Tarrant, orchestrated two consecutive mass shootings at mosques in a terrorist attack wherein he live streamed the first shooting on Facebook on 15th March 2019. In March 2020, he pleaded guilty to 51 murders and 40 attempted murders. Facebook had to remove 1.5 million copies of the massacre video[89] from the platform running weeks after the event.

- BBC: Facebook 'hosts' cybercrime marketplaces[90]: Facebook has been found by researchers at Cisco to have hosted no less than 74 groups openly trading stolen credit cards and bank account details, and that the groups had a regular membership of 385,000 people. Roman mosaics still in the ground were being offered for sale on Facebook. Facebook later said it removed 49 groups the investigation found 120 Facebook groups developed solely for looting and trafficking activity.

- BBC: Facebook bans 'loot-to-order' antiquities trade[91]: a 2020 investigation by BBC News uncovered how items looted from Syria were sold on Facebook. Facebook has since banned the sale of all such artefacts on the platform.

- BBC: FBI proclaims Capital Riots of the 6th of January 2021 as "domestic terrorism", noting that "bad actors" were mobilizing online using encrypted messaging platforms to evade authorities like the FBI. FBI boss Christopher Wray noted:

---

[87] 47 Facebook Stats That Matter to Marketers in 2021 (hootsuite.com)

[88] Christchurch mosque shootings - Wikipedia

[89] Christchurch attacks: Facebook curbs Live feature - BBC News (last accessed August 2021)

[90] Facebook 'hosts' cyber-crime marketplaces - BBC News

[91] Facebook bans 'loot-to-order' antiquities trade - BBC News

Terrorism today, and we saw it on January 6th, moves at the speed of social media. …If we don't collectively come up with some kind of solution, it's not going to matter how bulletproof the legal process is, or how horrific the crime is, or how heartbreaking the victims are,…we will not be able to get access to the content that we need to protect the American people. And then I think we will all rue the day. Source[92].

This is the Director of the pre-eminent FBI telling all that modern day terrorism moves at the speed of social media, as well as openly decrying encrypted technologies.

Can you the reader see the individual privacy vs. benefits to society balance here? Personal liberty vs. public good?

These are non-trivial policy lines to draw by policy makers. Where would you draw the line and how would you balance these two? Do not expect all the 193 nations[93] [sample] of the United Nations to all be clustered in the middle of the normal distribution. Of course, some would be at the extremes!

The answer to where one draws the line would be dictated by public policy positions taken by Governments on such polemic questions. Brittannica notes public policy

generally consists of the set of actions – plans, laws, and behaviours – adopted by a Government[94].

Indeed – plans, laws and/or behaviours adopted by various Governments would help steer their positions on this. In the USA for example, a 1905 Supreme Court decision – *Jacobson v Massachusetts*[95] - tackled the question

---

[92] FBI Director Wray Testifies On Riot, Role Of Right-Wing Extremism : NPR

[93] About Us | United Nations

[94] Governance - Public policy | Britannica

[95] Jacobson v Massachusetts: It's Not Your Great-Great-Grandfather's Public Health Law (nih.gov)

of the Constitution's protection of personal liberty vs. the power of the state government to protect the public's health [in the context of vaccination against smallpox during a smallpox epidemic]. The Court *upheld* the Cambridge, Mass., Board of Health's authority to require vaccination, i.e. in this case at least, it ruled the public's health trumped personal liberty. This is arguably the most relevant case with the Covid19 pandemic today in 2021 in the USA where some States oppose what they perceive as President Joe Biden vaccine mandates. Other countries would have their own law versions of *Jacobson v Massachusetts,* or plans and behaviours - and with their positions drawn differently! This is one of the challenges with such mega-digital platforms – different countries would want different content controls from them.

Returning to negative externalities that come with the Facebook platform, I proceed in this section with this rather long quote from Gretchen Peters and Amr Al-Azm of Morning Consult – because it well captures both the scale of Facebook's online criminality challenge, but also the immense responsibility on the shoulder of Facebook and its leaders to deal with it.

> The world's largest social media company does more than just connect people. Facebook has also become a repository for massive online criminal markets and terrorist groups. Outdated technology laws have created an environment where social media giants generate billions of dollars in revenue without any accountability for this and other illegal activity occurring on their platforms.
>
> One-third of the world's population logs onto Facebook platforms, benefiting from a digital space for shared ideas and a network for global activism. Those same platforms have become ground zero for organized crime syndicates to connect with buyers, market their illegal goods, and move money, using the same ease of connectivity enjoyed by ordinary users. Facebook and its related companies are also used by terrorist groups as a megaphone for propaganda, a platform for recruiting new members, and even a source of financing. This illegal activity often occurs out in the open through Facebook groups and pages, two staple features of the platform.
>
> Instead of acknowledging that their technology is being used for illegal purposes and fixing the problem, Facebook CEO Mark Zuckerberg has hidden behind immunity he claims is provided by Section 230 of the Communications Decency Act of 1996, which courts have interpreted to mean that tech companies shouldn't be held liable for content posted by third parties.

Authors: Gretchen Peters and Amr Al-Azm (2019), Morning Consult[96]

As I draw towards concluding this sub section with the pertinent position from Peters & Al-Azm of Morning Consult, I could not help but reflect of the Emperor Haile Selassie saying which I used to begin this subsection: "there is no power or authority without responsibility, and he who accepts the one cannot escape or evade the other".

Facebook – along with other mega-digital platforms – neither sought nor seeks the power they wield, nor the authority they hold. This though is not the point – we are where we are and so are they. As Selassie asserts, they clearly have the responsibility to society that goes with this immense power and authority, merited or not. Yet no one on Facebook's Board or leadership is elected – not even in America – yet alone in the scores of countries across the world which hosts the 2.853 Billion active Facebook users as of July 2021. The success Facebook enjoys has consequences – and believe me as we see in this Chapter - they include life and death ones. This is one of the toughest conundrums with Authorities regulating content on mega-digital platforms like Facebook.

They [Facebook] innocently set themselves up to create value and maximise profits (or producer surplus in economics speak) for their shareholders and staff. This they have achieved in the billions of dollars along with a trillion dollar market valuation as of September 2021. The Facebook Board rightly deserves and owns this incredulous success. However, unwittingly they arguably created even orders more benefits to citizens (or broader social value) including possibly hundreds of billions of dollars of criminal value too [if not more], i.e. negative externalities. This negative externality cannot clearly be owned – solely - by the unelected Board of a company sitting in one country of the 193 on the UN roster of countries. Part of the conundrum is that when the negative externality to society is potentially so humongous – think about a smelly polluting plant next to a major city like London – it becomes a societal problem. With the best will in the world, the

---

[96] Time to Clean Up Facebook's Dark Side (morningconsult.com) last accessed September 2021

Facebook Board cannot own the Facebook platform's negative externalities by itself. It needs societal help.

Part of the conundrum here is does society start interfering in the running of mega successful businesses? Do you even trust Governments not to make it worse? Who fanned the flames [the most] using social media [irresponsibly] leading to the biggest domestic terrorism scenes for decades in the USA with the January 6th 2021 US Capitol riots? I think you would agree Donald J. Trump not only fanned the flames – he probably had the lighter in his hands too, metaphorically speaking. And the last I checked, he was the sitting Head of State and Head of Government of the great United States well before and during when this happened. Blaming social media platforms may be too easy then. These platforms like Facebook [hosting a normal distribution of the order of 1/3rd of humanity] just ultimately reflect society - the very good, the good, the bad and the truly ugly! Perhaps holding them to a higher standard is plainly unreasonable, particularly when some of the "bad actors" using the platforms held/hold tremendous political power themselves. This is real ultimate conundrum – who polices and oversees these platforms?

I think you would agree we do not want some of those with political power anywhere near policing them – in just the same ways you do not want politicians controlling News editors, Newspaper editors, etc. However, if not them who are elected by society – who then? And what about the scores of countries who are impacted by these platforms and who would have no say? And how does society 'buy' its way into power and authority of a company like Facebook in order to share in the responsibility?

I believe Facebook is currently attempting *content self-regulation* with its Oversight Board[97] because it clear realizes "there is no power or authority without responsibility, and he who accepts the one cannot escape or evade the other". The jury is clearly out whether this would suffice.

---

[97] Oversight Board | Independent judgement. Transparency. Legitimacy.

However, *statutory content regulation* of such a mega-platform which reflects society and humanity's best and worst – whilst maintaining everyone's individual liberty and privacy – does not appear to me possible either. Unless humanity all become robots. Perhaps this is the biggest conundrum of it all.

2.3.4.7 Internet Zoning – where does 'acceptable' Internet zoning stop and Internet censorship begins?

Table 2 mentioned Internet Censorship and Surveillance whilst Figure 12 covered countries who practice some form of Internet censorship and surveillance. However, I believe I would be intellectually dishonest if I do not mention the concept of "zoning" the Internet.

At its most basic, zoning the Internet means creating an Internet where different groups of people can see different things, e.g. those searching for information on something originating from the USA would see results that those searching from France would not (because it is not allowed for example).

Zoning the Internet has been with us arguably since 2000 when there was a famous case in France – LICRA vs. Yahoo![98] [99] (Reidenberg, 2001/2). LICRA petitioned their French Court that their online auction service was being employed to enable Nazi period memorabilia contrary to a key article of the French Criminal Code. The facts of the case were not contested. Yahoo!'s defence argued that the auctions were being conducted under the laws of the USA, and that it was impossible to prevent French citizens from participating in such auctions and that this would compromise the essence of the Internet. Specifically, Yahoo! argued

    (i)   Its servers were located in the USA.

    (ii) Their services were primarily aimed at their USA citizens.

---

[98] Yahoo and Democracy on the Internet (core.ac.uk)

[99] LICRA v. Yahoo! - Wikipedia

(iii) That the First Amendment of the United States Constitution[100] guarantees freedom of speech and expression. Any enforcement in the USA of the LICRA positions would fail.

(iv) And that a French Court cannot possibly hear the case.

The French Court dismissed these complains asserting they had jurisdiction to hear the case. They ruled that Yahoo! must and should remove Nazi memorabilia from both Yahoo.com as well as from its local Yahoo.fr websites. Removing from Yahoo.com was particularly controversial because the Court argued that French citizens could get at it too!

In any case, Yahoo! did find ways to block most French users (from within France) from the Nazi auction sites or other sites deemed to have Nazi-related racist material. This is 'zoning' of the Internet. And Yahoo! did choose to eventually remove all Nazi memorabilia.

However, the case raised some core questions: (i) whose laws apply to websites viewable outside their home country? (ii) can a foreign court in Country A assume jurisdiction over online companies who are operating from Country B?

And Big Tech and Governments make controversial Internet content decisions daily:

- In September 2021, a smart voting app designed by Russian opposition leader Alexei Navalny was removed by Apple and Google from their App stores – just one day before Russians started voting on the 18th September 2021[101]. Russian Authorities had threatened to fine both gatekeeping companies. The Opposition expected their website to be blocked and so devised this voting app which could be downloaded from the two main App stores. The fact the Google and Apple acquiesced to Russian Government threats is a classic example of how Big Tech are

---

[100] First Amendment to the United States Constitution - Wikipedia

[101] Russian election: Opposition smart app removed as vote begins - BBC News

navigating stormy political waters across the globe. Do we really expect Big Tech to "help" in this way?

- Some Governments, e.g. India (not a country considered involved in Internet censorship as in Figure 12), block access to what they consider controversial blog sites (anything with gay and lesbian content, women's rights sites, etc.)

- Microsoft acceded to requests from the Chinese Government to remove blog posts that contain controversial political content[102]

- There are credible reports that Google still plans 'censored search engine' for China[103] after it abruptly stopped all activities there in 2006. China just simply blocks most top Western sites[104] like all of the main ones of Google's, YouTube's, Meta's (including Facebook, WhatsApp and Instagram), BBC etc. – even Wikipedia is blocked.

Where then does 'acceptable' Internet zoning stop and Internet censorship begins? Many have also asked - is it really wrong to create special "zones" online where it would be fine for "adult" material to reside, and other zones that would be children-friendly? Who told you policing and controlling Online content was easy?

2.3.5 Enabling Technologies and Services Segment Externalities

Enabling Technologies and Services as seen in Figure 1 covers the categories of Design and hosting, Payment platforms, M2M platforms, Advertising, Internet analytics and Managed bandwidth/content delivery.

The benefits of these technology-related categories are clear:

- design/hosting of online services sites like those e-Travel are obvious; managed bandwidth/content delivery by the likes of

---

[102] BBC NEWS | Technology | Microsoft censors Chinese blogs (last accessed September 2021)

[103] Google in China: Internet giant 'plans censored search engine' - BBC News

[104] List of websites blocked in mainland China - Wikipedia

Akamai with their edge servers to improve quality of service and reduce latency times are clear too;

- payment platforms are invaluable to the digital economy;
- and M2M platforms provide for applications such as connecting computer servers to gas meters, electricity meters or other remote sensor applications;
- Internet analytics is crucial for the advertising business model.

These categories hardly present massive negative externalities which require policy and regulatory concerns/interventions. Arguably, the one category that does raise significant potential concerns is that of the *advertising* category whose algorithms decide what we see when, for example, we do a Google search.

Recall that cloud computing services clearly fall under this segment too dominated by the big two of Amazon and Microsoft (Azure). Imagine the role of AI, Machine Learning (ML) and Big Data with these two players – they are two of the key leaders in these technologies.

2.3.5.1 Google Ads, Paid for Search & Competition Concerns –

This subsection covers a brief Overview on the Role of Advertising Algorithms (incl. AI, Big Data & ML) across the Enabling Technologies and Services Segment

In the last section covering the Online Services segment, I concluded with the role algorithms including AI, ML and other ones within the segment, using the organic reach of brand pages on Facebook versus paid-for distribution. It also showed how when Facebook prioritised brands/businesses in their algorithms over consumers/citizens, political misinformation and hate speech was arguably propagated faster across the Facebook platform – hence the significant changes Zuckerberg announced in early January 2018.

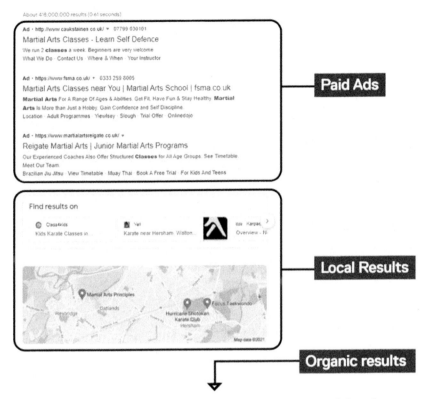

Figure 15 – Google Search for "karate classes" showing paid-for advertising and much lower ranked organic results

Advertising algorithms within the Enabling Technologies and Services segment present similar challenges too: paid-for Search items typically push down organic search results. Consider the case of *Google's Ads*[105] (formerly Google Adwords), Google's core online advertising platform where advertisers bid to pay to display brief advertisements, service offerings, product listings or videos to Internet users. If your business chooses not to go down the *paid-for* route for some keywords, then you would need to depend on Google's organic results and optimize your search using Google SEO[106], or search engine optimisation.

---

[105] Google Ads - Wikipedia

[106] Search engine optimization - Wikipedia

Let me clarify this a bit more with Figure 15 which shows the results of a typical Google search showing clearly the paid for ads, local results and the organic results at the bottom.

The results of my Google search for "karate classes" of Figure 15 shows how the Google Ads algorithm presents its results: usually with the paid-for search ads at the top or first, then Google tries to present some relevant local results next to where I live second (Google knows my local postcode/zip code), and only finally do the general *organic* search results appear – in this case none appeared on the first page!

The key words "karate classes" has clearly been bought or (paid for) by the reasonably nearby businesses at the top through a bidding process within the Google Ads algorithm. Google is paid on a pay-per-click (PPC) basis for these ad placements – there is no guarantee the clicker would buy anything. And some businesses can pay north of US $40 per click and much more. You now begin to see why Google is such a profitable business!

According to Financesonline[107], Google's revenue in 2020 amounted to $182.53 billion with year-over-year growth of 13%, with a net income of $41.22 billion in 2020. However get this: Alphabet, Google's parent company, gained $104.06 billion in revenues from Google searches and $19.77 billion from YouTube ads. Yes you read it right! $104.06 billion from searches like Figure 15. Searchers click on these paid-for ads, and Google knows that close to 4 out of 5 searchers (some say even up to 90%[108]) do not bother to go to the second page, as you would typically just refine your search keywords. And according to financeonline.com too, Google captures 92% of the search engine market as you also see in Figure 13b.

---

[107] 90 Google Search Statistics for 2021: Usage & User Behavior Data - Financesonline.com - https://financesonline.com/google-search-statistics/ (last accessed August 2021)

[108] 90% of people don't go past page 1 of the Google Search results when searching for you - The Conversion Guru

Why did I go on about Google Ads again? Yes, because it is the bread basket of Google's revenues as we see in the early figure - 57% of its revenues come from Google searches alone. However, I also cover this because Google Ads employs much AI, Big Data, Machine Learning (ML) and even Neural Networks (NN) techniques. Google announced[109] in 2018 several new ML-powered ad offerings to help brands and businesses run more effective campaigns across its Google Ads, YouTube and Google Maps properties. AI and ML assists in further determining which types of ads performed best down to the level of that first page since Google knows not many of us bother to go to page 2. It claimed ML-powered ad optimisations could realise 15% more clicks. More revenues for Google.

However, what about the competition concerns around Google on the Internet value chain? Google's ML derives from the massive data it collects from the 5.18 billion webpages it has indexed online and from the 80.93 billion visits to Google in February 2021[110] alone. This level of Big Data and its processing is simply incredulous, like with Facebook's 4 petabytes of data daily.

What is my core point of this section [yet again] as before with the Online Services segment? It is this. There are increasing and justifiable concerns about the role of algorithms within the Enabling Technologies and services segment, particularly in the Advertising category as exemplified with Google Ads above. These algorithms across Google Search, Google Maps and YouTube employ much Machine Learning, AI and Big Data that regulators must be aware of too. Policy makers and regulators have typically not bothered about algorithms in the past, yet alone AI/ML algorithms. However, those days are arguably over.

Do these algorithms entrench competition and concentration to the point where there is no other competitor to Google (some would argue we are

---

[109] Google Uses AI to Enhance Ad Campaigns (businessinsider.com) - https://www.businessinsider.com/google-uses-ai-to-enhance-ad-campaigns-2018-7?r=US&IR=T
[110] 90 Google Search Statistics for 2021: Usage & User Behavior Data - Financesonline.com
Ibid.

there already)? Is Google now not just an essential facility? Do brands and business truly have any bargaining power with Google on its pay-per-click (PPC) auction pricing embedded in Google's big data accumulation? Does the big data accumulation by the Googles and Facebooks not just add to their market concentrations (see Figure 13b again)? These are just the tip of the iceberg of the deep competition concerns in such areas?

2.3.5.2 The increasing concerns with the mega Digital Platforms

Avant-garde Governments and Regulators are increasingly concerned about the Market Power of the major Digital Platforms

In the last major section [on Online Services], I briefly covered Facebook's market power (with 2.85 Billion active users as of July 2021) and how it made some significant changes to its algorithms in early 2018. I also covered Facebook and the spread of misinformation.

In this section [Enabling Technologies & Services], I have briefly covered Google's almost absolute market Power in search. Much of the power of this mega-Digital platforms derive from their processing of the huge quantities of data they collect which they can enrich and exploit. I have covered the high degree of concentrations of such digital markets (see Figures 13a and 13b). Big data accumulation is only one of the key concerns with such mega-platforms, but other issues like multi-sided markets[111] and networks effects[112] add to their concentration. The barriers to switching from these

---

[111] Multi-sided platforms or markets connect two or more independent segments/groups using intermediation or matchmaking as we find with digital platforms. Groups/segments included (i) the billions of consumers that actively use the platforms like Facebook or Google (ii) the advertisers who flock to be matched with the consumers they seek (iii) suppliers of goods and services who are attracted to such platforms, (iv) media content creators, etc. The emergence of these different "sides" just reinforce the concentration of these platforms.

[112] Sometimes known as network externality, it refers to the phenomenon wherein the value of a product or service is dependent on the number of people using the service. The more of your friends and family who choose to join the Facebook platform encourages you too to join the platform to find more of your friends/family on it. Similarly, a world with only one telephone is pretty useless—no one else to phone! A world with a thousand telephone lines is

mega-platforms are just humongous - just think about the last time you used Bing instead of Google, or how difficult it is to switch from Google Android to Apple IoS and vice versa!

I hope it is therefore clear that I see significant [potential] policy and regulatory concerns with these mega-digital platforms enabled by the Internet value chain – and it is not only Google and Facebook. I would easily add Amazon, Tencent and a few others to this list of mega-platforms (or mega-platforms owners). Just suffice to say, some of the top avant-garde Governments and regulatory authorities in the world also have similar concerns and have commenced regulatory inquiries into these mega-platforms. I only mention three below and they include:

a) *The UK's Government Furman & Competition & Market Authority (CMA) Reviews*: The UK Government instigated an investigation into the possible changes to the UK's Government competition framework to address the concerns and challenges of digital platforms. The UK Government appointed former Chief Economist to President Barack Obama, Jason Furman, and the latter made six core recommendations that have all been accepted by the Government. First amongst the recommendations is the establishment of a UK Digital markets Unit (DMU) empowered with new tools and powers to regulate digital competition. The UK's CMA also carried out a high profile inquiry into online platforms and the digital advertising market[113] which concluded in July 2020. The summary of their report could not be clearer. Permit me to cite extensively from the its summary as it addresses and summaries some of the key IVC externalities I attempt to point out in this chapter:

> ... Google and Facebook are the largest such platforms by far, with over a third of UK internet users' time online spent on their sites. Google has more than a 90% share of the £7.3 billion search

---

more valuable, as each can telephone 999 others. This is clearly more valuable. A network of one hundred million numbers is clearly exponentially more valuable—this is the essence of the network effect.

[113] Online platforms and digital advertising market study - GOV.UK (www.gov.uk)

advertising market in UK, while Facebook has over 50% of the £5.5 billion display advertising market. Both companies have been highly profitable for many years.

Both Google and Facebook grew by offering better products than their rivals. However, they are now protected by such strong incumbency advantages – including network effects, economies of scale and unmatchable access to user data – that potential rivals can no longer compete on equal terms. These issues matter to consumers. Weak competition in search and social media leads to reduced innovation and choice and to consumers giving up more data than they would like. Weak competition in digital advertising increases the prices of goods and services across the economy and undermines the ability of newspapers and others to produce valuable content, to the detriment of broader society.

The concerns we have identified in these markets are so wide ranging and self-reinforcing that our existing powers are not sufficient to address them. We need a new, regulatory approach – one that can tackle a range of concerns simultaneously, with powers to act swiftly to address both the sources of market power and its effects, and with a dedicated regulator that can monitor and adjust its interventions in the light of evidence and changing market conditions.

We are therefore recommending that the government establish a pro-competition regulatory regime for online platforms. A Digital Markets Unit (DMU) would be empowered to enforce a code of conduct to govern the behaviour of platforms with market power, ensuring concerns can be dealt with swiftly, before irrevocable harm to competition can occur. The DMU should also have powers to tackle sources of market power and increase competition, including powers to increase interoperability and provide access to data, to increase consumer choice and to order the breakup of platforms where necessary.

We have identified a wide range of specific interventions that the DMU could introduce under this regime to tackle the market power of Google and Facebook, from ordering Google to open up data to rival search engines and separate aspects of its open display advertising business, to requiring Facebook to increase its interoperability with competing social media platforms and give consumers a choice over whether to receive personalised advertising. We are now taking forward further advice on the development of this pro-competition regulatory regime through the Digital Markets Taskforce

Source UK Government[114]

b) *The Australian Digital Platforms Inquiry by the Australian Competition & Consumer Commission (ACCC)[115]:* the Australian Government opened an inquiry into digital platforms in December 2017. Specifically the inquiry was into the effects that social media platforms, digital search engines and other digital content aggregation platforms have on competition in media and advertising services market. The ACCC had a particular remit to inquire into the impact of digital platforms on news and journalism in Australia, as well as their roles in promoting terrorist, extremist or other harmful content on these platforms. Do these read familiar with some of the externalities I have covered so far in this section? The inquiry also looked into social media and its influence on political advertising. This meant looking at the spread of political information on digital platforms when this information is presented as news and journalism. The final report was published in July 2019 covering more than 600 pages including annexes and 23 truly key recommendations[116] including changes to merger law, changes to search engine/internet browser defaults by Google, inquiry into ad tech services/advertising agencies, new codes of conduct to govern relationships between digital platforms and media business, etc.

c) *Italian Inquiry into the Big Data Sector:* I hope the themes, concerns and externalities I am highlighting are becoming clearer and clearer as I summarise the concerns of Governments across the world. The Italians instigated a Big Data Inquiry conducted jointly by three Authorities: the Italian Competition Authority (AGCM), the

---

[114] Final report (publishing.service.gov.uk) - https://assets.publishing.service.gov.uk/media/5fa557668fa8f5788db46efc/Final_report_Digital_ALT_TEXT.pdf

[115] Digital platforms inquiry | ACCC - https://www.accc.gov.au/focus-areas/inquiries-finalised/digital-platforms-inquiry-0

[116] Digital Platforms Inquiry - Final report - part 1.pdf (accc.gov.au) – see Chapters 3 to 7.

Communications Regulator (AGCOM), and the Data Protection Authority. Their authoritative report was published in February 2020. The inquiry started from the clear perspective of intensive and extensive use of Big Data in the economy and society of Italy and elsewhere. All three agencies agreed to some key positions going forward: (i) that protecting privacy [as a fundamental right] should neither hinder dynamic competition nor innovation; (ii) that though appropriate regulatory measures should be considered to mitigate the market power of mega-digital platforms, the risks of premature *ex ante* intervention in innovative markets must be minimised; (iii) that competition in "zero price" digital markets should be examined differently from that of traditional markets. 11 recommendations accrued from the Inquiry[117].

This section has hopefully shown that the externalities of the IVC are clearly providing new headaches to avant-garde Governments and regulators.

These examples have shown that areas and/or harms I have covered including social media, search, elections, big data, fake news, advertising, mega-digital platforms and more are truly the emerging concerns for the wider Digital Economy sector policy making and regulation.

2.3.5.3 Case Study: Amazon vs. European Commission (EC) – Conflicts of Interest

Amazon is one of the top Big Tech companies in the world dominating many key online segments. Amazon dominates the e-Commerce Online Services category of the IVC as no other company does with circa 50% of this category globally excluding China. Furthermore, Amazon is now a major player with Amazon Prime in both the Content Rights segment (Premium Rights) as well as in in the Online Services' streaming category.

117

https://en.agcm.it/dotcmsdoc/pressrelease/Italy%20Big%20Data%20Sector%20Inquiry%20-%20Summary.pdf (last accessed August 2021)

Amazon is also the number one Cloud Computing company in the world dominating the Enabling Technologies & Services segment of the IVC. Amazon is incredibly data driven and extremely automated using truly innovative algorithms based on its use of AI, Machine Learning and Big Data. These algorithms dictate Amazon's new product launches, how Amazon manages its inventories and even prices and choices of best suppliers for products. Amazon is also one of the Big 3 with Facebook and Google in the digital advertising market. Amazon runs – in the opinion of most experts – the most efficient logistics and delivery services in the world too, driven by its Big Data algorithms.

The EC rightly notes that Amazon has a dual role as a mega-digital platform:

- As a *marketplace* where individual sellers sell directly to producers, and
- as a *retailer* on the same market place, where Amazon sells products in competition with those same sellers .

Therefore, it is no surprise that Amazon has found itself being investigated by the European Commission (EC) for having breached EU antitrust rules by distorting competition in online retail markets[118].

This obviously presents a conflict when any major player effectively competes with its own customers. This has led the EC to open two cases against Amazon

- In September 2018, the EC sent out Requests For Information (RFIs) suspecting strong conflict of interests for Amazon between its upstream intermediation market for businesses (or Amazon's merchants marketplace) and downstream retail markets, i.e. shoppers on its market place. EU Commissioner for Competition, Margrethe Vestager, initiated an EU-wide e-commerce investigation[119] into the EU e-commerce sector in 2017 which led her raising her concern thus:

---

[118] Antitrust: Amazon (europa.eu)

[119] http://ec.europa.eu/competition/antitrust/sector_inquiries_e_commerce.html

If you as Amazon get the data from the smaller merchants that you host – which can be, of course, completely legitimate because you can improve your service to these smaller merchants – do you then also use this data to do your own calculations: as what is the new big thing, what is it that people want, what kind of offers do people like to receive, what makes them buy things (Source: Prof Thomas Hoppner[120]).

The suspected 'harm' is very clear: such conflict of interest and having data on your customers can lead a data-driven giant like Amazon to start new *downstream* product lines because they know what lines are working in their *upstream* marketplace – Ouch! Without clear "Chinese walls" inside Amazon, how can one avoid this? How will such walls work anyway?

- In November 2020, the EC opened a second formal antitrust investigation into Amazon alleging that Amazon prefers its own retail offers and those of its "customers" (i.e. marketplace sellers) who would use Amazon's logistics and delivery services. Margrethe Vestager noted yet again:

  We must ensure that dual role platforms with market power, such as Amazon, do not distort competition. Data on the activity of third party sellers should not be used to the benefit of Amazon when it acts as a competitor to these sellers. The conditions of competition on the Amazon platform must also be fair. Its rules should not artificially favour Amazon's own retail offers or advantage the offers of retailers using Amazon's logistics and delivery services. With e-commerce booming, and Amazon being the leading e-commerce platform, a fair and undistorted access to consumers online is important for all sellers.

  Specifically for this second case, the EC's focus is on how Amazon selects sellers to feature in its "Buy Box". The EC asserts that Buy Box prominently displays ads that "generates the vast majority of all sales". This second EC case is investigating whether Amazon "might artificially favour its own retail offers and offers of marketplace sellers that use Amazon's logistics and delivery services"[121].

---

[120] The EU's competition investigation into Amazon Marketplace - Kluwer Competition Law Blog

[121] Antitrust: Amazon (europa.eu)

I hope the reader can read into these two investigations how powerful Amazon's *own* collected Big Data is invaluable to Amazon itself, but even how more powerful the Big Data collected on *others* (i.e. merchants) could be to Amazon too.

2.3.6 Connectivity Segment Externalities and Concerns

This segment hardly needs much elaboration with respect to the IVC because it largely consists of the TMT sector's sub-categories of mobile access, fixed access (incl. Wi-Fi) and satellite access. I overview them briefly in the last chapter in Sections 1.4.1 and 1.4.2 and more fully in Chapter 3 (Section 3.9.2),

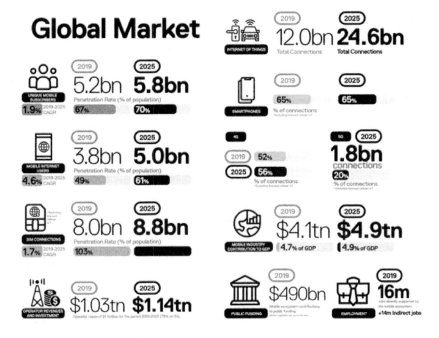

Figure 16 – The Global Mobile Market in 2020 and GSMA's projections to 2025

(Source – The GSMA[122])

---

[122] GSMA_MobileEconomy2020_Global.pdf

2.3.6.1 The Mobile/Cellular Industry has literally changed the world

Then positive externalities of mobile access (over the past 25 years) are completely proven for all to see: the mobile industry has more than changed the fortunes of the world – literally – particularly in developing countries.

The mobile/cellular industry's data speaks for themselves from GSMA's mobile economy report as seen in Figure 16:

- Unique mobile subscribers globally in 2019 totalled 5.2 billion projected to grow to 5.8 billion by 2025, or 70% of the world's population
- Mobile Internet users totalled 3.8 billion in 2019 and would grow to 5.0 billion by 2025
- SIM connections totalled 8.0 billion is 2019 and would grow to 8.8 billion by 2025
- Operator revenues and investment totalled US $1.03 trillion in 2019 growing to $1.14 trillion in 2025
- Smartphone penetration totalled 65% in 2019 and would grow to 80% in 2025
- Total connections through 4G was 52% globally in 2019 and would be 56% in 2025
- 5G would have 1.8 billion connection by 2025
- Mobile/cellular industry's contribution to GDP globally stood at US$ 4.1 trillion, i.e. 4.7% of GDP growing to $4.9 trillion in 2025 (4.9% of world GDP)
- Mobile ecosystem contribution to public funding stood at US $490 billion in 2019
- The mobile industry ecosystem is supporting 16 million direct jobs (+14 million indirect jobs) in 2019

I can quibble about some positive gloss the GSMA (the mobile industry's ardent and formidable advocate across the globe) puts in promoting the mobile industry in its annual Mobile Economy report. What is completely unarguable is that the mobile industry's positive externalities or benefits have literally changed the lives of billions of people so much for the better.

As someone who hails from Central/West Africa, it has just been a revolution to the lives of people there. For example, the ICT sector of the largest economy in Africa (Nigeria) is dominated by the telecoms industry which contributed 10.58% to total Nominal GDP in the Q4 2020, and the sector contribution to nominal GDP in 2020 was recorded as 11.03%[123]. For comparison, telecommunications contributed 0.06% to national GDP in Nigeria in 1999, just over 20 years ago and was 3.5% ten years ago in 2011 (Nwana, 2014, p. 10). No Nigerian would or should quibble about the positive externalities that have accrued from the mobile sector in Nigeria.

2.3.6.2 Wi-Fi's Positive Externalities are typically Underestimated

As for the fixed access subcategory (including Wi-Fi) of the Connectivity segment (see Figure 1), Wi-Fi is usually ignored at worst or grossly underrated at best. I usually spare no opportunity to shout out the contributions of Wi-Fi. The Wi-Fi industry does not have a formidable industry association and advocate of the caliber of the GSMA because it is an incredibly fragmented industry. This is more so because much of its contributions are not captured in the bulging profits (i.e. *producer surplus*) of the industry players like is the case with the world's mobile/cellular operators. Rather, much of Wi-Fi's contributions lie in the *consumer surplus* enjoyed by citizens (see Nwana 2014, p 475/476 or Economics Online[124]). Just imagine for a second – can you do without your Wi-Fi connection at home, at work or at other places? Your smartphone is connected to it – if you have Wi-Fi connection – practically all the time.

---

[123] NATIONAL BUREAU OF STATISTICS (nigerianstat.gov.ng) – The Information and Communication sector in Nigeria is composed of the four activities of Telecommunications and Information Services; Publishing; Motion Picture, Sound Recording and Music Production; and Broadcasting (last accessed August 2021)

[124] Consumer surplus | Producer surplus | Economics Online | Economics Online

The Wi-Fi Alliance® commissioned and published a seminal report that estimated the annual global economic contribution of Wi-Fi® at US$ 1.96 trillion, projecting that number to surpass 3.47 trillion by 2023[125]. These are not insignificant compared to the US$ 4.1 trillion contribution of the mobile industry to the world's GDP in 2019 (see Figure 16).

Quoting directly and extensively (and unapologetically too) from the Wi-Fi Alliance® commissioned-report's summary:

> Wi-Fi brings the greatest impact to the economy in four key categories: developing alternative technologies to expand consumer choice, creating innovative business models to deliver unique services, expanding access to communications services for fixed and mobile networks, and complementing wireline and cellular technologies to enhance their effectiveness. In addition to determining Wi-Fi's global impact, the study evaluates individual economies of six countries, highlighting the incredible value of Wi-Fi and underscoring the need for adequate unlicensed spectrum to ensure Wi-Fi continues to deliver benefits to consumers, business, and economies.
>
> Key findings of the report include:
>
> - United States: Wi-Fi contributes $499 billion in economic value today, $993 billion by 2023
>
> - United Kingdom: Wi-Fi contributes $54 billion in economic value today, $71 billion by 2023
>
> - France: Wi-Fi contributes $44 billion in economic value today, $64 billion by 2023
>
> - Germany: Wi-Fi contributes $94 billion in economic value today, $132 billion by 2023
>
> - Japan: Wi-Fi contributes $171 billion in economic value today, $248 billion by 2023
>
> - South Korea: Wi-Fi contributes $68 billion in economic value today, $138 billion by 2023

This study brings attention to the tremendous economic benefit from Wi-Fi, and underscores the importance of favorable spectrum policy to ensure Wi-Fi continues delivering even greater economic and societal benefits for many years to come.

---

[125] Wi-Fi® global economic value reaches $1.96 trillion in 2018 | Wi-Fi Alliance

I completely concur with this summary and I have been advocating for more Wi-Fi for a decade now. I also include the contributions of Wi-Fi to the six countries in the report as a further encouragement for all countries to take Wi-Fi much more seriously in their ICT and Digital Economy policy making and regulatory work. If Wi-Fi is this good for these developed countries, it would be good too for others.

2.3.6.3 The World's Fixed Submarine Cables are Invaluable

To round up on fixed and satellite access, can you imagine the world during the Covid19 pandemic without the world's fixed access submarine cables?

Telegeography notes there are some 447 cable systems and 1194 landing stations that were active, under construction or expected to be fully-funded by end of 2022. 99% of all Internet traffic travels through these undersea cables[126]. These cables can clearly not be taken for granted as they are just invaluable. Underwater cables are invisible to the modern Internet value chain, and the Internet giants like Google, Facebook, Microsoft and Amazon are increasingly funding these cables. It is a sad fact that in most developing countries, the national backbones to 'distribute' the terabytes/per secon of submarine cable capacity are very much still underdeveloped.

As for satellites, according to Union of Concerned Scientists (UCS) whose data I have always trusted most on all things satellite[127], there were 6,542 satellites orbiting the earth of which 3,372 satellites were active and 3,170 satellites were inactive. These data were as recorded by 1st January, 2021. The value of the world space economy is obviously much smaller than for the mobile sector and Wi-Fi at circa US $340 billion max in 2016[128].

---

[126] 99 Per Cent Of All Internet Traffic Travels Through These Undersea Cables (gizmodo.com.au)

[127] Satellite Database | Union of Concerned Scientists (ucsusa.org)

[128] Measuring the Space Economy: Estimating the Value of Economic Activities in and for Space (ida.org)

It would have increased by now with all the new LEO and MEO launches though from the likes of SpaceX Starlink, Amazon Project Kuiper, OneWeb and Telesat. The best information suggests that satellites carry less than 1% of the world's Internet traffic but I genuinely expect this to grow significantly with these more recent LEO launches. The fact remains that we rely on submarine cables entirely for Internet traffic because they are both faster and cheaper than satellites.

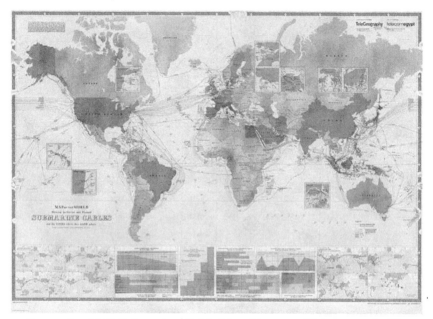

Image 3 – 2020 Submarine Cable Map (Source – Telegeography[129])

2.3.6.4 Negative Externalities of the Connectivity Segment

The Connectivity Segment's negative externalities that I would emphasise (over and above what was happening pre the Internet value chains of 2010/2016) stem from the *entrenchment and democratization* too of the Internet Protocol (IP). IP uses packet switching, rather than circuit switching.

---

[129] Interactive Cable Map Reveals 447 Cable Systems Under the Sea (terrapinn.com)

Circuit switching dominated the telecommunications industry pre the Iphone, i.e. before circa 2007. The package switching tidal wave came from the wider technology/computer industry with the likes of Microsoft, Cisco, etc. and there were no brakes possible by the telecoms sector to stop these invading standards coming from the technology/computer sector into the telecommunications sector.

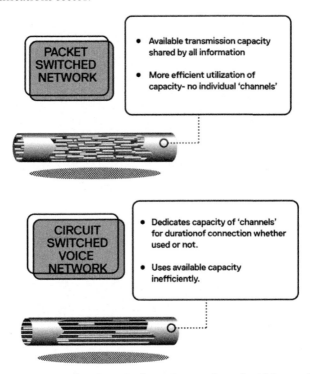

Figure 17 – Packet Switched vs. Circuit Switched Networks

Package switching is a mechanism of data transfer that offers advantages over circuit-switching that dominated non-IP fixed telephony and 2G/3G PSTN/TDM technologies. As Figure 17 shows, packets of data, addressed according to the Internet Protocol TCP/IP[130] are sent to the destination *in any order* along multiple network routes. Upon arrival the recipient

---

[130] Transmission Control Protocol/Internet Protocol – the communications protocol developed to enable computers of all kinds to share services and communicate directly as if part of a seamless network.

computer/server recompiles the data into the intended order. Networks are designed in such a manner that there are multiple routes available to the data, thereby ensuring there is no single points of weakness. The packets are 'routed' round the network until the destination is reached. As a packet switched network does not rely on the establishment and maintenance of a continuous circuit connection from origin to destination [as is the case with previous (circuit switched) telecommunications networks], the volume of data that can be transferred simultaneously through one link is far greater.

The revolution of packet IP networks combined with other standards such as HTTP, HTML and IP addressing led to a WWW information infrastructure where every computer server hosting information in the world sitting on other IP networks (like submarine cables and Wi-Fi) is addressable and possible to reach from anywhere in the world. As the numbers of computer/servers increased into the billions, the addressing number range had to be increased - hence the shift from IP version 4 or IPv4 to IPv6. Today in 2021, many countries are still operating IP addressing scheme IPv4, which is a thirty-two-bit number addressing system. This is an addressing scheme of thirty-two numbers consisting only of zeroes and ones whilst IPv6 uses 128 bits (see Nwana, 2014, p. 158/159).

This entrenchment and democratisation of IP's packet switching network has brought along some key challenges and harms for policy makers and regulators too as seen in Table 3 which is non-exhaustive.

Connectivity Services Externality	Brief Definition	Example(s)/Commentary
Cybercrime	Cybercrimes – enabled by IP and packet switching – is an unlawful activity using computers and the Internet where the computer is either a tool, or	• Hacking: illegal intrusion/alteration of computer systems (e.g. a Government's website), Virus, Botnets, Trojans • Spam: spyware, phishing, etc • Denial of Service (DoS) attacks

	target or both	
International Interconnect & International Gateway (IGW) Bypasses	There was a time when most countries had a simple international gateway into a country, a telephone number through which international long PSTN (and later even voice over IP) calls went through.	• IP-based technologies such as Skype, Google+, WhatsApp) and even satellites made it very easy to bypass such singular gateways into a country – and most such single-IGW and International Interconnect regimes have effectively broken down. Illegal bypass traffic accounts now typically accounts for more than 50% (at least) of incoming and outgoing international traffic (Nwana, 2014, p. 72).
Bypass/SIM Bank Frauds	A SIM box fraud/Bypass Fraud is a setup in which fraudsters install SIM boxes with multiple low-cost prepaid SIM cards. The fraudster then can terminate international calls through local phone numbers in the respective country to make it appear as if the call is a local call. This way, fraudsters bypass all international interconnect charges. A SIM Bank typically receives calls from an external IP address, i.e. a trunked call through the IP network. The	Bypass Fraud is intense and very dynamic: strongly linked to key "market" drivers • Regulation • International vs. national interconnection rate • Control on SIM distribution/activation • Competition on retail market and volume of international incoming traffic • The use of pre-paid SIM cards. Their ownership and address are much harder to trace. In Latin America – equipment costing less than $70,000 was making approximately $3 million in revenue fraud each month (Bitek, personal communication). Conservative estimates for several developing countries I have worked in for bypass fraud is circa 15% of Interconnect terminating revenues

	SIM bank is used to transmit the calls using the embedded numbers in the IP payload to the local landline or cell network.	
National Security & Critical National Infrastructure (CNI) Threats	Bypass frauds as defined above obviously present national security threats, as Governments neither know the provenance and destination of IP traffic.	• The USA has already witnessed disruption to its critical infrastructure: "Critical infrastructure systems like those driving power generation, water treatment, electricity production and other platforms are interconnected to form the energy "grid". Although beneficial to the public this grid is vulnerable to cyber-attack by "hacktivists" or terrorists"[131]. • Cyber attacks including cyber terrorism, cyber espionage, cyber extortion and cyber warfare, money laundering, etc. are rife.
Unlicensed Operators	IP has not only enabled bypass frauds, it has evolved full-fledged Unlicensed operators who set up bypass IP networks typically with SIM Banks.	• Such operators – both within countries and without do not bother to obtain any licenses from regulatory authorities and therefore can wantonly operate without paying any taxes and regulatory fees, whilst undercutting licensed operators.
Voice-Based Frauds	A voice-based communication fraud using voice telecoms products with the intention of illegally acquiring monies or failing to pay a telecoms company, state agencies and/or	• Sim Banks (see above) • Unlicensed operators • Hijacked PABXs voice switches without knowledge of owners typically to carry traffic • Bypass frauds • SIM routing frauds • Etc

---

[131] Cyber attacks on critical infrastructure (allianz.com)

	customers.	

Table 3 – Non Exhaustive Connectivity Segment Negative Externalities emanating from IP Entrenchment

2.3.6.5 Other New Concerns with the Connectivity Segment

The Connectivity Segment of the IVC encompasses much of the current telecoms and media sector as we know it today of our economies regulated by typical telecoms operators. The classic concerns of regulating for competition, regulating scarce radio spectrum resources, regulating traditional media, regulating traditional postal services, etc. all still remain key concerns, as covered in Nwana (2014). They are summarized in the next Chapter, Section 3.9.2.

However, there are new concerns too including the increasing concentration in mobile access competition with many countries having one or two dominant mobile/cellular operators (see Figures 13a and 13b).

Or what about the equipment sector to mobile/cellular operators increasing being concentrated, leading to a Tier 1 choices of either a Chinese supplier (Huawei typically and less so ZTE), Ericsson or a much smaller Nokia (compared to Huawei and Ericsson). This Radio Access Network (RAN) sector is becoming so concentrated, significantly lessening competition, that Governments like the UK's and Internet giants like Facebook[132] are funding RAN diversification projects[133] to promote more Tier 2 RAN players. I am a big advocate of such RAN diversification projects, not least because expensive RAN equipment would continue to contribute to ensuring rural Africa, rural South East Asia, rural Latin America, etc. remain unconnected.

---

[132] TIP Project Groups - Telecom Infra Project
[133] Future RAN: Diversifying the 5G Supply Chain - GOV.UK (www.gov.uk) – last accessed August 2020

2.3.7 User Interface Segment Externalities and Concerns

Recall that the user interface segment of the IVC is the last segment and that essential one that comprises two core sub-categories (i) *Devices* such as smartphones, PCs, tablets, game consoles, other mobile phones, connected TV set-top boxes, game consoles, etc. and (ii) *Systems and Software* that includes app stores, operating systems (such Play Store/Android vs. Apple Appstore/iOS vs. Windows 10), web browsers (Google, Bing, etc.), media players and games used to render services to end-users. This second category also includes the security and software and office productivity markets including software like McAfee Security and Office 360 productivity software. The profit truly stems from the User Interface segment too.

2.3.7.1 A Brief Overview of the Sources of the User Interface Segment Positive Externalities

The positive aspects of incredibly user-friendly smartphone interfaces is clear to all. In January 2007, Apple Founder the Late Steve Jobs changed the ICT world with the first iPhone. This is how he introduced and debuted it:

> Every once in a while, a revolutionary product comes along that changes everything and ... Apple has been very fortunate. It's been able to introduce a few of these into the world.
>
> - 1984 – we introduced the Macintosh. It didn't just change Apple. It changed the whole computer industry.
>
> - In 2001, we introduced the first iPod. And it didn't just change the way we all listen to music, it changed the entire music industry.
>
> - Well, today we're introducing three revolutionary products of this class. The first one is a *widescreen iPod with touch controls*. The second is *a revolutionary mobile phone*. And the third is a *breakthrough Internet communications device*.
>
> So, three things: a widescreen iPod with touch controls; a revolutionary mobile phone; and a breakthrough Internet communications device. An iPod, a phone, and an Internet communicator. An iPod, a phone... are you getting it?
>
> These are not three separate devices, this is one device, and we are calling it iPhone. Today, Apple is going to reinvent the phone, and here it is.

Yes indeed, Steve Jobs is in my humble opinion the biggest change agent and the most significant single individual behind the User Interface segment of the IVC.

The Apple Macintosh did indeed change the whole computer industry [and its-then terrible user interface] in 1984. I wrote/edited my first book on a Macintosh. The iPod changed the music industry with another change to the 'user interface' to access music. And on the 9th of January 2007, as noted in his transcript, he brought together the iPod, the phone and the Internet. The Iphone mainstreamed touchscreens to phones and this is now standard. It eliminated physical keyboards with some then-smartphones. However, it was an "Internet connection device". The rest as they say is history.

The ease, fun and usability (by practically all age groups including children) of Internet-connected smartphones, tablets, games, etc. is significantly thanks to Steve Jobs and Apple. These are some aspects of the core the massive positive externalities of the User Interface segment.

However there is more.

i. The Apps stores with the millions of apps in them meeting all kinds of needs for consumers. According to RiskIQ[135], users downloaded 218 billion apps in 2020 and spent more than US $240 billion in app stores globally. Mobile apps grew an astonishing 33% in 2020 relative to 2019. These facts are just incredible by all accounts.

ii. Tablets, smart TVs, connected set top boxes, consoles, fridges, connected homes, wearable devices, and so much more – all connected online.

iii. The ease with which users transact on these user interface and spend monies in their wallets or from their credit cards.

---

[134] Steve Jobs iPhone 2007 Presentation (Full Transcript) – The Singju Post

[135] RiskIQ's 2020 Mobile App Threat Landscape Report | RiskIQ - https://www.riskiq.com/resources/research/2020-mobile-threat-landscape-report/ (last accessed August 2021)

iv.   The hundreds of thousands of self-service kiosks for purchasing train or bus tickets, for self-service at supermarkets, at hospitals, at banks, employment kiosks, McDonalds food service kiosks, photo kiosks, airport kiosks, etc. These interfaces provide massive benefits today because all of these services are online.

v.   What would we do today without online navigation devices with easy-to-use user interfaces in our cars?

We could go on endlessly with how so many user interface devices, kiosks and more that keep many people so addicted to them.

2.3.7.2 A Brief Overview of the User Interface Segment Externalities and Concerns

However, there are many key concerns too. Having overviewed the other segments, I hope they are now predictable what some of the concerns with this segment are. Figures 13a and 13b clearly suggests some: the market concentration (and hence minimal competition) pertaining to mobile operating systems (OS), the market concentration around App stores and handsets, etc. Table 4 covers these and more.

User Interface Externality	Brief Definition	Example(s)/Commentary
Addictive Apps	Addiction to Online services happens via the very well designed apps and their user interfaces. These interfaces lead to behavioural addictions that is defined as being overly concerned about online apps	• Apps like Instagram, Tinder, Facebook, Twitter and more are sneakily designed to lure users and get them 'addicted' according to many experts[136]. It may just be time that they would have spent on TV or wasted in other ways that has been displaced to the online mediums, but it could be more concerning. Many apps are being "gamified" - as games typically grab users' interest and retain them, using clever tricks like changing colour of games icon. • Instagram is considered to be one of the most

---

[136] How App Developers Keep Us Addicted to Our Smartphones (businessinsider.com)

	like social media, online games, online gambling, etc. The interfaces drive uncontrollable urges to use them, negatively affecting other important areas of life like hobbies, spending time with family, etc. Again, AI is being used in many apps to keep users more engaged and minimise churn.	addicting, feeding on users forming a habit of taking pictures and videos, getting payoffs of "likes" and "views" and building 'intimate' networks. With 'push notifications' enabled on it, you get notified when a Facebook friend joins, when some friend's first story [right at top of the screen] or when someone you are following on Instagram is filming a video live on the platform. When Instagram launched in 2010, they courted very good photographers and designers with a high number of Twitter followers, leveraging users' popularity on other platforms. It is therefore no surprise that Facebook acquired them, and today more than 200 million Instagram users have over 50,000 followers each. I think that – unless you are a major celebrity or famous person, e.g. a major politician - you either serve your 50,000 followers as a true digital business, or you run the risk of being an addict.
		
		• Mobile Analytics firm Urban Airship's research suggest weekly push notifications can increase these social platforms' 90-day app retention by 190%[137] (i.e. almost double)
		
		• Just consider these legitimate and legal Urban Airship suggestions[138] on how "how push notifications boost ROI [Return on Investment]"
		
		    • "If you are not already sending push notifications, starting now could increase app retention by 190%
		
		    • Send push notifications to new app users within 90 days – or risk wasting 95 cents of every dollar you spent acquiring them
		
		    • Work to get opt-in: users opted in to push notifications are retained at nearly 2x the rate of those who aren't.
		
		    • Sending high value notifications can increase app retention rates by 3-10x
		
		    • Try rich push notifications – your direct open rates could increase by up to 56%
		
		    • Etc.
		
		Nothing illegal about these above, but consider the

[137] 7 Mobile Engagement Stats that Show How Push Notifications Boost ROI | Airship - https://www.airship.com/blog/7-mobile-engagement-statistics-that-show-how-push-notifications-boost-roi/ (last accessed August 2021).

[138] *Ibid.*

		potential negative externalities on the vulnerable, and all the "luring" steps above.
Age-Appropriate (Children) Apps Design Concerns	Leading countries like the UK are now beginning to effectively force leading tech companies to adapt and design their tech apps to be age-appropriate. This is in order to create a "better Internet for children"	• See later section on UK Children's Code or – the UK Age-Appropriate Design Code[139] – which came into force on the 2nd September 2021. The code is a set of 15 flexible standards that do not ban or specifically prescribe. Rather, they strongly push to the fore the best interests of children as new apps are designed and current ones adapted. • This code has for children apps are now enforceable in the UK as covered later
Mobile Operating Systems (OS) dominance	This refers to an OS for phones, smartphones, tablets, PCs and other User Interface segment devices. Figures 13a and 13b notes clearly that whether it is in Brazil, the UK or anywhere else for that matter, consumers have a choice globally of just two Mobile Operating systems. Is this sufficient and/or good for competition?	• Google Android dominates mobile OS segment followed by Apple's IoS. Even Internet and Cloud giant Microsoft hardly gets a look-in. There are countries though, like Japan and the USA, where Apple IoS dominates as of July 2020, whilst populous nations like China and India are largely Google Android[140] markets.
App Stores dominance	App Stores refers to a digital distribution platform where consumers can buy and download digital	Figures 13a and 13b depict – again clearly like for Mobile OS - the dominance of Google Android and Apple IoS. Many competition authorities are concerned about these two. See later.

---

[139] Age appropriate design: a code of practice for online services | ICO

[140] iOS More Popular in Japan and US, Android Dominates in China and India (pcmag.com)

	applications and software, typically just referred to as apps.	
Rogue Apps and App Stores	Rogue/Unsafe apps refers to apps that would compromise your device in one or multiple negative ways. Unsafe App stores refers to 3rd part app stores that support thousands of unauthorised and malicious software and/or apps.	The 218 billion apps that users downloaded in 2020 (as noted earlier) also sadly included millions of rogue apps as users increasing relied on their devices during the Covid19 pandemic. I always advise all who ask me never to install unauthorized apps and software from third-part app stores. In as much as I am concerned about the concentration of Android and Apple iOS, I am a hundred times more concerned with third-party App stores that deliberately allow the loading of malicious apps. RiskIQ's 2019 Mobile App[141] threat landscape Report found that a third-party free mobile app store, 9Game.com, offering Android games was the most dangerous store to download apps from. The report noted that there were almost 62,000 new malicious apps uploaded to the store in 2019 alone. Consumers must be protected from rogue mobile apps stores.
Ransomw are	This is a type of malicious software designed to block access to a computer system until a ransom – or a sum of money - is paid. Cybersecurity firm SonicWall reported an all-time high 78.4 million ransomware attacks globally in June 2021[142].	Ransomwares clearly fall under the Systems and Software category of the User Interface segment of the IVC. Ransomware attacks are typically targeted at major companies. However, I prefer to quote the following real story from India, to reminder the reader that – whilst the big multinational companies may be able to address ransomware attacks, I am truly more concerned for SMEs as demonstrated following: "Kiran Shetty was dumbfounded. A middle-aged owner of a small family-run jewellery store in Mysore, Shetty found himself unable to access the files he used to run his business on. It was only when he received an email from an unknown source did he realise that his PC had been hacked. The mail didn't claim responsibility for encrypting Shetty's files. Instead, it purported to be from a

[141] RiskIQ's 2019 Mobile App Threat Landscape Report | RiskIQ

[142] 5 Ransomware Attacks of 2021 That Blew The Internet - Analytics India Magazine (last accessed August 2021)

		vendor offering to help him access his files again as long as he paid $10,000 for a decryption solution. Shetty had just been rudely introduced to the world of ransomware" (Source[143]).

Table 4 – Negative Externalities of the User Interface Segment (non-exhaustive)

2.3.7.3 Case Studies: Four Brief Competition Cases at the User Interface Segment

These have been mentioned above and well depicted by Figures 13a and 13b clearly suggests some, i.e. the market concentration (and hence minimal competition) pertaining to mobile operating systems (OS), ditto around App stores and handsets, etc. These concerns are real.

2.3.7.3.1 Google Android vs. EC Case

Competition authorities around the world have been investigating mobile apps stores dominance. The European Commission (EC) found Google to be dominant with its Android mobile OS, Google Play Store, and fined the Internet giant €4.34 billion in 2018 for anti-competitive practices[144]. The EC argued that Google acted illegally [145]. The details of the found infringements matter to this manuscript: and are quoted in full following:

Google is (or has been):

    (1)   tying the Google Search app with its smart mobile app store, the Play Store;

---

[143] Why 2021 will be the year of ransomware for India | #cybersecurity | #cyberattack - National Cyber Security News Today

[144] The European Commission, Case numbered 40099 Google Android Decision, 40099_9993_3.pdf (europa.eu) - https://ec.europa.eu/competition/antitrust/cases/dec_docs/40099/40099_9993_3.pdf

[145] Antitrust: Commission fines Google €4.34 billion for abuse of dominance regarding Android devices (europa.eu)

(2) tying its mobile web browser, Google Chrome, with the Play Store and the Google Search app;

(3) making the licensing of the Play Store and the Google Search app conditional on agreements that contain anti-fragmentation obligations, i.e. preventing hardware manufacturers from:

    (i) selling devices based on modified versions of Android ("Android forks");

    (ii) taking actions that may cause or result in the fragmentation of Android; and

    (iii) distributing a software development kit ("SDK") derived from Android; and

(4) granting revenue share payments to original equipment manufacturers ("OEMs") and mobile network operators ("MNOs") on condition that they pre-install no competing general search service on any device within an agreed portfolio.

Source: The EC Google Android Decision, Case Number 40099 [146]

These infringements found by the EC speak for themselves and clearly demonstrate the risks to competition with such high concentrations seen across the IVC. These were serious: that Google was tying search (which it is clearly most dominant in) with its app store, Play Store – not good! Google was tying its web browser [Chrome] with its app store and its search app – even worse! Who knows how or whether these Google illegal actions led to the exit of the Windows Phone and Symbian devices that have fallen by the way side.

Such illegal steps by Google led to device manufacturers using operating systems based on Android – hence the so called "Android forks" above, and such forks would result in the fragmentation of Android, and played to Google's benefit. By the way – in case you ask – the EC found that Apple provides no device-level OS competition to constrain Google in this matter. Therefore a key part of the case (or as smart Economists call it – *theory of harm*) against Google by the EC was that Google exploited its dominant position on Android OS "cement its dominant position" in general Internet search.

---

[146] *Ibid.*

Google was firmly ordered by the EC decision to "cease and desist" such anti-competitive activities as well as pay the massive fine.

2.3.7.3.2 Apple Music vs. EC Case

Lest you the reader thinks Google is the only EC "bad boy", the EC has opened a case against Apple [Apple Music][147] after a competition complaint filed by Spotify under the banner "time to play fair". Spotify accuses Apple of exploiting its dominance of the apps store market to leverage its own music streaming service, Apple Music, against the interests of Spotify. For example, it argues that Apple uses its in-app purchase system to charge players like Spotify a 30% fee for using its payment system for users subscribing via Apple App store. Spotify calls this fee "unfair taxation" for other players in the market such as YouTube Music, Amazon, and Google Play Music. And that it effectively forces "artificial inflating" of membership prices above Apple Music's stated membership fees. This 30% IAP fees is currently (as of August 2021) being investigated in the USA too (see later).

Furthermore, Apple's rules prevent app developers from informing users who buy their apps on Apple App store that they could have alternative purchasing possibilities outside Apple App store, including from the websites of the apps developers themselves. The apps would be typically cheaper on the developers' websites than from App store, but woe betides the developers for informing users of this possibility. I do not think this is right [if true], and the EC is clearly right to investigate.

There are other allegations that I do not cover here – but permit me to rather summarise quoting from the current EC Executive VP responsible for Competition Policy, Margrethe Vestager on why she opened the competition case against Apple Inc:

> Mobile applications have fundamentally changed the way we access content. Apple sets the rules for the distribution of apps to users of iPhones and iPads. It appears that Apple obtained a "gatekeeper" role when it comes to the distribution of apps

---

[147] Antitrust: Commission opens investigations into Apple (europa.eu)

and content to users of Apple's popular devices. We need to ensure that Apple's rules do not distort competition in markets where Apple is competing with other app developers, for example with its music streaming service Apple Music or with Apple Books. I have therefore decided to take a close look at Apple's App Store rules and their compliance with EU competition rules."

Source: Margrethe Vestager, EC Executive Vice President & Commissioner for Competition and "Europe Fit for the Digital Age"[148]

2.3.7.3.3 Apple vs. U.S. App Developers

I note in the Apple Music – EC case above that Apple is being investigated in the USA too on the 30% in-app purchases (IAPs).

Well briefly, the case here is that a group of US App developers collectively filed what is called a class-action lawsuit[149] in 2019, asserting that Apple had been engaging in anti-competitive practices. The lawsuit alleged that App Store charged exorbitant commissions in IAPs by operating an illegal monopoly on iPhone apps. Apple was sued for unlawfully monopolising the post market (or aftermarket) for apps by ensuring App Store charges a 30% commission to developers, leading to inflated prices for consumers.

Apple has confirmed[150] that it would make significant changes to the App Store and its back-office systems and processes. The Apple press release[151] of August 26th, 2021 states:

> The agreement clarifies that developers can share purchase options with users outside of their iOS app; expands the price points developers can offer for subscriptions, in-app purchases, and paid apps; and establishes a new fund to assist qualifying US developers. The updates constitute the latest chapter of Apple's longstanding efforts to evolve the App Store into an even better marketplace for users and developers alike.

---

[148] *Ibid.*

[149] A class action lawsuit or class suit is a kind of lawsuit where one of the parties is a group of people represented collectively by a subset of the group, or by just one person.

[150] Apple, US developers agree to App Store updates - Apple

[151] *Ibid.*

This is clear acknowledgement Apple realises – not only that it lost the class action suit in court – but that it engaged in anti-competitive practices in stopping developers sharing "purchase options with users outside of their iOS app", for example. Apple also agreed to pay US 100 million into a Small Developers Assistance Fund in order to support independent developers with better terms on app commissions and transactions.

2.3.7.3.4 Google Apps and Apple Apps vs. South Korea

Just I was concluding this section, the prestigious London Financial Times published a story that both Google and Apple's app stores had been hit with a new South Korean law[152]. This law responds to exactly some of the concerns that the above EC – Apple Music case is about, as well as the class action lawsuit above between Apple and U.S. developers.

Apple and Google take a commission of up to 30% on digital sales from their apps stores, and for in-app purchases such as subscriptions. South Korean lawmakers see this as anti-competitive citing the frankly irreplicable gate-keeping roles that these stores now play. These App stores practices are incredibly profitable to these gatekeepers according to this FT article.

This new 2021 law bans Google, Apple as well as other app store operators from the *harm* of requiring Korean users to be forced to pay for apps with their own in-app purchasing systems, triggering this commission payments. It also addresses the *harms* of (i) delaying approvals of apps into the Google and Apple Apps stores (ii) and/or removing them "inappropriately".

This South Korean law is likely to be a major precedent for other jurisdictions to follow, particular in jurisdictions such as Australia, the UK, the EU and the USA.

---

[152] Google and Apple's app stores hit by new South Korean law | Financial Times (ft.com)

2.4 Are the Gatekeeping companies to the Internet already too big to regulate?

If your mind formulated this question after reading the four case studies above, you have [good] company – me! Are the gatekeeping companies to the Internet already too big to regulate? I am afraid to concede that I think the answer is largely Yes. Let me try to explain why – but before that I want to ensure you the reader is aligned with me on the gatekeeping companies in question.

Figures 13a and 13b depicts some of the top bottleneck companies, i.e. gateway or gatekeeping companies to the Internet, without whom the Internet as we know today does not operate. From these figures alone, it is obvious that (excluding Chinese Internet activities):

i.   Google is unquestionably the Search Engine gatekeeper to the Internet. It has a circa 92% market share in most EU states, 90.3% in the UK as shown in Figure 13b and much higher in Brazil at 99.5% (Figure 13a).

ii.   Google Android and Apple iOS are the only two "go to" Mobile Operating systems (OS), i.e. the two gateway OSs which practically all tech app developers develop apps for.

iii. On App stores, consumers really only have a choice of mainly Google Apps or Apple Apps. It is good to see another category "Other Android" in Figure 13a

These above are not the only *de facto* gateways to Online services, but they suffice for the purposes of my arguments of this section.

2.4.1 Google Shopping/Google Search vs. EC

In 2017, Google was fined a whopping €2.42bn by the EU/EC for abusing its dominance in Online shopping. It was found to have done so by having consistently promoted its own shopping comparison service at the top of its own search results!

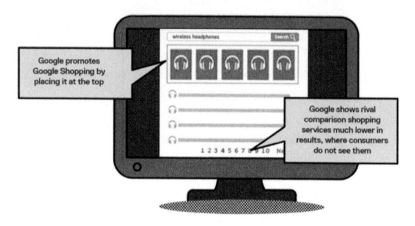

Image 4 – Illustration of how Google abused its dominant position in Google Search to give advantage to Google Shopping

Source: [153]

This broke EU antitrust competition rules. Commissioner Vestager requested Google remedies this breach within 90 days or further penalties would be imposed of up to 5% of average daily worldwide turnover of Alphabet, Google's parent company. She noted

> Google has come up with many innovative products and services that have made a difference to our lives. That's a good thing. But Google's strategy for its comparison shopping service wasn't just about attracting customers by making its product better than those of its rivals. Instead, Google abused its market dominance as a search engine by promoting its own comparison shopping service in its search results, and demoting those of competitors.

> What Google has done is illegal under EU antitrust rules. It denied other companies the chance to compete on the merits and to innovate. And most

---

[153] Google Shopping €2.42 Billion Fine - Right or Wrong? (datafeedwatch.com)

importantly, it denied European consumers a genuine choice of services and the full benefits of innovation[154].

Well what do you think happened after such a clear finding? Some argue not much has changed and that the market has even deteriorated further, whilst most of the "abused" companies (i.e. the numerous comparison websites that entered the market) have exited the market[155]. Some argue Google has played the European regulatory system[156], buying time with the array of expensive lawyers it hired – and even worse, that Google may have engaged in propagating fake comparison sites to give the impression that the market is more competitive. Others have argued that the EC case was very weak.

However wait for it, 3 years later in 2020, Google started its appeal against the shopping fine of 2017[157], arguing that the case has neither legal nor economic merit. It argued that the EC excluded key players such as Amazon out of its antitrust analyses, thereby dragging another big West Coast (of USA) giant into the case.

In a statement to the BBC, Google said:

> We're appealing [against] the European Commission's 2017 Google Shopping decision because it is wrong on the law, the facts, and the economics. Shopping ads have always helped people find the products they are looking for quickly and easily, and helped merchants to reach potential customers…we look forward to making our case in court and demonstrating that we have improved quality and increased choice for consumers [158].

Well here is what I think. This big giants can drag cases out whilst some of those that brought the antitrust complaints against them just fall by the way side. As the BBC article notes, one of the lead complainant in this Google

---

[154] Antitrust: Commission fines Google €2.42 billion (europa.eu)

[155] Time to bring Google Shopping case to a close (theparliamentmagazine.eu)

[156] Competition Policy (europa.eu) – see the process and investigations dating back to 2010 on this site on just this case

[157] Google starts appeal against £2bn shopping fine - BBC News

[158] *Ibid.*

Shopping [Foundem] case filed its complaint about Google as far back as 2009! Google was finally fined in 2017. Google starts appealing the fine in 2020.

I live in Europe, and it is factual that the numerous comparison web sites that emerged after 2010 have literally all disappeared. However, it is also factually true that Google innovated and innovates their Google Shopping service much better than the imitation comparison sites that came up, and so they fell away because consumers 'voted' with their clicks for a better Comparison service in Google.

Nevertheless, we do not know how many truly innovative and potentially competitive comparison websites fell away too because their marketing budgets dried out as they tried to get themselves from page 4 (see Image 4) to the first page on Google search. So I think the Google Shopping argument of – hey 'look over there too, consumers compare using Amazon' is just convenient. Pointing to yet another American Internet behemoth when the major harm is the thousands of EU comparison websites who did not stand a chance is a convenient diversion.

In the meantime Google has changed the shopping box to both show its own ads and the ads of other shopping comparison services who can bid for these advertising slots. Google's slots are of course assured.

What I really want you the reader to take away from this excursion on the Google (Search) Shopping case is threefold:
  (i)   how difficult it is for even some of the best-resourced antitrust agencies (the EC) to check and control the Internet giants;
  (ii) how long it takes and what happens to the "abused" firms in that time; and
  (iii) how nuanced some of the arguments are.

As an addendum to this case, this record €2.42bn Google antitrust fine was upheld by Europe's second-highest court who dismissed Google's challenge to the fine. "The General Court largely dismisses Google's action against the decision of the Commission finding that Google abused its dominant position by favouring its own comparison shopping service over competing comparison shopping services," the Court said, according to Reuters[159]. Google is likely to appeal to the higher EU Court of Justice (CJEU). The saga continues after an already seven year investigation.

2.4.2 Google AdSense vs. EC

I cover the Google Android vs. EC case earlier, but it is also relevant here so I cover it briefly because Google Android OS is a clear gateway operating system. Recall that in essence, the main charge is that bundling Search with the Google Play Store results in most manufacturers installing Google Search and Chrome – and therefore consumers using Google Search by default, restricting the ability of rival search providers to compete on their merits. Therefore, Google is accused of using its *gateway* dominance in Mobile OS to even further cement the dominance of its Search engine. Google naturally appealed in October 2018 after it was imposed in July the same year, and also changed the procedures and processes for Google Play Store and Android, and manufacturers would also be able to use "forked" Android OSs

Google AdSense vs. the EC presents a similar competition challenge. Google AdSense allows Google to provide search adverts to owners of "publisher" websites. Essentially, Google is an intermediary advertising broker between advertisers and website owners that leverage the horizon around Google search results pages. Therefore, AdSense for Search works as an online search advertising intermediation platform - a market that the EC asserts Google has a market share above 70% from 2006 to 2016 within European Economic Area (EEA). This is on top of its 90%+ market share in Search. In 2019 the EC fined Google again €1.5bn over Google AdSense, for blocking adverts from rival search engines.

Again what I think? You know what I think for the Google Shopping case above. All those views apply to these too. Google has made some changes with the three cases, but I personally remain unconvinced as to whether

---

[159] Google's Record $2.8B Antitrust Fine Upheld By EU Court – Deadline

competition has been restored in these relevant markets that the EC has opened these cases.

Megan Gray, general counsel of rival search engine DuckDuckGo who was a complainant on the Android case sagely commented in an interview:

> "The bad actor gets to decide what their medicine is going to be. And that's just crazy, right?"[160]

I can feel Ms. Gray's pain.

2.4.3 EC Competition Policy vs. Politics

The European Commission is proposing new legislation to the European Parliament to help "address more effectively" competition problems in the tech sector. I am unconvinced this is an issue of the Commission not having sufficient powers.

I submit we are arguably at the boundary between competition policy and politics. To address Ms. Gray's clearly identified conflict above of Google being expected to *behave* better whilst deciding "what their medicine is going to be" frankly requires a structural remedy, i.e. breaking up an American company. This is where Politics sets in. The EU will rightly tread very carefully in such a minefield, leaving such a possible move to their US antitrust counterparts such as the Department of Justice (DoJ). The DoJ has already filed its own suit against Google covering similar grounds joined by more than 11 Federal US States[161].

These gateway companies are already too big to regulate and control properly. This certainly seems to be the case from the perspective of the

---

[160] European antitrust investigations failed to curb Google dominance of search - The Washington Post

[161] Justice Department Sues Monopolist Google For Violating Antitrust Laws: Google Complaint

EU/EC. During the US elections, Senator Elizabeth Warren strongly advocated and still advocates for breaking up Big Tech - asserting

> Today's big tech companies have too much power – too much power over our economy, our society, and our democracy[162].

If the problem is stated this way, no competition authority can possibly address it because it is highly political. Yes indeed – again – big tech gateway companies are arguably much too powerful to control with traditional antitrust instruments.

2.5 UK's Age-Appropriate Design for Apps for a "better Internet for Children" – positive externalities well beyond the UK

I decided to include this 'catch-all' section because I genuinely think one of the biggest challenges Digital Economy policy and regulation is the protection of vulnerable consumers and citizens, and they do not come more vulnerable than children. I did mention I would do so earlier when I covered the scourge of child-on-child sexual abuse in the UK earlier. This section goes beyond child-on-child abuse.

I note in this chapter the challenge of addictive apps by illustrating it with Instagram and its notifications. I note inappropriate ads which children stumble upon frequently online. Such inappropriate stumbling is very rare offline. Earlier on in the chapter, I note how Pakistan has also banned Tinder, Grindr and three other dating apps for "immoral content" and how Pakistan's Telecom and Media regulator – the PTA - asked video-sharing platform YouTube "to immediately block vulgar, indecent, immoral, nude and hate speech content for viewing in Pakistan". Earlier too in this chapter, I note other harms like child sexual exploitation, child grooming online and much worse. Much worse because, I note earlier too the very sad example of

---

[162] Break Up Big Tech | Elizabeth Warren

a UK Teenager Molly Russell, 14, killing herself in 2017 after seeing graphic images of self-harm and suicide on Instagram.

Absent new policies and regulations, these online apps (whether social media, gaming platforms, video apps, music apps, etc.) use and share children's personal information and data to engage them. They are "gamified" keeping them online for longer and present to them inappropriate content for their ages. Inappropriate advertising to children such as auto-playing one video on a website after the other, and abuses of their privacy are just rife with so many apps that children use routinely. There is much evidence emerging that this is leading to societal harms including physical (harming others and self-harm), emotional and financial harms.

These harms not only present high risks to this vulnerable class called children, but frankly in some cases are being clearly linked to mortal harms.

What these multiple harms and risks to children collectively speak to in the UK context is a clear initiative for what the UK's independent data authority – the Information Commissioner's Office[163] (ICO) – calls the creating "a better Internet for children". Therefore, the UK's ICO introduced the Age-Appropriate Design Code in September 2020 and gave a year's notice for tech companies to comply.

I think the UK's Information Commissioner's (the boss of the ICO) Foreword to the code eloquently introduces the code much better than I ever could:

> Data sits at the heart of the digital services children use every day. From the moment a young person opens an app, plays a game or loads a website, data begins to be gathered. Who's using the service? How are they using it? How frequently? Where from? On what device?
>
> That information may then inform techniques used to persuade young people to spend more time using services, to shape the content they are encouraged to engage with, and to tailor the advertisements they see.
>
> For all the benefits the digital economy can offer children, we are not currently creating a safe space for them to learn, explore and play.

---

[163] Home | ICO - https://ico.org.uk/

This statutory code of practice looks to change that, not by seeking to protect children from the digital world, but by protecting them within it.

Source (UK ICO Commissioner's Foreward to Children's Code[164])

As noted in the quote, the code seeks to pre-empt the designing apps for children protection - "not seeking to protect children from the digital world, but by protecting them in it". The code's set of fifteen flexible standards do not ban or specifically prescribe, but rather strongly push to the fore the best interests of children when apps are designed and/or adapted.

I have included here the entire set of standards for the ICO's Age appropriate design: a code of practice for online services[165] - because they truly speak to much of what this entire chapter covers. The wordings of the fifteen standards are verbatim from this ICO consultation[166].

1. Best interests of the child: The best interests of the child should be a primary consideration when you design and develop online services likely to be accessed by a child.

2. Data protection impact assessments [DPIA]: Undertake a DPIA specifically to assess and mitigate risks to children who are likely to access your service, taking into account differing ages, capacities and development needs. Ensure that your DPIA builds in compliance with this code.

3. Age-appropriate application: Consider the age range of your audience and the needs of children of different ages. Apply the standards in this code to all users, unless you have robust age-verification mechanisms to distinguish adults from children.

4. Transparency: The privacy information you provide to users, and other published terms, policies and community standards, must be concise, prominent and in clear language suited to the age of the child. Provide additional specific 'bite-sized' explanations about how you use personal data at the point that use is activated.

5. Detrimental use of data: Do not use children's personal data in ways that have been shown to be detrimental to their wellbeing, or that go against industry codes of practice, other regulatory provisions or Government advice.

6. Policies and community standards: Uphold your own published terms, policies and community standards (including but not limited to privacy policies, age restriction, behaviour rules and content policies).

---

[164] *Ibid*

[165] Age appropriate design: a code of practice for online services | ICO

[166] age-appropriate-design-code-for-public-consultation.pdf (ico.org.uk)

7. Default settings: Settings must be 'high privacy' by default (unless you can demonstrate a compelling reason for a different default setting, taking account of the best interests of the child).

8. Data minimisation: Collect and retain only the minimum amount of personal data you need to provide the elements of your service in which a child is actively and knowingly engaged. Give children separate choices over which elements they wish to activate.

9. Data sharing: Do not disclose children's data unless you can demonstrate a compelling reason to do so, taking account of the best interests of the child.

10. Geolocation: Switch geolocation options off by default (unless you can demonstrate a compelling reason for geolocation, taking account of the best interests of the child), and provide an obvious sign for children when location tracking is active. Options which make a child's location visible to others must default back to off at the end of each session.

11. Parental controls: If you provide parental controls, give the child age appropriate information about this. If your online service allows a parent or carer to monitor their child's online activity or track their location, provide an obvious sign to the child when they are being monitored.

12. Profiling: Switch options which use profiling off by default (unless you can demonstrate a compelling reason for profiling, taking account of the best interests of the child). Only allow profiling if you have appropriate measures in place to protect the child from any harmful effects (in particular, being fed content that is detrimental to their health or wellbeing).

13. Nudge techniques: Do not use nudge techniques to lead or encourage children to provide unnecessary personal data, weaken or turn off their privacy protections, or extend their use.

14. Connected toys and devices: If you provide a connected toy or device ensure you include effective tools to enable compliance with this code.

15. Online tools: Provide prominent and accessible tools to help children exercise their data protection rights and report concerns.

These standards are really both germane and much needed. Some – including me – suggested they were unclear when they were published in September 2020 because we were unsure about whether it would move the dial with these mega-digital West Coast (of America) Corporations.

However, I may have been wrong to be too skeptical. There has been a series of policy changes by some of these companies over the last several months [as I concluded this book] suggesting they are taking the code more seriously than I expected. They include:

- August 2021: Just before the September 2nd 2021 deadline date when the UK Children's code would come into force, TikTok announced that it will stop sending notifications after 9pm (the UK watershed[167] hour) to 13 to 15 years olds, and after 10pm for 16 to 17 year olds168. All users under 16 will be prompted to decide/choose those who can see their videos the first time they post them. This is to ensure children do not accidentally broadcast to a much wider audience than they intended.

- August 2021: YouTube will turn off default auto-play on videos, block ad targeting for all children as well as all personalisation[169]. The Irish Times announced that "Google has announced a raft of privacy changes for children who use its search engine and YouTube platform designed to give minors more control over their digital footprint". Any videos uploaded by an under 18 will be set to private by default. This means only him/her would be able to view or whoever he/she chooses at first. He/she would be able to adjust the settings though, but at least it would no longer be default publishing to the world. Google's new rules would even allow for under 18s and/or their parents to request their photos to be taken down from image searches.

- 31st August 2021: Facebook announced that Instagram is defaulting all child accounts to private and requiring users to login in by entering their date of birth[170]. Instagram is also preventing adults messaging children who do not follow them in order to minimise child grooming amongst other harms. As the Guardian Newspaper notes[171], "the requirement has been introduced just two days before the UK begins enforcing the age appropriate

---

[167] The watershed means the time when broadcast TV programmes which might be unsuitable for children can be broadcast. There are strict rules in the UK about what can be shown on TV before the 9pm watershed.

[168] TikTok acts on teen safety with 'bedtime' block on app alerts | TikTok | The Guardian

[169] Google boosts privacy protections for children on search and YouTube - The Irish News

[170] Instagram to require all users to enter birthdate | Instagram | The Guardian (last accessed September 2021)

[171] *Ibid.*

design code. The code requires companies to identify child users and take special effort to safeguard their personal data, limit attempts to alter their behaviour, and prioritise their wellbeing". Instagram is stopping targeting under 18s using any information other than their demographic information.

Skeptical me! The age-appropriate design code is already working as I write this section on the day it came into force in the UK, i.e. 2nd September 2021. It is almost certainly due to the fact that these changes are happening because companies found in breach of the code are subject to the same penalties as those that apply when they infringe the GDPR regulations, including up to 4% of their global turnover. Consider the following.

Suddenly TikTok's Alexandra Evans and Aruna Sharma have now discovered that

> We want to help our younger teens in particular develop positive digital habits early on[172].

And Instagram's Pavni Diwanji writing in a statement[173]:

> This information allows us to create new safety features for young people, and helps ensure we provide the right experiences to the right age group. Recent examples include changes we made in March [2021] to prevent adults from sending messages to people under 18 who don't follow them, and last month we started to default new accounts belonging to people under the age of 16 into a private setting.

Better late than never I say!

2.5.1 The Online Age Identification Conundrum

One big challenge rest I can almost hear you the reader shouting back at me. "H – children would lie about their age!!" I completely agree. The ICO has

---

[172] Furthering our safety and privacy commitments for teens on TikTok | TikTok Newsroom (last accessed September 2021)

[173] Asking People for Their Birthdays | Instagram Blog (last accessed September 2021)

thought about this issue too, and age assurance would be part of the process of determining whether the code is being followed correctly. The details would be left to the tech industry, but the ICO is setting out some proposals on age-verification methods[174] soon including:

i. *Self-declaration* – depending on the user to simply state their age without providing any evidence to confirm it. Of course children may just *not* be truthful about their age using this method.

ii. *Artificial intelligence* – AI makes it possible to make an estimate of a user's age by analysing the way in which the user interacts with your service. One could use this type of profiling to check that the way a user interacts with your service is consistent with their self-declared age. This technique will be better than just self-declaration.

iii. *Third party age verification services* – Companies may choose to use a third party service to provide them with an assurance of the age of your users. These services typically work using an 'attribute' system where the company requests confirmation of a particular online user's attribute (in this case age or age range) and the 3rd party service provider provides a 'yes' or 'no' answer.

iv. *Account holder confirmation* – this method would rely on confirmation of user's age from an existing account holder who you know to be an adult. For example, the ICO suggests companies could provide a logged-in or subscription based service wherein the main (confirmed adult) account holder sets up children's profiles. These responsible adults could restrict further access with a password or PIN, or simply confirm the age range of additional account users.

v. *Technical measures* – Technical measures can discourage false declarations of age, or identify and close under age accounts. These would be useful to support or strengthen self-declaration mechanisms. The ICO suggests examples like presenting neutral age declaration screens or preventing users from immediately resubmitting a new age if they are denied access to the service when they first self-declare their age.

---

[174] age-appropriate-design-a-code-of-practice-for-online-services-2-1.pdf (ico.org.uk)

vi.   *Hard identifiers* – these confirm age using solutions which link back to formal identify documents or 'hard identifiers' such as a passport. The ICO does not prefer this to be the default way though.

Companies may use a combination of the above too in order to corroborate each other.

There are other tricky circular-risks to achieve age verification though like this one: do you collect even more personal data to establish age? Particularly when a key part of the problem the ICO Office is trying to address user's privacy?

2.5.2 Tencent using Facial Recognition to Protect Children Online

Well China has its unique answer to the age-identification challenge and protecting children online. Tech behemoth Tencent began (in July 2021) blocking Chinese children[175] from playing a number of its hit games after 10pm. However, Tencent's method is controversial as it uses facial analysis technology designed to ensure children do not pretend to be adults while using the app.

2.5.3 The UK's Children Code Potential Positive Externalities beyond its shores

One reason I have consumed so many pages explaining the UK's age-appropriate design code for online apps is because I believe the UK's Online Children Code is clearly providing much benefits not only in the UK (as the examples I cite above from TikTok, YouTube and Instagram), but also because its influence would be definitely felt well-beyond the shores of the UK:

---

[175] Tencent Uses Facial Recognition to Ban Kids Gaming Past Bedtime - Bloomberg

- The Data Protection Commission of UK's neighbour - the Republic of Ireland - is already preparing similar regulations. It is called the ' "Children's Fundamentals" – a guide to protecting children's personal data[176]' which proposes 14 key principles.

- It stands to reason that when TikTok, Facebook, Instagram and Google/YouTube roll out these changes to their apps – in order to meet the UK's Age-Appropriate Design Code – they would almost certainly roll out these changes to many other countries in the world, and help protect children in these countries too. Why would they not? It would be ethically untenable to protect UK children more than Pakistan's/Indian's children.

- Recall, Pakistan regulator (PTA) asked video-sharing platform YouTube "to immediately block vulgar, indecent, immoral, nude and hate speech content for viewing in Pakistan". However, to the best of my research, the PTA did not consult and roll out a Children's code like the UK's ICO has done along with clear ways to enforce it. Google/YouTube has clearly reacted to the UK ICO's code. Pakistan would like get some of its wishes without its own clear Children code through YouTube rolling out what it is doing in the UK. Alternatively, it could develop and enact its own code too like the UK's.

Either way, I believe the UK's ICO has done the rest of the world a major service with this Children's code in order to "create a better Internet for Children".

It is clearly not the best in the eyes of some including the Coalition for a Digital Economy[177]. I did subscribe to their skepticism about this code ever working. They also wrote in their response to the consultation

> If the UK truly wants to lead the way in online child protection, it should do so on a global scale through open standards, not on a national level through closed

---

[176] The "Children's Fundamentals" – A guide to protecting children's personal data | 18/03/2021 | Data Protection Commission

[177] Microsoft Word - COADEC age appropriate design code - consultation response (ico.org.uk) (last accessed September 2021)

legislation. ICO should either alter the nomenclature of the plan away from "code standards" or - to be truly bold in the Digital Charter's vision of making the internet safer[178].

We may have been both been wrong to be skeptical. It appears to have started working already. The UK's code influence portends to be far reaching – because protecting children is not an option, it should be a must. And any code that is working – without resorting to a surveillance Internet – must be welcomed. This is not one of those situations where we should pitch the good against the best. We start with the good and we continuously iterate towards the best. For our children are worth it.

2.6 Summary

I have hopefully taken you in this Chapter through the top-level takeaways and externalities of the IVC, and begun to give you more than a flavour of the implications on new Digital Economy Policy making and regulation that comes with the Internet value chain.

All the different segments of the value chain come with an array of positive and negative externalities, and with different players who sometimes overlap two or more segments of the value chain, e.g. Google/Alphabet spans across Online Services, Enabling Technology/Services, Connectivity and User Interface segments.

Hopefully you the reader now recognise that many of the regulatory concerns (e.g. market dominance and market concentration challenges) and other negative externalities (fake new, disinformation, etc.) can hardly be addressed in most national jurisdictions, against some Internet giants who are literally bigger in revenue terms than the GDP of most countries combined.

Also - as I note at the introduction to this chapter, I hope this 'excursion' in this chapter provides some sort of *structure* and *categorisation* of the externalities that come with the IVC. I hope this is useful to the reader, as opposed to having no such structuring and categorisation. This chapter realises one of the core contributions of this books.

---

[178] *Ibid.*

Part II — Defining the New Digital Economy Policy & Regulatory Challenges Landscape *with the Internet Value Chain*

Chapter 3 Punchline: If the expansive Digital Economy that all countries crave in order to power their economies has consequences, how does one define – clearly - the combined challenges across the old Offline TMT/ICT sector and the new Online (IVC) one?

Chapter 3

A Definition of the New Digital Economy Policy and Regulatory Landscape

"A problem well stated is half solved."

— *Charles Kettering, Head of Research at General Motors from 1920 to 1947*

I would grossly summarise the first two chapters that form Part I of this book as this: the [expansive] Digital Economy that most if not all countries crave in order to power their economies has consequences. This singular chapter of Part II of this book attempts to answer this important follow up question: if the expansive Digital Economy that all countries crave has consequences, how does one define – clearly - the combined challenges across the old largely *offline* TMT Economy of Nwana (2014) and the new *online* one?

3.1 Introduction to the Digital Economy Problem Definition

This is another *core* chapter of this book along with the previous chapter, i.e. Chapter 2. This is a new Part of this book, Part II, so permit me to remind you the reader of this book's goals, and where this chapter sits in it. In my preface I noted three broad goals and a supplementary one.

1. Introduce the Internet Value Chain (IVC) and why it is most pertinent to Digital Economy Policy makers, regulators and network operators. Chapter 1 covers this.

2. Provide some sort of *structure* and *characterisation* of the positive - and especially too - the negative externalities, along with as many

illustrations of the new risks and harms as possible using min-case studies in order to explain them clearly. I hope you the reader believe that Chapter 2 achieves this.

3. Provide as best as possible a definition of the combined *offline* (as in offline TMT/ICT), Big Tech and other digital platform harms/risks and the numerous other *online* (IVC) harms. My hope is that this would accrue to defining the *problem statement* of the overall policy and regulatory challenges that face Digital Economy Policy makers, regulators and network operators going forward. Once again, as I try and define the problem statement, I have again set myself the goal of providing as many illustrations of the risks and harms as possible by using min-case studies in order to explain them clearly. I assume current ICT policy makers, regulators and network operators would have to morph into the Digital Economy ones – as they are overlaps between the two, and they are the natural ones to start addressing the combined set of challenges.

This last goal (i.e. 3rd) is the subject and challenge of this current chapter, and Part II of this book.

I have chosen to start this chapter by citing Charles Kettering's famous maxim, a problem well-stated is a problem half-solved. If I vaguely succeed with the last Chapter and this one, then I hope this manuscript would have succeeded in *half-solving* the new Digital Economy 'problem definition' [c.f. Charles Kettering] – i.e. by *well-stating* them and illustrating the new challenges through min-case studies wherever possible.

Since this chapter is about defining the problem statement for Digital Economy policy makers, regulators and network operators, I also introduce and cover the problem statement challenges of Big Tech regulation. For good or ill, these Big Tech players have shaped our industry like no other over the past decade. Like in the last chapter, I use mini-case studies or recent 2020/2021 actions by competition and/or anti-trust authorities across the world to both illustrate and reinforce the problem definition statements of this chapter.

I truly believe that ICT Ministers, Digital Economy Ministers, ICT regulators, ICT policy makers, ICT and Digital Economy regulators, Digital Economy students and the rest of us practitioners need to understand this problem statement carefully – and would truly benefit from it – because otherwise it truly gets most confusing to so many stakeholders of the Digital Economy and ICT ecosystems. Furthermore, we can only start prioritising the Digital Economy priorities for each of our countries once we have defined them clearly.

3.2 Key Lessons from Part I of this Book

Before I expound on the lessons of Chapters 1 and 2, I think I should remind the reader what a typical ICT sector of [developing] national economies comprises of. Indeed, I mentioned in Part I that the Information and Communication sector in Nigeria is composed of the four activities of (i) Telecommunications and Information Services (ii) Publishing (iii) Motion Picture/Films, Sound Recording and Music Production and (iv) Broadcasting[1]. I chose Nigeria[2]'s because it is broadly similar to what comprises the ICT sector in most other [developing] countries, e.g. Thailand's which I mention later. You the reader should have these four activities in mind as you read the lessons following.

There are 10 key lessons that I would like to draw from Part I of this book in order to start the definition of the combined offline ICT (including TMT) and online IVC-inspired Digital Economy challenges. I suspect you the reader may draw some further key lessons too. This is because your local country context would typically help you perceive some new and/or slightly different lessons to mine below. The lessons I draw and would like to highlight from Part I of this book follow.

1. *The TMT/ICT Value Chains and the IVC are not mutually exclusive:* we see that the current TMT/ICT value chains (see Figures 4, 5, 6 and 7) and the IVC value chain (see Figure 1) are *not mutually*

---

[1] NATIONAL BUREAU OF STATISTICS (nigerianstat.gov.ng) (last accessed August 2021)

[2] Nigeria is also Africa's biggest economy by GDP.

exclusive. This is because I hope I establish in Chapter 1 that though much of the current TMT/ICT value chains are still off the Internet, i.e. *offline.* Case in point, the terrestrial and satellite broadcasting value chains are largely offline, though there are some aspects of the TMT/ICT value chains that are effectively online.

For example, I explained that the connectivity segment of the IVC includes the IP-based elements of the radio access (e.g. 4G), any fibre-based core and international network elements that contribute to providing Internet services to some home office user in Pakistan say, from Internet servers in California say (see Figure 7). These connectivity elements – if it includes 4G and/or Wi-Fi – would *all* sit on the IVC, as they are all IP. Conversely, much ICT 'publishing' would be offline as in publishing of physical books, periodicals and newspapers – but some would happening both offline and online (see Figure 4).

2. *TMT/ICT Policy makers and regulators cannot divorce themselves from the encroaching IVC-inspired Digital Economy.* Clearly, with the value chains not being mutually exclusive, TMT/ICT Policy makers and regulators are already implicated in both offline and online sectors. Plus, the IVC would continue to be all pervasive, "absorbing" and/or increasingly substituting some TMT value chains over the current decade to the 2030s and beyond. This suggests current ICT Policy makers and regulators are the natural ones to continue to engage the 'encroachment' problem of the IVC, i.e. evolve to be the Digital Economy policy makers and regulators too. I do not think this is an easy task as they are already busy enough as it is, and their skills need to be significantly enhanced.

3. *Increased Risks of Asymmetric Policies and Regulations:* as the IVC online tidal wave washes over the ICT/TMT offline sectors slowly but surely, there are increasing risks of asymmetric policies and regulations over different platforms. What you may ask is asymmetric policy/regulation?

Consider what asymmetric regulation over different platforms means for the same content? So in India, watching a Bollywood movie over the terrestrial broadcast platform is subject to a different set of policies/regulations from watching the *same* movie *streamed* over Wi-Fi or fibre, or over the Internet? Another example - offline

149

advertising regulations being completely orthogonal to their online counterparts without clear reasons beyond that they have different laws/statutes underpinning them? My key point here is IP creates opportunities for differential and inconsistent policies and regulations from disparate regulators, or even the same one because of different statutes governing offline and online activities. Indeed, there would be more 'turf wars' as to whether some issues (e.g. telecoms cybersecurity or privacy concerns) should sit with the Data Protection Agency or with the telecoms regulator? This is one of the reasons I have always argued that, at the very least, a single converged regulator (or fewer digital regulators) is a first step to addressing differential regulation by different entities. Digital Economy policy makers and regulators would need to start harmonising regulations across different platforms, e.g. advertising rules across broadcast, SVOD, AVOD and Online platforms would clearly need harmonising.

4. *Some similar Policy and Regulatory Concerns apply both across the [offline] TMT/ICT and the [online] IVC Value Chains*: in Chapter 2, we observed recurring (but similar) set of challenges across both the offline and online worlds. For examples,

  • *Worries about increasing market concentration*[3] where some telecom operators in countries like Myanmar (MPT), India (Jio), Kenya (Safaricom), Nigeria (MTN), South Africa (Vodacom), etc. have growing [and more 'sticky', i.e. hardly any churn] market shares. These present worries from a competition perspective. We see in Chapter 2 that we also have concentration issues galore with digital platforms like Google Ads, Google Search, Google AdSense, Facebook, Amazon, Apps Stores, Operating Systems (OSs) and so on. Figure 13a clearly shows that for Internet search in Brazil, only Google truly matters. The market concentration issues

---

[3] Market concentration worries accrue when a small number firms (sometime just one firm) account/s for large percentage of the total market of specific services like voice, data, broadband, fiber, etc.. It measures the extent of domination of sales by one or more firms in a particular market. The market concentration ratio measures the combined market share of all the top firms in the industry sector/subsector.

with digital platforms are almost totally global though, not just national (e.g. for services like Search outside China).

- *Worries about Consolidations across the IVC as well as Cultural Concerns*: Just revisit Chapter 2's Figure 14 which shows Meta has three of the top five apps by number of active users (Facebook, WhatsApp and Facebook Messenger). Even in China, Chinese conglomerate Tencent owns both WeChat, or Weixin in China (1.24 billion active users) and QQ (606 million active users). These are data as of July 2021. What would your view be Facebook or its parent Meta were to attempt purchase TikTok? Many competition authorities now know enough about the IVC to be fully concerned about such a potential acquisition.

Chapter 2 also shows that clear consolidations are happening involving significant Content Rights segment actors and Connectivity sector players which evidently derive from the new IVC as seen in Figure 10: the ATT (Connectivity segment) and Time Warner (Premium Content Rights segment) transaction with the Connectivity player in the lead; the Walt Disney and 21st Century Fox transaction (both of Content Rights segment); and the Comcast (Content Rights segment) and Sky (Content Rights/Connectivity) transaction. This is further evidence of the dynamic the IVC is driving. In Chapter 2's Figure 10, Augusto Pretta clearly highlights how the consolidations in the picture create data and content packages (via quad plays across voice, data, fixed, mobile Internet access and video/TV). However, he also highlights the greater role of Big Data and Artificial Intelligence in the identification and servicing of subscribers (i.e. shifting from a B2B strategy to a direct consumer offerings) in order to compete with emerging future content behemoths like Netflix and Amazon (see Figure 11b).

Chapter's 2 Figure 11a shows mostly American companies leading on Content rights production and acquisition. From a *cultural and competition* perspective, this is hardly healthy even from the European Content Rights segment vantage point, yet alone from the vantage points of African countries, South East Asian countries, India, Caribbean and elsewhere. *Cultural concerns* and cultural imperialism[4] are looming even larger than ever with the Content Rights segment of the IVC – with fears that not only American culture, but also American technological imperialism are being exported worldwide unchecked[5].

- *Worries about promoting true competition*: in India for example, a new entrant called Reliance Jio entered the Indian telecoms scene in 2016 and has clearly 'shaken up' the telecoms market there, arguably leading to at least two bankruptcies of other big telecoms names. This is on the downside. On the upside, prices in India tumbled, subscriptions to data services grew exponentially, monthly data consumption per subscriber grew exponentially, etc. However, there have been many cries of "foul play" in India about Jio's rise to top by its competitors, alleging she is not playing "by fair rules". Pricing below costs and/or cross sector subsidies allegations abounded and still abound. Arguably, the lack of a truly independent regulator in India allowed for Jio's rise – but I must say the consumers and citizens benefits of Jio's entry have been humongous. I mention this Reliance Jio example because we see in Chapter 2 too, that similar anti-competitive complaints are being filed about the way the mega-digital platforms compete across the globe, whether it is in South Korea, Australia, the UK, the EU - or even in the USA where most of these mega platforms derive from.

- *Worries about Protecting Consumers*: TMT/ICT [Offline] regulators worry about this today, whether it is about traditional broadcasters' duty to protect children/minors from the certain tasteless content [e.g. before a 9pm watershed say] on TV terrestrial broadcast platforms. Guess what? There is unlimited and far more tasteless content online, inspired by

---

[4] Cultural Imperialism: Hollywoodization – communicationtechnology101 (wordpress.com)

[5] Are tech companies Africa's new colonialists? | Financial Times (ft.com)

the IVC - unlimited content that is patently not appropriate for minors/children. Therefore, current offline TMT/ICT regulators address consumer protection issues by (i) enforcing national consumer laws including addressing unfair terms/contracts (ii) enforcing offline advertising protection, e.g. minimising 'junk food' adverts that children see (iii) providing consumers as much information as possible for them to make informed choices (iv) regulating Quality of Service/Experience (QoS/QoE), etc. Having seen the non-exhaustive but numerous list of online harms of Chapter 2, I hope it is obvious how much more important consumer protection/empowerment is required with online activities. Just recall the section on the UK's children code of the previous chapter.

Allocating and managing Scarce Resources: Many TMT/ICT [Offline] regulators exist because they need to efficiently manage scarce resources. Can you remember what some are? I am sure you do. The big one is wireless radio frequency Spectrum, these scarce and irreplaceable public assets that every country needs to build a significant part of their digital economies on. Spectrum is not only nationally managed – it is also internationally managed through the ITU [6]. You remember any other scarce resources that ICT/TMT regulators manage? Of course, they manage the allocation and assignment of telephone numbers too.

The online world also has its own assets to allocate and manage carefully. Computers, servers and devices across the Internet have to be addressed, in just the same way as we are addressed by our *individual* names. Computers and servers online are addressed by numbers. I note in Chapter 2 that as the numbers of computer/servers increased into the billions, the addressing number range had to be increased - hence the shift from IP version

---

[6] The ITU denotes the International Telecommunication Union. It is a United Nations specialised agency for information and communication technologies (ICT). Most importantly, it coordinates the shared global use of the radio spectrum and supports/facilitates the development and coordination of worldwide technical standards for radio and non-radio-based equipment.

4 or IPv4 (32 '0's and '1's) to IPv6 (128 '0's and '1's), see Nwana, 2014, p. 158/159. The more than 20 billion devices/servers connected to the Internet all need their identities, or *IP addresses*. This is an example of allocating finite Internet 'resources'. *Domain names* (like www.cenerva.com or www.bbc.com) all need management through being registered, etc. On behalf of the Internet Assigned Numbers Authority (IANA), ICANN allocates IP address blocks to five Regional Internet Registering (RIRs) around the world, who in turn issue and manage the generic TLDs (gTLDs) such as www.bbc.com or country code TLDs (ccTLDs) such as www.icasa.za (.za is the country code TLD for South Africa). What again is my point here? Simply that the Internet has its own resources too, to allocate and manage.

Public Policy challenges: Public policy generally consists of the set of actions—plans, laws, and behaviours—adopted by a government[7]. TMT/ICT [Offline] regulators typically work in partnership with their Governments to address many public policy challenges. They could include (i) access and inclusion to all (or most) to connectivity services (ii) financial inclusion (iii) digital literacy (iv) coverage of voice and data networks (v) broadcasting to inform, educate and entertain all citizens of a country like the BBC does in the UK (vi) postal policy and implementation. Well – guess what? The IVC-based online public policy challenges are just numerous: online regulation challenges, cybercrimes, OTTs, cyber-frauds, Tax frauds, data protection and privacy, grooming, national security, internet addiction, spam emails, the use of AI, the use of facial recognition, etc. You recognise this unfinished list? All the harms and potential harms of the last chapter are mostly issues too of public policy. Ultimately, a country can decide to have no Internet at all – and avoid all the harms, risks and concerns of the last chapter – or have the Internet and deal with all these consequences as public policy challenges. Politicians must lead on such public policy concerns: they have been elected to deal with

---

[7] Governance - Public policy | Britannica

them. Most independent regulators have never been elected, so they should ideally play supporting roles on such issues.

So we see similar offline and online policy and regulatory challenges.

5. *Mobile/Cellular operators have suddenly found themselves delineated to the Connectivity layer/segment of the Internet value chain whilst other players dominate other layers* – and *all Online Segment services are OTT services*: these are truly two seminal lessons of the IVC. Mobile/cellular operators who dominate the telecoms sector (and hence the ICT sectors) of most economies now sit in a different segment (Connectivity) of the Internet value Chain (IVC). This consequence of this seemingly innocuous 'reclassification' is quite fundamental: different segments of the IVC have different players, risks, opportunities and would have different policies and regulations to address any issues they face.

Digital Economy policy makers and regulators have to contend with this new reality. There must be *consistency* in policy making and regulation within the same segment (or segment categories) of the value chain, and there would be clear *differences* across different segments. Current mobile/cellular operators hate this inescapable conclusion. Furthermore, OTTs sit in a totally different segment (Online Services), and practically all the services of the Online Services segment are OTT services. So if mobile/cellular operators complain to Digital Economy policy makers and regulators about social media apps like Facebook and WhatsApp, they should equally complain hard about Google Search, Amazon, Ebay, YouTube, etc. which drive more data usage, and hence more revenues for operators. I would add to this list too smartphones suppliers and App stores which make access to online services so seamless and easy to use.

6. *TMT/ICT policy making and regulation can no longer ignore the 'online' and the IVC:* as Chapter 2 shows, the digital IVC world and digitisation in general has consequences. It is not just a matter (as I note in Lesson number 2 above) of the policy makers and regulators

evolving into Digital Economy personnel, but also the whole new raft of policies, regulations and codes that need to be developed.

Just consider the UK's age-appropriate design code for online children apps of the last chapter which takes many pages to summarise. Consider the numerous other harms/risks of Chapter 2 and imagine the amount of work and effort required to develop new sets of policies and regulations to tackle the ones your country judges need to be tackled.

7. *The Long Tail theory and Anderson (2006) three drivers appear to be exactly at the core of the IVC's positive externalities, and sadly as well as the negative ones too. Elections and democracies are at risk with Online services*: the democratisation of (i) digital production (ii) distribution and (iii) and the bringing matching of supply and demand – are core drivers to the *Online Services* segment of the IVC.

The Internet's global nature supports *long tail* economics, i.e. relatively small numbers of "geographically dispersed readers, viewers, or listeners with a common interest can now be aggregated to form a sizeable audience". We observe this long tail economics daily today on all platforms such as Twitter, Facebook, YouTube and more. And both benefits and harms derive too because of the aggregation of geographically dispersed consumers/citizens with similar interests, whether good or bad. If the long tail dynamic brings together geographically dispersed 'bad actors' (read conspiracy theorists say) who amplify their craziness within their echo chambers, we then see in Chapter 2 the terrible consequences to society including, e.g. the case of a Californian dad killing his children over QAnon/serpent DNA nonsense.

We also see that how former President Donald Trump incredibly picked up conspiracy theories online, used the Twitter to help propagate and amplify them – and how it galvanised a "stop the steal" movement who attacked to the US Capitol on the 6th January 2021. Elections and democracies truly do face risks with Online services – and they truly need to be checked. Do not listen to me –

listen to Facebook's Founder and CEO Mark Zuckerberg who has called for elections to be regulated on Online platforms [8]. Specifically, Mr Zuckerberg requests stronger laws around the world to protect the integrity of elections with common standards for all websites to identify political actors. He asked for this amongst other things in 2019! Just reflect on this date for a moment. After what happened at the 2020 elections, who can refuse this? Lest the reader forgets, former U.S. President Trump was banned off digital platforms including Twitter and Facebook[9] – truly surreal!

8. *The Mega-digital Platforms, Operating Systems (OSs) and App Stores are being slowly but surely 'checked' across the world. Avant-garde regulators'/consumers' actions in one country may have disproportionally positive externalities in multiple countries. However, it is true too that these mega digital platforms are already too big to control, and perhaps even more worrying, it is not obvious how to truly regulate mega social platforms like Facebook*: Chapter 2 covers many case studies and cases covering digital platforms and services like Google Ads, Google Search, Facebook, Instagram, TikTok, Amazon, etc. and App Stores such as Google Apps and Apple Apps. The chapter also covered the concentration issues with OSs like Google Android and Apple iOS.

It is clear from Chapter 2 that the risks, concerns and harms that are already being inflicted on consumers and citizens using these IVC digital platforms/services. It is also clear how stakeholders – i.e., regions (e.g. EC), countries (e.g. South Korea, USA, UK, Australia, Italy, India, Pakistan, Indonesia, Bangladesh, etc.) and even developers/consumers (via class action lawsuits) – are fighting back for the benefits of their consumers and citizens. Some countries like India and Pakistan have actually banned platforms: the former (India) banned TikTok, WeChat and 58 other apps,

---

[8] Mark Zuckerberg asks governments to help control internet content - BBC News (last accessed September 2021)

[9] Donald Trump's 'communications' platform permanently taken offline - BBC News (last accessed September 2021)

whilst the latter (Pakistan) has banned Tinder, Grindr and three other dating apps for "immoral content".

Competition Authorities across the world such as the UK's CMA, Australia's ACCC, the European Commission (EC), Italy's AGCM/AGCOM and more are either carrying out investigations/studies into these digital platforms and/or setting up new policies/institutions to regulate them. I think these are wholly necessary too.

In Chapter 2, we also see how the UK's age-appropriate design code for online apps has already forced TikTok, Google's YouTube and Meta's Instagram to make significant pro-children protection changes to these platforms, and how these benefits are very likely to ripple through to many other countries and regions. I predict the UK's ICO children code will be replicated in essence in many other countries.

Consider as well South Korea's law [August 2021] to counter the power of Google App Store and Apple Store. I am confident other competition authorities like the EC, Australia's ACCC, the UK's CMA and even back in the USA are taking keen notice. Even class action lawsuits by citizen developers against App Stores would have a ripple effect across the globe.

All the above said, I conclude that the big tech gateway companies are mostly already too big to control using traditional antitrust/competition instruments – because most non-US authorities would tread very carefully in proceeding with any structural (i.e. breakup) proposals about US behemoths. It is just too hot politically. Big tech knows this better than most.

As I noted in the last chapter, this [and talk of breaking up big tech] would have to be left to US politicians like Senator Elizabeth

Warren who has strongly advocated and still advocates for breaking up Big Tech[10].

Furthermore, in the last chapter discussed what I termed the Facebook content conundrum, i.e. how to regulate such a mega platform where its broader social value contributions to society are arguably multiples of its private value (i.e. profits and consumer surplus), i.e. valued at a multiple of Facebook's public value to circa US $1.0 Trillion (as of 3rd Sept 2021). Sadly, its negative externalities' total value may arguably in the hundreds of billions of dollars, if not orders bigger.

9. *Internet Censorship and Surveillance – a Bifurcation of the Internet?* Chapter 2's Figure 12 highlights a likely trend of a 'bifurcated' Internet of either a more *Open* Internet or a more *censored* one. Figure 12 depicts that Internet censorship and surveillance is already *pervasive* not only in China, but Bahrain, Iran, Kuwait, North Korea, Oman, Pakistan, Qatar, Saudi Arabia, Syria, Turkmenistan, UAE, Uzbekistan and Vietnam. This makes fifteen countries under pervasive censorship and surveillance.

Indeed I note China's emerging Internet. I allude that China may be drawing the line between individual liberty/privacy vs. public good in a very different place – and it appears to me worth repeating because of its core implications. I note that that some argue China is arguably creating a different kind of Internet. Consider these:

- monitoring millions via the Internet using close to 200 million surveillance cameras across the country
- using advanced AI facial recognition technology, online systems allegedly collecting voice recognition samples to boost surveillance[11]
- connecting to a DNA database of millions of people "to help solve crimes"[12]
- moderators deciding on what people post/not post, etc.

---

[10] Break Up Big Tech | Elizabeth Warren

[11] China: Voice Biometric Collection Threatens Privacy | Human Rights Watch (hrw.org)

[12] China's massive effort to collect its people's DNA concerns scientists (nature.com)

- Etc.

This is truly Frankenstein in approach compared to the Western view of an Open Internet.

This 'bifurcation' appears to me to be at the heart of all the spying fears [13] [14] by some Western Governments/ pro-Western Governments against Chinese behemoth technology firms, specifically Huawei, ZTE, StarTimes and more.

Indeed, since 2019 the USA has been warning allies and partners [15] that having Chinese telecom giant Huawei build their 5G networks risks exposing their citizens' and even their countries official information/data to Chinese State surveillance. Therefore the Trump administration heavily lobbied other countries to keep Huawei out of their networks.

Huawei has consistently asserted its independence from China's Government – but sadly Chapter 2 report on how major Chinese behemoths like Tencent have acquiesced to the Chinese Government inside China. This does not portend well for most including me who study these closely; however, it is neither proof-positive either that Huawei is doing anything nefarious with its 5G networks. In this vein, I must also add that Australia banned Huawei and ZTE over anything 5G since August 2018 [16]. Indeed, there are persistent *rumours* Australia would prefer the Chinese do not buy telecoms assets in its backyard in the Pacific as is evidenced by the title of this Reuters' article: *Telstra in talks to buy Digicel Pacific in Australian Govt-backed bid* [17]. The Indian Government have banned Chinese apps. Indeed by late October 2021, it was

---

[13] China dismisses 'absurd' African Union HQ spying claim - BBC News

[14] China spied on African Union headquarters for five years — Quartz Africa (qz.com)

[15] How America Turned the Tables on Huawei | Voice of America - English (voanews.com)

[16] Huawei and ZTE handed 5G network ban in Australia - BBC News

[17] Telstra in talks to buy Digicel Pacific in Australian govt-backed bid | Reuters

confirmed that Australia's Telstra had bought Digicel Pacific "to block China"[18].

Chapter 2 also covers the reality of the zoning of the Internet, and asks the question where acceptable zoning ends and where Internet censorship starts?

Why are all of these USA, Indian and Australian intrigues against China relevant – I hear you ask? Simply because they matter for [public] policy and regulation. At its apex, does your Government buy into Internet surveillance (like the 15 countries listed above do) or does it buy into the Open Internet? It seems to me this decision is massively fundamental to *free speech, privacy and anonymity* online. Either way as a Digital Economy policy maker and/or regulator, it appears to me you should not allow your country to sleepwalk into a surveillance Internet with your "eyes shut".

10. *Online Risks and Harms that emanate from the IVC are both numerous and some truly deadly:* Disinformation and conspiracy theories are truly bad for society, and sometimes deadly.

---

[18] Digicel Pacific: Australia's Telstra buys Pacific firm 'to block China' - BBC News

Figure 18 – Content Rights Segment Negative Externalities (from Chapter 2)

I hope Chapter 2 demonstrates the numerous harms and risks amply and I would not add much to this narrative here. However, I summarise them as best as I can in the following word cloud of Figures 18 to 22 - segment by segment. I hope these figures provide another form of summary of the harms, risks and concerns per IVC segment of Chapter 2.

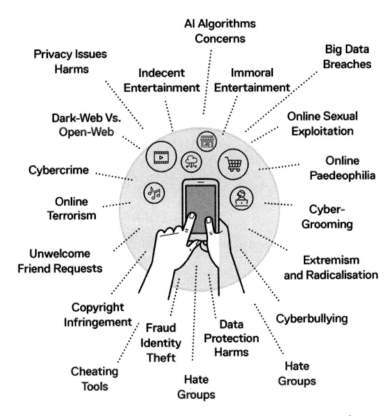

Figure 19 – Online Services Segment Negative Externalities (from Chapter 2)

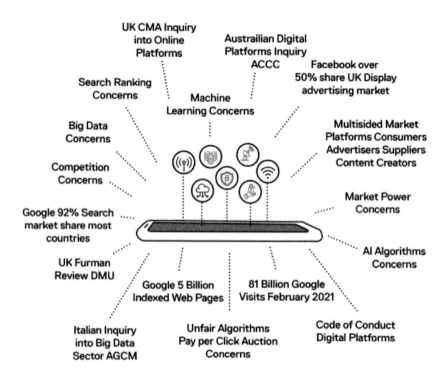

Figure 20 – Enabling Technologies & Services Segment Negative
Externalities (from Chapter 2)

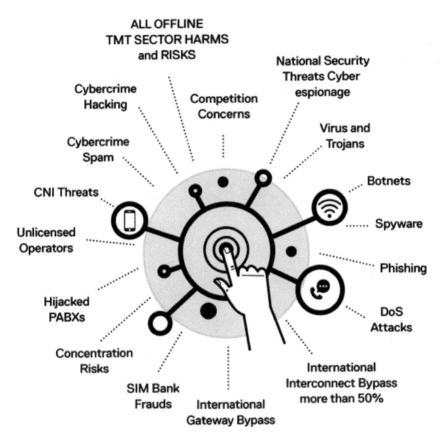

Figure 21 – Connectivity Segment Negative Externalities (from Chapter 2)

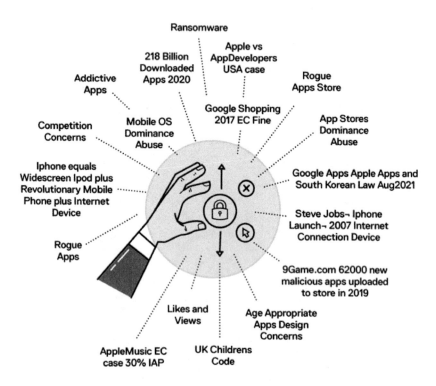

Figure 22 – User Interface Segment Externalities (from Chapter 2)

What Figures 18 to 22 graphically depict is how *literally* numerous the concerns, risks and harms that come with the IVC are.

I have also been at pains to emphasise that these risk, harms and concerns are not exhaustive, but hopefully you note how difficult many of them are too from a policy and regulatory standpoint.

3.3 A Summary set of Assumptions and Top-Level Exam Questions for Digital Economy Policy Makers & Regulators

Often I emphasise across this book that digitalising economies has consequences. I hope the consequences are clearly illustrated (summarized from Chapter 2) in Figures 18 to 22 above.

I cover next a summary narrative on some key assumptions and what I term the top-level exam questions for Digital Economy policy makers and regulators. Here they follow.

1. *Most countries are digitalising their economies:* this is a key assumption of this manuscript. The efforts to do this digitalising are typically led by ICT/TMT or Post & Telecommunications ministries and ministers. Their ministries are being rebranded as Ministries of 'Digital Economy' or of 'Digital Technologies' or something similar.

   Alternatively in some other countries, Ministers are appointed under largely *un-rebranded* ministries and given 'Digital', 'Innovation', etc. responsibilities. See the following examples to illustrate.
   - Jordan – Ministry of Digital Economy and Entrepreneurship[1]
   - Nigeria (2019) – Ministry of Communications and Digital Economy[2]
   - Thailand – Ministry of Digital Economy and Society[3]
   - South Africa (2020) – Ministry of Communications & Digital Technologies
   - UK (2017) – Minister for Digital and the Creative Industries[4] (under a slightly rebranded Department for *Digital*, Culture, Media and Sport)

---

[1] Home Page - Minister of Digital Economy and Entrepreneurship (modee.gov.jo)

[2] Federal Ministry of Communications and Digital Economy, Nigeria - Home | Facebook

[3] Ministry of Digital Economy and Society – Thailand

- Benin (2019) – Ministry of Digital Economy and Communication[5]

- European Union – Vice President for the Digital Single Market, European Commission

- Malaysia – Ministry of Science, Technology & Innovation

There is even an OECD 'Digital Economy Ministerial Meeting' series[6]. Those civil servants and policy makers in previously or currently named Ministries of Post & Telecommunications, ICT, etc. have now *de facto* become Digital Economy policy makers and regulators.

2. *Most countries [particularly developing ones] are still set up largely to regulate the Offline ICT/TMT sector:* in fact, their regulators still largely regulate as they have been for the past 20 years, assuming a relatively static ICT/TMT sector. Admittedly, it is true some countries are *incrementally* enacting some digital economy laws, e.g. on Privacy laws, or E-Commerce laws, etc. However, I contend this incremental approach is sub-optimal to the challenges of the risks, harms and concerns of Figures 18 to 22.

3. *The largely offline ICT/TMT Sector has been significantly evolving already into the online Internet Value Chain in some countries who were not quite ready:* some of this is happening slowly and perhaps going unnoticed, bypassing existing industry structures. The next section covers a mini-case study of the "Netflix effect" in Thailand to illustrate this point. I deliberately draw some key lessons from this interesting mini-case study.

4. *The Internet Value Chain (IVC) is already with us in most countries:* there is hardly a country in the globe who has not started facing the *online* challenges, harms, risks and/or concerns of Figures 18 to 22.

5. *Therefore, Digital Economy ministers, policy makers and regulators have to start grappling with all these new Online harms in addition to the old Offline ICT/TMT ones too:* a key further challenge is that these new digital economy policy makers and regulators are already very

---

[4] Minister for Digital and the Creative Industries - GOV.UK (www.gov.uk)

[5] The Ministry of Digital Economy and Communication (Ministère du Numérique et de la Digitalisation) (MND) (Benin) | Devex

[6] Digital Economy Ministerial Meeting - Organisation for Economic Co-operation and Development (oecd.org)

overworked and yet they have to deal, mostly untrained, with these new online harms.

This short narrative – as I explained in my preface at the start of this book – is at the core of why I penned it.

3.4 Introducing Big Tech and other Emerging Online Change Makers

It would be impossible to define the challenge for the new Digital Economy Policy and Regulatory challenges going forward without formally defining/identifying Big Tech and other key emerging Online change makers. I have already covered several of them in the previous chapter, but not collectively as a group in the case of Big Tech. I have certainly covered Amazon, Facebook, Google and Apple as mini-case studies in the previous chapter.

Let me start with who Big Tech is or are. Wikipedia defines Big Tech (or Tech Giants) as the name given to the four or five most dominant companies in the ICT industry of the USA, namely Amazon, Apple, Google (Alphabet), Facebook/Meta[7] and Microsoft[8].

Wikipedia defines Big Tech as "dominant companies in the ICT Industry of the USA", but frankly we will agree – China aside - that these companies are truly global. These five companies – for good or for ill – have come dominate our *online* lives:

- *Amazon* is the undisputed dominant player of the e-Commerce market of Online Services segment of the IVC with almost 50% of all online sales going through this platform. Amazon has changed the value chains of many sectors and has revolutionised just-in-time logistics worldwide. Amazon has set up value chains in developed economies like the UK, USA and France which completely bypasses

---

[7] In October 2021, Facebook formally became part of a new parent holding company called Meta.

[8] Big Tech - Wikipedia

those of the traditional sectors, e.g. postal, books, food, etc. Amazon is the a cloud computing leader – and it is also in video streaming now with Amazon Prime. Amazon is also one of the world leaders in the use of AI-based digital assistants.

- *Apple* is a dominant player of the User Interface segment of the IVC, not only with its devices but also with Apple Apps Store. Apple – as we see in the last chapter too – is one of the duopoly players in mobile Operating systems (OSs) market.

- *Google (Alphabet)* needs no introduction. So profound is this company to our online lives that the venerable Oxford English Dictionary included 'google' as a verb in their dictionary on June 15th, 2006[9]. To google means to search the Internet. Google also owns YouTube.

- *Facebook (now part of Meta)* is virtually a synonym with social networking and social media. Need I add more than reminding the reader to look at Figure 14 showing that more than 1/3rd of humanity use this platform? Meta also dominates the IVC categories of the sharing of images/videos with Instagram and messaging communications with WhatsApp.

- *Microsoft* is the undisputed leader with desktop operating systems (OSs), office productivity software and a major leader of the cloud computing industry (Microsoft Azure), second only to Amazon.

As I wrote the above, I was literally a bit jolted not only how these Big Tech companies influence economy and society today and shape the way society progresses or the way society is harmed, I was also jolted on how I personally rely on their products and services. I suspect you are in the same position too.

Drawing again from Wikipedia's Big Tech[10], let me throw in a few other relevant acronyms and names pertaining to these Big Tech companies. Note that the acronyms below have not been updated to accommodate Meta - Facebook's, Instagram's and WhatsApp's new parent company.

---

[9] Google Now A Verb In The Oxford English Dictionary - Search Engine Watch
[10] Big Tech - Wikipedia

- *Big Five (Big 5) Tech* refers to all five companies above – sometimes referred to as GAFAM (Google, Apple, Facebook, Amazon and Microsoft) of FAAMG. Sometimes the Big 5 stocks are referred to as FAAAM stocks (Facebook, Amazon, Alphabet, Apple and Microsoft).

- *Big Four (Big 4) Tech* is typically used to refer to Facebook, Alphabet (Google), Facebook and Apple – or GAFA. Microsoft – though currently bigger than Google and Facebook in terms of market capitalisation – is typically excluded from the Big 4 because it does not drive online consumer revolution in the minds of online users as these big 4 do.

- *The Digital Advertising Big Three (Big 3):* Google, Facebook and Amazon form this group. As we see in the last chapter, competition authorities around the world (e.g. in the USA, UK, France, EU and Australia) are all very concerned about the dominance of these Big 3 in the online advertising market.

- *FAANG* – permit me to also mention this other acronym which introduces another new and clear emerging player, Netflix, i.e. Facebook, Amazon, Apple, *Netflix* and Google (Alphabet). For this reason, I introduce a mini-case study on Netflix next.

- *FANGAM* – stands for Facebook, Amazon, Netflix, Google (Alphabet), Apple and Microsoft. These six companies are the household names across the IVC and cloud value chain.

- *Chinese Big Tech (BATX)[11]:* to conclude this section, I briefly mention the Chinese Big Tech which includes Baidu, Alibaba, Tencent and Xiaomi collectively known as BATX. Baidu is simply the 'Google' of China, and has benefitted from Google's ban in China. Alibaba is roughly the 'Amazon' of China. Tencent as I note in Chapter 2 owns both WeChat, or Weixin in China (1.24 billion active users) and QQ (606 million active users) – see Figure 14. WeChat provides an incredible array of offerings range from sending text messages, playing games, processing digital payments to making video calls. QQ is the WhatsApp and more of China.

---

[11] BATX - Wikipedia

Xiaomi is roughly the 'Apple' of China and is dominant in consumer electronics and related software company.

In the same way as FANGAM dominates our online (and offline) lives outside China, BATX do likewise in China. The same competition and harms concerns we have with FANGAM and other online players in the West, China has similar concerns with BATX inside China too.

3.5 Case Study: The "Netflix Effect" on the Film and Broadcasting Industry in Thailand[12]

I cover all FAANG companies in one way or the other in Chapter 2 bar Netflix. I take the opportunity to address this here and now.

Netflix brands itself as "the global Internet TV network". Ramasoota & Kitikamdhhorn (2021) published a most interesting paper on Netflix with the above section title in the Telecommunications Policy journal. Their paper presents a most intriguing case study on how Netflix is enabling the bypassing of the monopoly in the Thai film industry.

---

[12] "The Netflix effect" in Thailand: Industry and regulatory implications - ScienceDirect

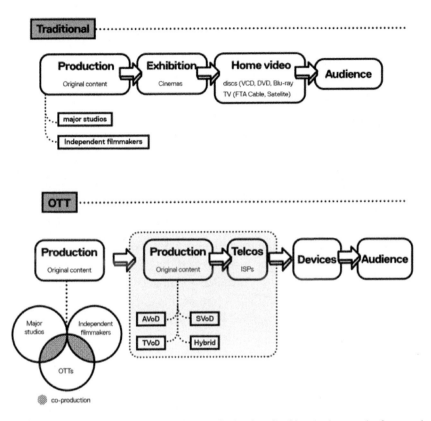

Figure 23 - Comparative value chain of Thailand's film industry, before and after OTTs (e.g. Netflix) arrived [Source: Illustrated from Ramasoota & Kitikamdhhorn (2021), p. 12]

Once again, bear in mind that Thailand's ICT sector is *broadly* constituted similarly to Nigeria', i.e. comprising of (i) Telecommunications and Information Services (ii) Publishing (iii) Motion Picture/Films, Sound Recording and Music Production and (iv) Broadcasting.

Figure 23 shows how the traditional Thai film industry is being disrupted by the OTTs in Thailand. It portends key lessons for other top content-producing markets like Nigeria (Nollywood) and India (Bollywood).

I believe some of the key lessons I draw below are truly illustrative and supportive of some of the assumptions and main arguments I argue for in this manuscript.

1. The first thing to note is that Thailand's online digital infrastructure is one of the best and with one of the highest fixed network subscribers numbers in South East Asia. Recall too that I note with Figure 7 in Chapter 1 that the IP-based *fixed* infrastructure [including the national fiber backbone and IP-Based Internet connections into subscribers' home (either by 4G, FWA or Wi-Fi)] would sit on the Internet value chain. This is exactly the case in Thailand.

   Ramasoota & Kitikamdhhorn (2021) report that fixed broadband has been expanding steadily to circa 10.1 million subscribers (circa 47% of Thai homes[13]) by the last quarter of 2019, driven by low prices for broadband Internet services from four major service providers for the fixed broadband service segment. There are also 17 International Internet Gateway (IIG) operators as well as a well-functioning National Internet eXchange (NIX). In fact, more recent data shows that Internet penetration in Thailand has increased to 48.59 million in January 2021[14], i.e. 69.5% (vs. 62% in January 2020).

   Other January 2021 data[15] proves the maturity of the Thai digital infrastructure: average daily Internet use (all devices) at 8 hours 44 minutes; average time spent watching TV (broadcast and streaming) at 3 hours 30 minutes; time spent using social media at 2 hours 48 minutes; time spent listening to music streaming services at 1 hour 34 minutes; time spent playing video games on a games console at 1 hour and 38 minutes; and *average download speed of fixed Internet connection at 308.34Mbs.* This last data point truly speaks to the increasingly robust digital infrastructure in Thailand – a key prerequisite for the digital economy.

2. Thanks to the increasingly robust Thai digital infrastructure, it is not surprising Netflix chose to enter the market early. As at October 2020, Netflix had already notched up 546,000

---

[13] This is quite high given that Thailand has a population of just under 70 million people.

[14] Digital in Thailand: All the Statistics You Need in 2021 — DataReportal – Global Digital Insights

[15] *Ibid.*

subscribers[16] in Thailand, i.e. 25% of the SVOD Thai market, along with a 3-month revenue of US $182.86 million for the first three months of 2020.

3. *Broadcasting & Film Industry Impact by Netflix in Thailand:* Ramasoota & Kitikamdhhorn (2021) find that Netflix has already significantly affected both the films and broadcasting value chains in Thailand.

For films, Netflix is reported to have reduced the monopolistic power that long dominated the Thai industry, giving the small film producers a globalized taste [movie production, distribution and theatres were previously a monopoly in Thailand under singular ownership dominated by two national chains in SF and Major]. Hence Netflix is enabling small Thai production houses and independent film makers to thrive and expose their talents internationally.

As Figure 24 depicts, an OTT platform like Netflix is replacing the erstwhile monopoly Thai home video and DVD markets of the traditional film value chain. Such disruption is welcomed by small movie producers and directors, and their films can now also be released on multi-platforms (i.e. cinema, broadcast TV and online). This reduction in monopoly power of Thai film industry is also leading to the shortening of the usual 90-day window between cinema and online OTT releases, as movie producers have stronger bargaining power.

As regards broadcasting, the authors note that Netflix is largely in control of production, distribution and presentation of content broadcasted now in Thailand. Netflix is acquiring streaming content in Thailand across various genres: movies, series, documentaries, animations and cartoons. Consider what they write about Netflix's impact on broadcasting:

> In the Thai context, Netflix has acquired a great number of local content into its catalogues from local content providers, television broadcasters and movie studios.... On the one hand, small broadcasters that are also content producers find themselves... having to adjust their content timetable to Netflix which holds a more prevalent platform This is exactly the case with True Visions, a digital TV operator, which had to

---

[16] Thailand Netflix subscribers 2020 | Statista (last accessed September 2021)

postpone its series to follow that of Netflix... On the other hand, content providers whose content have been licensed to stream on Netflix platform feel that they benefit from capitalizing on the same content product, while expanding their audience's base to international fronts. With regard to audience's consumption behavior, Netflix has reconceptualized TV-watching by dictating how the content is supposed to be viewed. In a nutshell, Netflix's release model ... is a factor contributing to ... self-scheduling and binge-watching. Netflix's algorithm..., particularly the autoplay, also contribute towards binge-watching by making it more flexible to resume the watch. In addition, Netflix has active collaboration with telcos... and device providers such as Samsung.. this again reflects the platform's influence over related actors in the value chain.

Ramasoota & Kitikamdhhorn (2021), p. 10.

There is clearly no doubt from the above quote – and looking at Figure 24 – that Netflix in Thailand is completely dominating the broadcast and film value chains, from production, to providing a "preferred" platform for distribution in addition to international opportunities (such as Thais in the USA), to devices, to binge-watching behaviours and more.

In summary, Netflix has triggered major Thai broadcasters to move online and to diversify as content providers to other South East Asian markets. Netflix has also emerged as an important distribution platform for filmmakers wishing to bypass the erstwhile monopoly in Thai film industry.

4. *Asymmetric regulation & a "rather relaxed regulatory environment"* (Ramasoota & Kitikamdhhorn, 2021, p. 2). I love the authors' use of the phrase "rather relaxed regulatory environment". What it really means is that Thai's broadcasting and telecoms regulations in force could not really 'catch' and control Netflix. The authors write, almost in passing, in a footnote:

The country's communications regulator, the National Broadcasting and Telecommunications Commission (NBTC) only regulates licensees that are local operators of broadcasting and telecommunications services on business and content issues. Meanwhile, the Ministry of Digital Economy and Society has legal authority over computer-related offences which spans over online content. However, cross-border streaming data like video-on-demand has not been clearly addressed in terms of jurisdiction and regulatory oversight since they are not registered businesses in Thailand and not license holders of the NBTC.

The last sentence of the quote above says it all: foreign VoD players have not been addressed in Thailand in terms of jurisdiction and regulatory oversight as they are not license holders in Thailand.

This is the rather "relaxed regulatory environment". Furthermore, this clearly means that the same content would be regulated differently on different platforms in Thailand, e.g. on broadcast TV vs. online with Netflix. I noted this as one of the lessons from Part I of this manuscript.

It is clear with international VOD players like Netflix and Amazon Prime that that value chain resource competition at the level of independent producers commences fairly early on at entry. This is because international VOD can make use of global significant market power to exercise influence in domestic markets, even prior to growth in audience in those domestic markets

I started this section by noting that Netflix brands itself as "the global Internet TV network". I think this brief case study from Thailand suggests that this branding may be merited. Netflix – as of the first quarter of 2021, had 207.64 million paid subscribers across the globe[17]. I would not bet against them doubling this within five years. This is another serious digital platform emerging.

3.6 Online and Big Tech Regulation – how has it come to this?

Well – I do not believe there is any other way to say what I say next. Both Online and Big Tech regulation are both necessary and needed now. I believe it is as simple as this.

I firmly believe this considering the following non-exhaustive reasons:

---

[17] Netflix: number of subscribers worldwide 2020 | Statista

(i)   The market dominance and concentration of Big Tech firms in key but yet to be clearly defined 'relevant' regulatory markets (e.g. digital advertising, App Stores, Mobile operating systems, social media, search, streaming video, e-Commerce, etc.) is clear. The 'abuse of their dominance' as seen in many jurisdictions across the world and covered in many of the case studies in this book is also clear to most who observe FANGAM closely.

(ii) The absolute gatekeeping roles to the digital world of Big Tech – see for example again Figures 13a and 13b – is worrying. Such concentrations and gatekeeping would hardly be allowed free reign by regulators in most other regulated sectors, or if they were, they would be firmly regulated monopolies.

(iii) The sheer conflict of interest challenges they face daily is clear, e.g. in the use and 'misuse' of big data on consumers and other merchants as is apparent in Amazon case study of the previous chapter. Data breaches also abound.

(iv) The numerous and proven harms summarized in this Chapter's Figures 18-22 (derived from Chapter 2) can no longer be ignored, particularly harms to the vulnerable and impressionable in society like children, teenagers and the old – harms whose consequences fall on the rest of society. This means whilst on the one hand Big Tech make incredible and well-deserved profits, on the other hand Big Tech negative externalities are socialized with the rest of society.

(v)   The "black box" nature of their algorithms using sophisticated AI, Machine Learning and Big Data analyses and techniques. Algorithms whose training sets are neither transparent to their unsuspecting users nor to any external regulators, algorithms allegedly maximizing user "engagement" at high costs to society, e.g. ranking extremist content higher and recommending this to users. I elaborate on these later in this chapter.

I do not decry for one second the absolute genius of the Big Tech founding entrepreneurs and their successors – the late Steve Jobs (Apple), Jeff Bezos (Amazon), Mark Zuckerberg (Facebook), Larry Page/Sergey Brin (Google), Bill Gates (Microsoft) and more. They have been deservedly been incredibly successful entrepreneurs who have literally changed the world. They have set of the rules of the digital economy and society. The rest of society largely and correctly allowed them the room to innovate – but when the negative externalities of their success start being socialized with an unsuspecting society (e.g. electronic waste, teenage suicides, Internet addiction, online terrorism, etc.), then it is time society takes over the setting of the rules. These brilliant entrepreneurs may decry this view, but online regulation and regulation/control of Big Tech is no longer optional – it is a must!

See if you agree after I cover three further mini-case studies in this section (on Instagram, Facebook and Twitter successively) concerning my fourth and fifth reasons above why I believe Big Tech and Online regulation is now a must, i.e. Reasons (iv) and (v) above.

And indeed, even both Big Tech and founders of the Internet are *meekly* demanding regulation as we see next.

Sir Tim Berners-Lee, Creator of the World Wide Web (WWW)[18]

1. The acknowledged creator of the World Wide Web opined in 2018:

   The changes we've managed to bring have created a better and more connected world. But for all the good we've achieved, the web has evolved into an engine of inequity and division; swayed by powerful forces who use it for their own agendas.

2. Mark Zuckerberg, Founder and CEO of Facebook in an answer at a US Senate hearing:

   My position is not that there should be no regulation.... I think the real question as the Internet becomes more important in people's lives is 'What is the right regulation, not whether there should be or not[19]. April 10th 2018.

   Note what the Facebook CEO says at the end: "not whether there should be or not". He was then asked by whether he would submit some proposed regulations to the Senate to which he agreed.

---

[18] Sir Tim Berners-Lee, 'One Small Step for the Web…', *Medium* (29 September 2018): https://medium.com/@timberners_lee/one-small-step-for-the-web-87f92217d085 [accessed September 2021]

[19] 'Marks Zuckerberg's testimony to Congress: Facebook boss admits company working with Mueller's Russia probe' Transcript of Mark Zuckerberg's Senate hearing - The Washington Post (last accessed September 2021)

Eventually, in March 2019, Facebook identified four areas where to start regulating the Internet[20]:

> Technology is a major part of our lives, and companies such as Facebook have immense responsibilities. Every day, we make decisions about what speech is harmful, what constitutes political advertising, and how to prevent sophisticated cyberattacks. These are important for keeping our community safe. But if we were starting from scratch, we wouldn't ask companies to make these judgments alone.
>
> I believe we need a more active role for governments and regulators. By updating the rules for the Internet, we can preserve what's best about it — the freedom for people to express themselves and for entrepreneurs to build new things — while also protecting society from broader harms.
>
> From what I've learned, I believe we need new regulation in four areas: harmful content, election integrity, privacy and data portability.

There we are – not only is Big Tech requesting regulation, but they have suggested some areas to start from.

Case Study: Instagram and Teenage Girls

Following on from Big Tech itself requesting new rules for the Internet, Instagram came into sharp focus in the press as I was penning this chapter. In Chapter 2, I note briefly the case of how one unfortunate UK Teenager, Molly Russell, 14, killed herself in 2017 after seeing graphic images of self-harm and suicide on Instagram (source BBC)[21]. Instagram was purchased in 2012 and is owned by Meta, which yet again brings Mark Zuckerberg into this story.

To Meta's credit, perhaps after sad events like the UK's Molly Russell I note above, it has been carrying out internal research on the impact of this platform on its users over the past several years. This is good that Meta carries out such research. However in September 2021, the *Wall Street*

---

[20] Opinion | Mark Zuckerberg: The Internet needs new rules. Let's start in these four areas. - The Washington Post (last accessed September 2021)

[21] Molly Russell: Social media users 'at risk' over self-harm inquest delay - BBC News - https://www.bbc.co.uk/news/uk-england-london-55986728 (last accessed August 2021)

Journal (WSJ) laid its hands on some Facebook internal research on Instagram and went on to report that 'Facebook Knows Instagram is Toxic for Teen Girls, Company Documents Show'[22]. The sub-title to the article also damningly reads "its own in-depth research shows a significant teen mental-health issue that Facebook plays down in public".

What did some of the internal research findings state? Here are a few highlights from the WSJ article.

- Allegedly, one presentation slide states "we make body image issues worse for one in three teen girls".

- Allegedly, the research showed that "thirty-two percent of teen girls said that when they felt bad about their bodies, Instagram made them feel worse," and that the research found that 14% of US teen boys said Instagram made them feel worse about themselves too.

- Teenagers reported suicidal thoughts, with 13% of British users and 6% of American users tracing their desire to kill themselves to the Instagram platform.

- Allegedly too, the report states that "aspects of Instagram exacerbate each other to create a perfect storm". Instagram's Explore page is a page where posts from a range of other Instagram are served, and the researchers suggest that this could push impressionable teenagers into harmful content pages.

What is Instagram's side of the story? Instagram on 14th September 2021 published a statement acknowledging the WSJ story and the above findings amongst others. Instagram stated:

> The Wall Street Journal published a story today about internal research we're doing to understand young people's experiences on Instagram. While the story focuses on a limited set of findings and casts them in a negative light, we stand by this research. It demonstrates our commitment to understanding complex and difficult issues young people may struggle with, and informs all the work we do to help those experiencing these issues.
>
> The question on many people's minds is if social media is good or bad for people. The research on this is mixed; it can be both. At Instagram, we look at the benefits

---

[22] Facebook Knows Instagram Is Toxic for Teen Girls, Company Documents Show - WSJ

and the risks of what we do. We're proud that our app can give voice to those who have been marginalized, that it can help friends and families stay connected from all corners of the world, that it can prompt societal change; but we also know it can be a place where people have negative experiences, as the Journal called out today. Our job is to make sure people feel good about the experience they have on Instagram, and achieving that is something we care a great deal about.

Karina Newton, Head of Public Policy, Instagram[23]

Instagram [Karina Newton] above generalises the issue from Instagram's specific [potential] harms to one of "if social media is good or bad for people". This is frankly a very weak response. It is akin to me querying why ordinary people should be allowed to buy an AK47 assault weapon and the response is that of studying whether guns are good or bad for ordinary people. No! There are specifics of the AK47 rifle that makes it (particularly) potentially dangerous in the wrong hands. Similarly, there are specifics about Instagram's design – e.g. its Explore page which could be a "perfect storm" – that may/would need redesigning for teenagers.

It is true that - if "thirty-two percent of teen girls said that when they felt bad about their bodies, Instagram made them feel worse" – then it also means 68% (maximum) of teens do not feel likewise. However, 32% is not insignificant either.

The above all said, perhaps the main issue here is one of the fact that these research was shown to CEO Mark Zuckerberg in 2020, and allegedly, then-Facebook was building a version of Instagram for children under thirteen which the company was urged to scrap[24], which Facebook did in late September 2021. Should Mark Zuckerberg alone be ultimately responsible for deciding alone what to do with such research? These are very difficult and complex public policy areas where the negative externalities fall back on society.

US Senator Richard Blumenthal twitted stating that Facebook has known for years of Instagram's

---

[23] Using research to improve your experience (instagram.com)
[24] Facebook urged to scrap Instagram for children plans - BBC News

damaging effect on young people …[they] shoved aside in favor of growth…..I'm appalled and alarmed by Facebook's targeting of teens with dangerous products while hiding the science of its toxic impact… Through hearings and legislation my Commerce subcommittee will act to protect children and support parents[25].

With the best will in the world, it is difficult for Instagram and Facebook to argue about what the Senator states in his tweet because this is the arena of public policy – and Instagram/Facebook would find it difficult to mount arguments against why Instagram should not be closely scrutinised – if not regulated – after this internal report's findings. At the very least, Instagram/Facebook should be fully report transparently on what it has done with these findings - and at the other extreme, statutory online regulation of Instagram is on its way.

Case Study: AI, Ethics, Privacy, Facebook, YouTube & Misinformation

When you're in the business of maximizing engagement, you're not interested in truth. You're not interested in harm, divisiveness, conspiracy. In fact, those are your friends… they [Facebook] always do enough to be able to put the press release out. But with a few exceptions, I don't think it's actually translated into better policies. They're never really dealing with the fundamental problems.

Hany Farid, Professor, University of California, Berkeley, as quoted in Hao (2021)

In Chapter 2, I note how Facebook greatly employs AI and Machine Learning (ML) techniques in its News Feed algorithm [which does the core rankings] called EdgeRank[26]. I note how Facebook has been iterating its ranking algorithms with some key changes to them in January 2018[27]. This happened after it came under much scrutiny post the 2016 US Presidential elections on its role with the online propagation of "political misinformation and hate speech".

---

[25] Facebook knows Instagram is toxic for teen girls, mental health, body image, company documents reveal - ABC7 New York (abc7ny.com)

[26] EdgeRank - http://edgerank.net/ (last accessed August 2021)

[27] Facebook Is Making Big Changes To Your News Feed (buzzfeednews.com)

Well the story – from a policy and regulatory perspective - is much deeper than just a company iterating its algorithms. This is just normal. The real big policy and regulatory story here is about AI, ethics and privacy.

Hao (2021) published an article in the well-regarded MIT Technology Review on Facebook and Misinformation[28]. Karen Hao titled the article *He got Facebook hooked on AI. Now he can't fix its misinformation addiction.* The sub-title of the article reads – *the company's AI algorithms gave it an insatiable habit for lies and hate speech. Now the man who built them can't fix the problem.*

Hao interviewed many former and current members of Facebook's AI team for her investigative piece, and her core conclusion is that AI models drive Fakebook's recommendation algorithms, algorithms that ferment misinformation and abuse, fuelling societal political polarisation. Most tellingly, her investigations conclude Facebook knew all about this – that these AI models driving Facebook's recommendation algorithms maximising social media user engagement (and profits of course) also increased political polarisation in society. Maximising engagement equals growth. If there are negative externalities to society – tough. The allegation is that Facebook does not really have an incentive to solve the misinformation problem. This is the essence of Hao's investigative reporting on Facebook, AI and misinformation. CEO Mark Zuckerberg was even quizzed about this at a congressional hearing in March 2021[29].

I have not seen much disputing on the record of the details of the facts of Hao's case. I summarise below for the benefit of emphasising my argument that – 100% accurate or less – I do not think Facebook should be dealing with this humongous problem of misinformation and disinformation by itself. It is both (i) too hard in terms of its harms or negative externality to society and (ii) too replete with conflicts of interest on the part of Facebook.

---

[28] He got Facebook hooked on AI. Now he can't fix its misinformation addiction | MIT Technology Review

[29] Mark Zuckerberg still won't address the root cause of Facebook's misinformation problem | MIT Technology Review

When both of these issues come together – it shouts "Regulate Regulate" – or it should do, irrespective of what Facebook thinks.

Just re-read the quote from Professor Hany Farid that I use to start this section. He asserts – "when you are in the business of maximising engagement, you're not interested in truth. You're interested in harm, divisiveness, conspiracy. In fact, those are your friends". And this is from a professor who collaborates with Facebook "to understand image-and-video-based misinformation on the platform" (Hao, 2021).

Hao's story starts with Joaquin Candela who joined Facebook in 2012 to help set up the AI team, and later these AI algorithms later started to find their way into helping target users with content precisely tailored to their interests. Traditional hard-coded algorithms were replaced by machine learning algorithms. These algorithms are "trained" on ad click data – massive amounts of such Big Data collected by Facebook daily. Countless trained models then accrue covering fine-grained categories like "women between 25 and 34 who liked Facebook pages related to yoga" would have specific ads targeted at them. Such finer-grained targeting is great for advertisers, and they would rightly pay for more such clicks.

My doctorate was in AI, so I understand the true challenge Facebook faces here. Imagine the countless number of such AI trained mini-models like women between 25-34 years old and yoga. There would be thousands others – if not up to a hundred thousand. There would be mini-models determining that if a person likes dogs, friend's posts about dogs would rank higher up in the their Facebook's News Feed. There are many problems with this – including maintaining these thousands of mini-models which is already hard enough. Harder still is what we call *AI bias* – which is technical speak for the models are only as good as the training sets you used to train them on.

Maybe the user does not like dogs at all – it is the user's son or daughter that does. The training nearly got it *right* with the user, but not quite right. More training would improve it. However when is enough training enough – before it is deployed in Facebook's ranking algorithms? The point is that the more the content recommended "speaks to the user", the more they are engaged. Facebook (according to Karen Hao) apparently seeks to maximise a metric called L6/7, the fraction of people who log into Facebook six of the previous seven days. This is allegedly one of the "engagement" metrics – the propensity of the platform to keep the user engaged on the platform, and even better still use them to keep others too on the platform, by really knowing their interests, dislikes and likes. These algorithms are tweaked as more data is collected daily. So far so good – if all is benign.

However, like your kitchen knife, the good can come with the bad if the incentive to use the knife is different, i.e. more than just giving the user the best recommendations on his/her news feeds *neutrally*. If the incentive becomes maximising L6/7 engagement at all costs, then do not be surprised if the thousands of trained AI mini-models in the ranking algorithms favour controversy, misinformation and extremism.

Allegedly, this is what Facebook's AI-powered algorithms have been doing. Hao (2021) explains how the most devastating example of this was with Myanmar where viral fake news and hate speech about the Rohingya Muslim minority [instigated by the ruling military junta] helped escalate the Myanmar's erstwhile religious conflict into a full-blown genocide. As the BBC confirmed, Facebook has since admitted it was used to "incite offline violence" in Myanmar[30]. Facebook largely equals the Internet in Myanmar like in many other countries, and an independent report commissioned by Facebook noted that it created an "enabling environment" for fomenting offline violence. Facebook acknowledged it had not done enough "to help prevent our platform from being used to foment division and incite offline violence" (Hao, 2021).

---

[30] Facebook admits it was used to 'incite offline violence' in Myanmar - BBC News

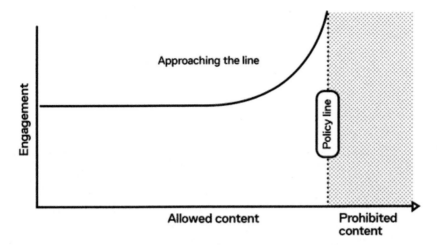

Figure 24 – Natural Enagagement Pattern on Facebook vs. Policy Line - Source: Facebook[31]

Mark Zuckerberg fully acknowledges this problem of AI-based ranking models favouring controversy, misinformation and extremism when he allegedly internally used the chart shown in Figure 24 within Facebook. He allegedly showed (or was shown) clearly that the more a post approaches the Facebook prohibited content policy line, the greater the user engagement.

In plain English, the algorithms that maximise engagement reward more inflammatory, controversial and/or extremist content. You think about it for a second, it makes much sense. It is easier to inspire people to anger than to other emotions. Disinformation and angry content are enticing to people and keeps them on the platform more. Therefore, *echo chambers* with extremist content in it would have the highest user engagements. According to Hao (2021), a Wall Street Journal researcher [Monica Lee] found from an internal presentation that Facebook was not only hosting a large number of extremist groups, but also *promoting* them to its users.

Pause here a bit and reflect – the Facebook platform is [allegedly] promoting extremist groups! The Facebook presentation apparently noted that "64% of

---

[31] https://www.facebook.com/notes/mark-zuckerberg/a-blueprint-for-content-governance-and-enforcement/10156443129621634/

all extremist group joins are due to our recommendation tools", thanks to the AI models behind "Groups You Should Join" and "Discover" platform features. Ergo – as from Myanmar and this latter extremists groups example – maximising engagement increases society polarisation.

Permit me to return to my key point of this case study – AI, Ethics, Privacy and Misinformation – by noting again that as someone who knows a bit about both the problem and about AI, this misinformation and hate speech problem is very hard. Worse, its harms or negative externality to society when got wrong is deadly as shown by the Myanmar Rohingya story. Worst, in my humble view from a policy and regulatory perspective, the problem is too replete with conflicts of interest on the part of Facebook.

Facebook not only has to decide on where the Policy line in Figure 24 lies, but has to optimise where it draws that line with its [Facebook's] profitability. If a foreign company is provably creating national security problems in a 3rd country – just as it is accused to have done in the USA itself with the January 6th 2021 Capitol Riots – then the wider [negative] externalities of the platform have not only *not* been pre-assessed by national regulators, they are being socialised well beyond the boundaries of the USA to unsuspecting countries like Myanmar. How much do such concerns in political hotspot countries Myanmar, Nigeria, Cameroon, Pakistan, India, Afghanistan, Syria, etc. feature in the Board rooms of Facebook? And – as smart as Facebook founders and staff are – why should they continue to be judge on jury on such socially-challenging and ethical issues?

You know what is worse? If users (Facebook Businesses, Brands, Facebook Groups, etc.) work out that extremism, controversial views and hate speech drives even more engagement (as per Figure 24), guess what they do. They ramp up these negatives. Russian hacks used it to meddle in US elections by fomenting polarisation to thousands of Facebook groups to benefit their preferred candidate. I have no doubt Facebook is counteracting these – but the conflict of interest challenge is huge and also ethically non-trivial.

The intersection of AI, Ethics, Privacy and Society is a new area for policy makers, regulators and network operators. They should innovate and understand it fast enough in order to provide the regulatory oversight that companies like Facebook, Google and Instagram increasingly need. The case for algorithms transparency is becoming stronger and stronger.

As an addendum to this section, the whistle-blower who leaked much of this internal information about Facebook and hate speech/misinformation to the WSJ unveiled herself after she resigned and quit Facebook. She also admitted having leaked much internal information about Instagram too, i.e. Instagram and teenage girls. Her name is Frances Haugen. Ms Haugen has since given evidence to both the US Senate[32] and the UK House of Commons[33]. She has since her quitting Facebook released thousands more pages which allegedly support all what I cover in this section and more. She alleges blatant disregard by Facebook executives when they learned their platform could have harmful effects on democracy and on the mental health of children by prioritising its profits over people. She warned the UK Parliament who are working on the Online Safety Bill that Instagram was

> is more dangerous than other forms of social media... Instagram is about social comparison and about bodies... about people's lifestyles, and that's what ends up being worse for kids... I am deeply worried that it may not be possible to make Instagram safe for a 14-year-old, and I sincerely doubt that it is possible to make it safe for a 10-year-old. Source: BBC[34]

There is so much more to Whistle-blower Frances Haugen's allegations that I do not expound upon here, but the ethical algorithms and conflicts of interest challenges with these social media platforms are now most clear – thanks to the likes of Ms Haugen.

To be crystal, this is not just about Facebook and its algorithms. It is about the other major social media and video platforms too. Consider the following BBC story about someone called Mike who found himself captive by algorithms on Facebook, but on YouTube too (see what I highlight in particular).

---

[32] Key takeaways from Facebook whistleblower Frances Haugen's Senate testimony - ABC News (go.com)

[33] Frances Haugen says Facebook is 'making hate worse' - BBC News

[34] Ibid.

Encouraged by the father of a friend, Mike began listening to right-wing talk show host Sean Hannity, and when he searched for similar content online he found alt-right videos and podcasts on Facebook and YouTube. *Social media algorithms were already creating what is known as the rabbit-hole effect - leading him to content that became more and more extreme....*

Eventually Mike migrated to the darkest corners of the internet - to white nationalist message boards on 4chan and 8chan. These sites were like a social club for racists, Nazis and white nationalists, where people could say the N-word while getting to know one another, Mike says. He started exchanging messages with a group of neo-Nazis in the San Francisco Bay area and that is how he ended up on Paul's doorstep that summer afternoon. "I was just looking for a place to put all my anger," Mike says. "And it found a perfect home."

Source BBC[35]

These algorithms create the "rabbit-hole" effect. Mike was rescued but he confesses "I could have been a racist killer". How many killers are being created through similar rabbit-hole effects online?

Case Study: Twitter, Fake News and Bots

Lest the reader believes that challenges with algorithms only afflict Meta-held companies such as at Facebook and Instagram, recall that in Chapter 2 I note the research on Twitter and Fake News. The research showed that Factual news takes 6x longer than fake news to be seen by 1500 people on Twitter. This is according to according to a 2018 MIT study published in the journal *Science*[36].

This particular study found that the spread of false information was not due to bots[37]; rather, false news travels 6x faster around Twitter due to people

---

[35] 'I could have been a racist killer' - BBC News - https://www.bbc.co.uk/news/stories-59171107

[36] *Science*, DOI: 10.1126/science.aao4960 & Fake news travels six times faster than the truth on Twitter | New Scientist

[37] Bots are short for "robots". A bot is a piece of software that perform automated, repetitive and pre-defined tasks. A news bot may mimic a human being and post and forward news as if it is being done by a human being.

190

retweeting inaccurate items of news. What surprised me even more was the finding that the Twitter cascade depth of falsehoods reach depths of about 10. A cascade depth is the length (or depth) of an unbroken retweet chain. This fake news cascade depth of 10 was also found to be some 20 times faster than that for the depth of facts.

It is no wonder one of the MIT study authors concluded:

> We found that falsehood diffuses significantly farther, faster, deeper, and more broadly than the truth, in all categories of information, and in many cases by an order of magnitude.
>
> Sinan Aral, Professor, MIT Sloan School of Management[38]

However though the MIT study found that humans, not bots, are primarily responsible for propagating fake news, Twitter told the US Congress in October 2018 that it had discovered 36,746 Russian bot accounts that posted *automated* material about the US election, and that Russian state operatives were behind at least 2,752. Twitter later revised the latter number to more than 3,800 accounts that had been traced back to Russian state operatives attacking Hillary Clinton and her performances in the presidential debates[39].

Clearly the harm to democratic elections by bots could be huge.

So do you agree after these three case studies on Instagram and Facebook Misinformation [and this reminder on Twitter and Fake News] that Big Tech and Online regulation is now a must?

---

[38] Study: On Twitter, false news travels faster than true stories | MIT News | Massachusetts Institute of Technology

[39] Twitter admits far more Russian bots posted on election than it had disclosed | Twitter | The Guardian

3.7 Case Studies: USA, EU, UK, Australia and South Korea Bills to Regulate Big Tech

As I cover in Chapter 2, there are also many regulatory actions on Big Tech and on Online regulation in progress from across the world. Perhaps those coming out of the US Congress are most significant.

USA Big Tech Bills: The US Congress is pursuing several different Bills as of June 2021: Congress unveiled 5 bipartisan Bills that mark the biggest steps yet in regulating Big Tech[40]

- *The Access Act (Augmenting Compatibility and Competition by Enabling Service Switching)*: this covers a new framework for data portability and interoperability. This aims to allow users to leave a social media platform and take their data to a competing platform.

- *The Merger Filing Fee Modernization Act*: this gives the Federal Trade Commission and the Justice Department more monies to take on competition or antitrust cases against Big Tech. It increases the filing fees for tech mergers above $500 million and lowers fees for those under that level.

- *The State Antitrust Enforcement Venue Act*: this would give states greater powers in deciding the courts where tech antitrust cases are heard. Over the last several years, it has been rather confusing with State Attorneys Generals, the US Justice Department and the FTC all suing dominant US technology companies.

- *The Platform Competition and Opportunity Act*: this would prevent Big Tech from buying up early stage competitors, like the Facebook acquisition of Instagram in 2012. This will also stop buy-to-kill-off.

- *The Ending Platform Monopolies Act*: this would force Big Tech companies to sever lines of business that conflict with one another and hurt competitors, i.e. stop Big Tech monopolies from selling in marketplaces they control – like App Stores.

---

[40] US lawmakers introduce bills targeting Big Tech - BBC News

- *The American Choice and Innovation Act*: this would seeks to stop Big Tech like Google and Amazon from giving preference to their products on their own platforms.

These Bills emerged after a 16-month investigation into the market power of Amazon, Apple, Facebook and Google. If these bills gather momentum, the US could make landmark changes in the tech industry – but no one should doubt the counter-lobbying power of Big Tech either.

EU/EC: The *EU Digital Markets Act (DMA) Bill* of December 2020[41]: this evolving Act from the EU is narrowly aimed at dealing with antitrust issues with Big Tech online platforms that the EU denotes as "gatekeepers" in digital markets. It strives to ensure that these platforms behave in fair ways online. This Act will give the Commission wide-ranging investigatory powers as well as the ability to levy fines of up to 10% of global turnover when infringements are determined following market investigations. This Bill is furthermore a clear move towards *ex-ante* rules with these Big Tech gatekeeper platforms than ex-post investigations and enforcement. The EU would like to see more *contestability* and *fairness* with these gatekeeper platforms.

In addition, the EC is also progressing a *Digital Services Act[42] (DSA) Bill* which was also introduced in December 2020. Whilst the DMA aims to tackle the lack of competition in digital markets by targeting "gatekeepers", the DSA is primarily concerned with transparency, user safety and consumer protection. It proposes to address both illegal and harmful content. The DSA targets "intermediaries" (conduit, caching and hosting providers), online platforms (e.g. marketplaces, social media, app stores, etc.). It proposes special rules for "very large" online platforms, which they define as greater than 45 million monthly active EU users (e.g. YouTube). The Bill introduces liability rules, reporting obligations and due diligence obligations too. It would be enforced through national regulators supported by a new

---

[41] The Digital Markets Act: ensuring fair and open digital markets | European Commission (europa.eu)

[42] The Digital Services Act: ensuring a safe and accountable online environment | European Commission (europa.eu)

proposed independent advisory group, a new European Board for Digital Services (EBDS). The Bill also proposed fines of up to 6% of global turnover and in extreme cases restriction of access to platforms. Both the DMA and DSA are yet to become EC laws as of November 2021.

Australia Emerging Big Tech Laws and Codes: In the last chapter, I note how the Australian Government via ACCC[43] opened an inquiry into digital platforms in December 2017, specifically into the effects that social media platforms, digital search engines and other digital content aggregation platforms have on competition in media and advertising services market. I note the final report was published in July 2019 covering more than 600 pages and made 23 truly key recommendations[44] including changes to merger law, changes to search engine/internet browser defaults by Google, inquiry into ad tech services/advertising agencies, new codes of conduct to govern relationships between digital platforms and media business, etc.

UK Emerging Big Tech Laws and Codes: as I pen this section in late September 2021, the UK Government is conducting on a "new pro-competition regime for digital markets"[45] which closes in October 2021. The consultation mentions " our approach to 'pro-competitive intervention' that will address the root causes of market power". This very much reads to me like working towards proposing *ex-ante* digital market rules like the EU is working on too, which would underpin powers to the new Digital Markets Unit (DMU) that will implement any such rules. The consultation also covers new proposed 'codes of conduct' to "promote open choices, fair trading and trust and transparency", as well as proposed changes to mergers involving Big Tech players. The UK consultation may result in similar recommendations like Australia's.

South Korea Law on Gatekeeping App Stores: in the last chapter, I note how a new (August 2021) South Korean law[46] is responding to exactly some

---

[43] Digital platforms inquiry | ACCC - https://www.accc.gov.au/focus-areas/inquiries-finalised/digital-platforms-inquiry-0

[44] Digital Platforms Inquiry - Final report - part 1.pdf (accc.gov.au) – see Chapters 3 to 7.

[45] A new pro-competition regime for digital markets - GOV.UK (www.gov.uk)

[46] Google and Apple's app stores hit by new South Korean law | Financial Times (ft.com)

of the concerns that the EC has with Apple Music, as well as a similar class action lawsuit between Apple and U.S. developers in the United States. South Korean lawmakers saw anti-competitive practices resulting from Apple and Google's irreplicable gate-keeping roles that they have with App stores.

China Big Tech Laws: lest you believe that *only* Western countries are concerned about these major Big Tech companies and platforms, that is not the case at all. In April 2021, the Chinese Government fined Alibaba the equivalent of $USD 2.8 Billion (4% of 2019 revenues) for antitrust violations[47] for having found Alibaba to be behaving monopolistically. Recall like with Amazon case study of the previous chapter that Alibaba operates both an upstream wholesale merchants marketplace and a downstream retail set of operations. The Chinese State Administration for Market Regulation had found "exclusive dealing arrangements" that prevented upstream merchants on Alibaba's platform being able to sell their products on other rival platforms, a practice called "choosing one from two". Unlike what happens in the EU, UK, Australia or the USA, Alibaba did not appeal and accepted the penalty "with sincerity and will ensure our compliance with determination[48]". Wow! According to CNN, TikTok owner, Bytedance, and Baidu have both been fined for monopolistic behaviours including in corporate acquisitions. WeChat is under scrutiny as I write too.

3.8 Digital Economy Platforms – the foundations of your Digital Economy

One finding that clearly emerges as I have researched the Digital Economy efforts in developing and developed markets is the following: the former [developing markets] who are striving to digitalise their economies are largely in the dark of the need to evolve the necessary pillar platforms on

---

[47] China fines Alibaba $2.8 billion for behaving like a monopoly - CNN
[48] *Ibid.*

which to build their digital economies - yet they pronounce their 'Digital X'[49] ambitions loudly.

The developed economies largely have these platforms in place. It is absolutely imperative for developing economies to build these platforms. The Internet Value Chain (IVC) would not deliver these platforms organically in your country.

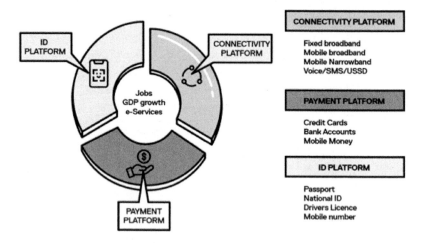

Figure 25 – The Three Pillar Digital Economy Platforms
Source: Illustrated from Dr Christophe Stork & Steve Esselaar[50]

What are these three pillar Digital Economy platforms? Why are they so important? And why are developing economies lacking them?

Well Figure 25 clarifies what these platforms are. Any country building a digital economy require these three pillar platforms to base their digital economies:

- *Connectivity Platform* (part of the Connectivity Segment of the IVC): the connectivity platform consists of a combination of fixed broadband, mobile broadband, mobile narrowband and

---

[49] E.g. Digital Nigeria, Digital Nepal, Digital Thailand, etc.

[50] Dubai_ITU_31Oct18 (researchictsolutions.com) - https://researchictsolutions.com/home/wp-content/uploads/2019/01/ITU_PP_2018_Dubai_ICT_Taxes.pdf

voice/SMS/USSD. Without connectivity to a maximum percentage of your citizens, they would hardly be part of the digital economy. What would be the point?

- *Payment Platform* (part of the Enabling Technologies and Services segment): this core platform consists of a combination of credit cards, bank accounts and mobile money (for developing markets typically). Without a widescale payments platform or payment gateways, there is no real Digital Economy in your country. How can there be?

- *Identity (ID) Platform* (part of the Enabling Technologies and Services segment): the ID Platform is a combination of citizen's platform, National ID, Drivers Licence and/or a unique mobile/cellular number. India in my opinion has the most sophisticated ID programme in the world with their Aadhaar ID[51] system. As of September 2021, Indian had 1.305 Billion holders[52] of the Aadhar card – this is virtually a universal ID ownership in India. You want every citizen in your country to have one identity, no matter how many bank accounts they may hold, how many SIM cards they may hold, how many credit cards they may hold, etc. This should be clear.

---

[51] Aadhaar - Wikipedia

[52] *Ibid.*

World's Most Unbanked Countries

Country	Total Population (Millions)	Unbanked Population (%)	Cash Transactions (%)	Card Transactions (%)	# of ATMs per 100,000 Adults	Internet Penetration (%)
Morocco	36.9	71	41	27	28.6	62
Vietnam	97.3	69	26	35	25.9	66
Egypt	102.3	67	55	27	20.1	45
Philippines	109.6	66	37	22	29.0	60
Mexico	128.9	63	21	44	61.5	66
Nigeria	206.1	60	24	27	16.9	70
Peru	33.0	57	22	62	126.7	49
Colombia	50.9	54	15	55	41.3	62
Indonesia	273.5	51	13	34	53.3	55
Argentina	45.2	51	18	45	60.9	76
Kenya	53.8	44	40	25	7.7	83
Romania	19.2	42	78	19	64.4	64
Kazakhstan	18.8	41	60	20	85.9	76
Ukraine	43.7	37	60	28	96.3	57
Uruguay	3.5	36	26	53	120.1	68
South Africa	59.3	31	11	43	65.3	56
Turkey	84.3	31	8	71	84.0	65
Brazil	212.6	30	18	62	101.7	67

Figure 26 – World's Most Unbanked Countries

Source: Merchant Machine, 2021[53]

Typically when I visit many developing countries or when we train Digital Economy policy makers from developing countries, I ask them about their progress on these three platforms. Typically, they do *not* even realise they are

---

[53] World's Most Unbanked Countries 2021 | Global Finance Magazine (gfmag.com)

the pillars of any digital economy. When we get past this realisation and delve into any progress on such three platforms in their countries, it is usually clear very quickly that progress is at best perfunctory. This is because in most cases there is no policy and regulatory drive behind these platforms.

You see – in developed countries – these platforms are largely taken for granted. Most of their citizens (frankly close to 100%) are connected on both fixed and/or mobile broadband. Most of their citizens are banked (i.e. have bank accounts) and a significant proportion have credit cards. Finally, most of their citizens can use a combination of driving licences, passports, national IDs, etc. – along with their home addresses, utility bills, etc. – to identify themselves.

Therefore, if developed countries' citizens are all connected, virtually all banked and all have clear forms of State-issued IDs – they have all the ingredients to participate in the IVC-inspired Digital Economy.

I do not need to provide the reader with any data to prove that the story on the equivalent three platforms in most developing economies is very different. However, Figure 26 proves my point to a large degree.

Take Kenya from Figure 26, for example with 44% unbanked as of January 2021. Broadband connections (3G-5G) as a percentage of all mobile connections as of January 2021 stood at 57.7%[54]. Luckily for Kenya, 72.9% of Kenyans have a mobile money M-PESA account[55]. Kenya's connectivity is improving – hence the conditions for having a digital economy in Kenya is arguably one of the best in sub-Saharan Africa. Nevertheless, there is a minor problem in M-PESA being based on 2G/3G USSD which strictly speaking makes it not sit on the IVC. USSD payment does not enable easier transactions on the Online Internet as much as payment apps and credit cards do – but it is a very good place to start.

Philippines is 60% unbanked with 60% penetration to the Internet. They have a long way to go to develop these core digital platforms.

---

[54] Digital in Kenya: All the Statistics You Need in 2021 — DataReportal – Global Digital Insights

[55] Ibid.

All the countries in Figure 26 and more clearly require major efforts to develop their three foundational digital economy platforms.

3.9 What Outcomes do Digital Economy Policy Makers & Regulators want then?

I have done a bit of a much-needed *tour* so far [after the assumptions of this chapter] into Big Tech, Netflix, the need for Big Tech and Online regulation, how various jurisdictions are already beginning to tackle Big Tech and all these mega-digital gatekeeper platforms. I also cover the three foundational platforms required for any true digital economy.

I hope you the reader would agree it was necessary to do this in order to 'round out' what the new Digital Economy policy makers, regulators and network operators have to deal with. They have to deal with the offline as well as the online - and with the latter, they cannot escape the Big Techs, Netflix and Online Regulation. Overviewing what other jurisdictions are doing hopefully shows other policy makers, regulators and network operators that these problems are largely common too.

As I start listing the outcomes sought, I would like to state clearly what I emphasise with regulators and policy makers - what good regulation (irrespective of the sector of the economy) truly addresses. Good regulation primarily addresses

- *Market failures* (which leads to high prices, low choice, low quality of service (QoS), low innovation, high barriers to entry, etc.)
- *Market power* - it checks on market power via carrying out market assessments/inquiries and if companies are found to have abused their dominant position, there are consequent remedies to correct their market behaviours and/or fines too.

The reader can see that the previous section on Case Studies on Big Tech across the world are mostly about achieving these two top outcomes: correcting market failures where possible or, at the very least, checking the market power of the Big Tech players and their gatekeeping platforms.

Broad Categories of Digital Economy Outcomes Sought

Therefore returning to the key goal of this section on what outcomes we need, I believe from the lessons learnt of this chapter so far that we have three broad ones. They include:

1. *Offline ICT/TMT Outcomes:* continue to regulate to realise the outcomes desired of the Offline ICT/TMT world. These have not changed. The fact much of this Offline ICT/TMT world has been delineated to the Connectivity segmented of the Internet value chain does not mean the outcomes sought of the Offline world are still not needed.. This includes addressing offline market failures and/or checking the market power of dominant companies. They continue to be very relevant and much needed indeed

2. *Good Competition Outcomes from Big Tech in particular* (i.e., more choices, fair trading, trust, transparency, and contestability): the last chapter shows amply the very high levels of market concentration that players have across the segments of the IVC value chain and its categories: Facebook in social networking; Google in search and Mobile OS; Amazon in e-Commerce; Apple in App Store and Mobile OS, etc. (see Figures 13a and 13b).

   I have to be honest to say the markets/countries where FANGAM players - either (i) earn miniscule percentages of their global revenues (ii) or markets that are not strategically key to them in other ways - have very little chance to influence these mega-digital players' behaviours. So if Sub-Saharan Africa (SSA) collectively is less than 1% or 2% of Google's global revenues, business reality suggests that SSA countries would not change Google's [alleged] anti-competitive practices anytime soon. They can collectively speak with "one voice" through other entities who can truly influence FANGAM players like the EC, the UK, Australia, India, France and the most key – the USA. I cover many examples where these latter entities are seeking to "promote open choices, fair trading and trust and transparency" with Digital platforms like the UK or the EU/EC seek. In short, most countries already have the tool of Competition Law used *ex-post* to address dominance abuses, but we saw earlier that countries are moving towards *ex-ante* rules for these platforms too, e.g. One would not compete with their competitors – which is what *the Ending Platform Monopolies Act Bill* in the USA is seeking to do (see previous section).

3. *Better Outcomes from Online Regulation against Egregious and Deadly Harms*: in this chapter, I argue earlier that both Online and Big Tech regulation are both necessary and needed now. The UK's Age-Appropriate Design for Apps for a "better Internet for Children" (cf. Chapter 2) which came into force in September 2021 is a good example of such Online regulation in order to mitigate online harms to UK children. In general, the numerous harms depicted in Figures 18-22 (drawn from Chapter 2) are in many cases just too egregious - if not deadly – for Governments and their policy makers/regulators to ignore. These could cover illegal/harmful content or Annual reporting on how these digital platforms deal with complaints in your country.

Recall from earlier that Facebook has offered up four areas that even Facebook concedes needs Government policies and regulations: harmful content, election integrity, privacy and data portability.

Note that I specifically used the word phrase 'better outcomes from online regulation' to start this paragraph because Governments cannot possibly insulate their citizens from all online harms. This is just not possible – no different from the knife in your kitchen not being used by a deranged person to commit a murder. The Government cannot ban knives for fear of this possibility with such a low probability.

And as for the previous paragraph, non-strategic countries to these Big Tech digital platforms and companies would like need to band together regionally e.g. all Caribbean Islands, all sub-Saharan African (SSA) countries, all African countries under the AU banner to influence these platforms on Online harms.

I will now overview these broad outcomes briefly.

Offline ICT/TMT Outcomes

Nwana (2014) covers this, but perhaps I can give the reader a quick reminder here of what goes on with Offline ICT/TMT Regulation today. Figure 27 attempts to capture what happens with offline Telecoms, Media and Technology (TMT) policy making and regulation today.

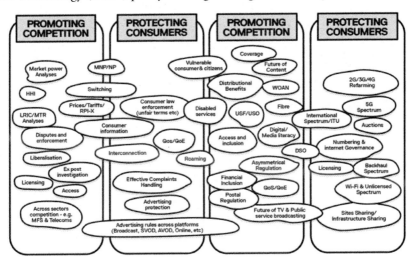

Figure 27 – Typical Key Areas of Offline TMT/ICT Regulation

As Figure 27 depicts, offline TMT Policy makers and regulators broadly seek four outcomes for their consumers and citizens.

- *Competitive TMT Markets:* they want competition to thrive in their offline telecoms, media and technology markets (cf. Figure 4 in Chapter 1). Such markets would offer their consumers more choice, lower prices, better QoS/QoE, more innovation, more new entrants into the market, lower barriers to entry, more switching by citizens and consumers between suppliers, more coverage and more. Clearly policy makers and regulators desire these.

- *Protected and Empowered Consumers and Citizens:* Policy makers and regulators seek to minimise consumers falling prey to say unfair contracts, want their complaints handled fairly speedily, want them to have good QoS/QoE and want them empowered with more information to make informed choices, and switch to other providers as they see fit.

- *Efficient Allocation of Scarce Resources to Stakeholders:* Scarce resources such as radio frequency spectrum must be allocated and assigned to those companies that would make the maximum use of it to society, translating to creating the maximum GDP contribution. They should also maximise broader social value benefits that accrue from unlicensed spectrum like Wi-Fi. Telephone numbers are also scarce resources that policy makers and regulators allocate and must assign efficiently too. Regulators also may choose to mandate sites and infrastructure sharing so as to maximise efficient use of such clearly scarce assets.

- *Good Public Policy Outcomes Sought by Government:* in the offline world, there are usually too many other public policy goals that require Governments to work with regulators to achieve. As shown in Figure 27, typical amongst these are access and inclusion to telecoms and broadcasting services, widespread coverage, digital literacy, access to post offices, disabled services, financial inclusion and more. Governments may set up Universal Service Funds (USFs) to achieve some or all of these.

Some of the methods and activities (not exhaustive) involved in achieving these broad offline outcomes are shown in Figure 27. I do not elaborate on them any further beyond that some activities straddle two or more broad outcome buckets. So for example, interconnection – which is an *ex ante* instrument which ensures no telecom operator refuses to connect to another (this will be very bad for competition) – is both necessary to promote competition and to protect consumers. Without networks being interconnected, consumers cannot switch suppliers without effectively giving up their numbers which they cherish.

Today's TMT/ICT Policy makers and regulators are already familiar with most (if not all) of the activities and challenges in Figure 27.

Big Tech Good Competition Outcomes and Typical Harms

I note earlier that the good competition outcomes from Big Tech include – like with offline too - more choices, fair trading, trust, transparency and contestability. I hope it is clear from the case studies of the previous chapter and some in this one that regulating Big Tech is proving most non-trivial.

I hope the reader is by now already convinced that these mega-platforms, these digital gatekeeping companies to the Internet are already too big to regulate. Practically, most of the case studies of Chapter 2 and this chapter attest to this. And as I note earlier in this chapter, unlike what happens in China where Alibaba [the Amazon of China] is fined and does not appeal - indeed accepts the penalty "with sincerity and will ensure our compliance with determination[56]" – I have never known this to happen with the Big 5 anywhere in the EU, UK, Australia or the USA.

I covered earlier the US Bills that have been proposed to regulate Big Tech. The outcomes that the USA Department of Commerce (DoC) are trying to achieve in the USA with Big Tech are very laudable – if they are ever achieved, given the sheer lobbying and fire power of the Big 5 or FANGAM individually and collectively. The outcomes sought for some of the key DoC bipartisan Bills include:

Proposed Bipartisan Bill	Outcome Sought
The Access Act (Augmenting Compatibility and Competition by Enabling Service Switching) Act Bill	To achieve data portability and interoperability between platforms
The Platform Competition and Opportunity Act Bill:	To prevent Big Tech from buying up early stage competitors, like the Facebook acquisition of Instagram in 2012. To stop buy-to-kill-off

---

[56] *Ibid.*

	competitors too.
The Ending Platform Monopolies Act Bill	To [possibly] stop Big Tech from operating upstream marketplaces at the same time as operating downstream retail activities, as this clearly raises conflicts of interests. E.g. stop Big Tech monopolies from selling in the same marketplaces they control – like App Stores.
The American Choice and Innovation Act Bill	To stop Big Tech like Google and Amazon from giving preference to their products on their own platforms.

These sort of outcomes all make much sense and are routinely "designed in" and enforced in the offline TMT world using *ex-ante* regulations and enforcement powers. We are playing a big catchup now with Big Tech.

Similarly, all the EC cases (including Australian, UK, South Korean and Italian investigations) against Big Tech that I cover in this book are seeking outcomes identical to those of the USA DoC Bills and/or other similar outcomes too.

For example, permit me to take the EC vs. Amazon case of Chapter 2. We can tease out what is called the *theory of harm*[57], and therefore the outcomes (or remedies) sought.

In a competition law case like this one or any of the EC cases I cover in this book, a theory of harm of a case explains why a particular type of conduct on the part of the accused entity constitutes a breach of competition law -

---

[57] 4_-DFF-Factsheet-Theories-of-harm-in-competition-law-cases.pdf (digitalfreedomfund.org)

with reference to the relevant legal tests set out in the law. In particular, it explains why that conduct causes harm to competition in the said relevant market/jurisdiction, and why it should be prohibited. Next, I look at the specific theories of harm and what outcomes I believe the EC is seeking for the said EV vs. Amazon case [feel free to reread the brief case studies into the two formal cases against Amazon in Chapter 2].

As a gentle brief reminder, I cover it in Chapter 2, Section 2.3.5.3. The context is Amazon has found itself being investigated by the European Commission (EC) for having breached EU antitrust rules by distorting competition in online retail markets. The EC alleges a competition conflict of interest since a major player like Amazon frequently effectively competes with its own customers on its platform. This has led the EC to open two cases against Amazon.

Theories of Harm of Amazon vs. EC Case (see Chapter 2)	Outcome Sought
The theory of harm of the first formal case is that of the *conflict of interest* on the part of Amazon – that of having *upstream* data on their merchants [as Amazon customers] that allegedly leads a data-driven giant like Amazon to start new *downstream* product lines because they know what lines are working in their *upstream* marketplace that they control.	The outcome the EC would/may like to see may be one of the following non-exhaustive options: • *Behavioral Remedy* "Chinese walls" inside Amazon where their upstream and downstream businesses do not interact with one another at all. Would this work? • *Structural Remedy*: Or does the EC hope the DoC's Ending Platform Monopolies Act Bill solves this problem for them *structurally?* This means the upstream and downstream businesses would be formally separated and perhaps owned by

	separate owners.
The theory of harm for the second formal concerns the fact that Amazon alone selects sellers to feature in its "Buy Box", and that these recommendations "generates the vast majority of all sales". Specifically that this selection allegedly prefers Amazon's own retail offers and those of its "customers" (i.e. specifically marketplace sellers who would use Amazon's logistics and delivery services).	The outcome the EC would like to see may be one or more of the following non-exhaustive options: • *Behavioral* – Amazon must stop preferring its own retail offers and those of its "customers" • *Transparency* on what features in the "Buy Box" • Or does the EC hope the DoC's Ending Platform Monopolies Act Bill solves this problem for them *structurally?* This means the upstream and downstream businesses would be formally separated and perhaps owned by separate owners.

Figure 28 – Some Typical Big Tech Competition Harms

I could proceed similarly with all antitrust cases against Big Tech across the globe that I cover in this manuscript, highlighting some of the proposed outcomes sought as I do with the EC vs. Amazon case above, but I think you the reader gets the point.

In Figure 28, I capture some of the typical Big Tech theories of harms. Indeed, I have derived them from the Big Tech-related case studies I cover across Chapter 2 and this chapter too.

I cover a sub-set of the harms of Figure 28 below in some more detail because I want to reader to be able to better appreciate how the harms could really affect players in their digital economies.

- *Conflicts of Interest:* I have covered many of these in the book. In the EC vs. Amazon case of Chapter 2, the EC alleges strong conflict of interests against Amazon between its upstream intermediation market for businesses, i.e. Amazon's merchants marketplace and downstream retail markets, i.e. shoppers on its market place.

- *Refusal to Deal:* practically all of the Big Tech dominant platforms like Google, Facebook or Amazon have been accused at one time of refusing to deal with rivals in adjacent markets. This is discrimination, and it is anti-competitive. An example is Google Search's alleged discrimination against Google's vertical rivals. Google Search has clear-cut monopoly power for general-purpose – or horizontal – online search. The allegation here is whether Google is *abusing* this horizontal search market power in specialised – or vertical – search areas? So does Goggle unfairly promote its own vertical properties like Google Maps, Google Local and Google Trips over competitors over others like MapQuest, Yelp and Expedia respectively?

- *Self-preferencing:* Is it really right that Google Search always prioritises higher its own products and properties? Should this be prohibited?

- *Tying:* in the Google Android EC case of Chapter 2, Google was charged with tying Google Search (which it is clearly most dominant in) with its Google Play app store – bad. Google was also allegedly of not only tying Google Search to its Google Play app store, but also its web browser [Google Chrome] too – even worse. These Google actions allegedly led to the exit of Windows Phone and Symbian devices that have fallen by the way side.

- *Unfair commissions:* Apple and Google typically take a commission of up to 30% on digital sales from their apps stores, and for in-app purchases such as subscriptions. In the Google/Apple Apps Store vs. South Korea in Chapter 2, I note that South Korean lawmakers see this as anti-competitive and have banned this practice there.

- *Predatory Pricing:* a monopolist that prices its products or services below costs to drive out competitors is engaging in predatory pricing. Amazon, for example, has been accused of this unfair practice during its acquisition attempt of Quidsi, the parent company of online baby-products retailer Diapers.com. After

Quidsi refused Amazon's initial offer to purchase it, Amazon allegedly cuts its prices for substitute baby products below costs, and this move started impeding Quidsi's growth. Quidsi relented and accepted Amazon's offer, after which Amazon allegedly increased its prices for baby products[58]. This is classic predatory pricing – and it can happen in your market too with these dominant platforms.

- *Abuse of dominant networks effects:* a digital platform benefits from network effects when its value to its users increases as more online users use it. The network effects could be "same side" when value of users on one side of the market increases as other users join that side of the market. Mobile operating systems stores like iOS and Android are marketplaces that bring together app developers who list their apps in these marketplaces and app buyers who buy and download the apps. The value of the market to buyers increase as more apps are listed on the marketplace, i.e. same side value increase. Apple iOS and Google Android have been accused of having used dominant network same side effects to accelerate the convergence to just two operating systems. Other smartphone manufacturers can hardly deviate from these two OSs including previous ones like Blackberry.

- *Abuse of multisided market platform power:* in addition to "same side" network effects above, digital platforms typically also benefit from "cross-side" network effects too wherein the value to users on one side of the market increases as the number of users on the other side of the market. In the Google Search/Shopping vs. EC case (see Chapter 2), Google allegedly abused its dominant position in Google Search to give advantage to Google Shopping.

- *Dividing regions,* e.g. tacit agreements between two forms not to compete against one another in some geographies or some relevant markets whilst competing in others.

- *Exclusive deals,* e.g. in the Apple Music vs. EC case (see Chapter 2), Apple's rules allegedly prevent app developers from informing users who buy their apps on the Apple App store that they could have alternative purchasing possibilities outside Apple App store,

---

[58] Antitrust and "Big Tech" (fas.org)

including from the websites of the apps developers themselves. The apps would be typically cheaper on the developers' websites than from App store. Similarly, in the Google Android vs. EC case (see Chapter 2), the EC also concluded that Google had exclusive deals made with certain large device manufacturers wherein Google made illegal payments them in exchange for them pre-installing Google Search on their Android devices.

- *Buy competitors to kill off*: Big Tech are typically accused of this. For example, Microsoft (dominant in the desktop productivity market with Office) was scrutinised when it bought task management app Wunderlist and mobile calendar Sunrise in 2015[59]. Both companies were highly regarded by Silicon Valley, but both apps were later scrapped by Microsoft. Indeed, some new research suggests that when a Big Tech acquires a startup or an app, it creates a kill area or kill zone and stifles further innovation in the entire area[60]. This speaks to stricter merger control and acquisition rules for Big Tech.

- *IPR Theft*: IPR is obviously more easily stolen online than offline.

As I note earlier, it was not my intention to fully cover all the non-exhaustive Big Tech harms of Figure 28, but to get you the reader to appreciate that these harms would be truly real in your markets too. Such harms are at the core of the many investigations against Big Tech from across the world, particularly in the USA, UK, Australia, South Korea, France and the EU.

To some degree it goes without much discussion and debate that such investigations are very costly and specialised. Bluntly, it is not realistic that my native country of Cameroon (located in Central West Africa) can possibly mount a credible competition case against a Google or an Apple. Firstly, Cameroon would hardly be a market that registers with these behemoths anyway. Secondly, such companies are not even registered or licensed in countries like Cameroon, and so there is no legal loci to do an investigation against Big Tech there too.

---

[59] Big Tech's 'buy and kill' tactics come under scrutiny | Financial Times (ft.com)

[60] Why big-tech mergers stifle innovation | Chicago Booth Review

However, it does not mean some of these harms would not materialise in your country. Do you want one of the Big Tech to buy and kill off promising and innovative Internet businesses in your jurisdictions? Do you want Big Tech platforms operating in your country to exclude some local businesses unfairly with exclusive deals? Do you want Big Tech platforms to use their same-side and/or cross-side network effects snuff out fledgling digital online businesses in your country? Digital Economy policy makers and regulators need to be aware such harms.

The next question then is that of how much leverage does your country have with the Big Tech 5 or 6? Australia, the EC, the UK, France, Russia, India, South Korea and the USA and China of course clearly do. They are large and/or strategic countries to these Big Tech players. Is your country strategic to the Big 6? If you judge you are not, my advice is to group your 'weight' with that others to get the leverage you may need to 'control' the competition harms with Big Tech you perceive in your market place.

Online Regulation is Indispensable Now

It is now clear – I hope – that the IVC-inspired online harms are real, many very egregious and some truly deadly. They are captured in Figures 18 to 22.

For brevity, I attempt to capture the main "categories" or classification of Online Harms that I have surmised [I make no apologies for the fact that this is just one classification and does not seek to be definitive in any way]. I start with Zuckerberg's four categories and proceed to add more:

1. Harmful Content	23. Internet Addiction/Addictive Apps/Social Disconnect Depression
2. Election Integrity (I add - Democracy and Botnets, Political Misinformation, Spread of Disinformation, Harmful Echo Chambers, and Decreased Trust in Government Risks to this one)	24. Dark Web – enabling terrorist communications and funding
3. Privacy	25. Critical National

4. Data Portability
5. Illegal Content/Pornography/Violent Graphic Content
6. Disinformation/Misinformation
7. Hate Speech/Offense Harms
8. Fake News, Rumours & Conspiracy Theories
9. Breaking News Risks
10. Online Harms not tolerated offline (Trolling, Online bullying, Unwelcome Friend Requests, Indecent Entertainment, Offensive Language, Bullying, Stalking, Obscene Content, etc.)
11. Security of Online Big Data/Data Breaches, e.g. Cambridge Analytica scandal[61]
12. Cybercrime (e.g. trafficking narcotics, money laundering, tax evasion, criminal groups, Organised crime, Drug crimes, Gang crimes)
13. Distributed Denial of Service Attacks (DDOS)
14. Rogue Apps
15. Telecom frauds
16. Identity Theft
17. Keystroke logging
18. Grey Services

Infrastructure[63] Threats/Cyber warfare
26. Online Terrorism
27. Extremism and Radicalisation
28. Cyberthreats (e.g. cyberbullying)
29. Cyber-harms (e.g. Online paedophilia, child sexual abuse, cyber grooming)
30. Copyright/Intellectual Property Rights Infringements
31. Algorithms Concerns (AI, ML and Big Data) with spreading Misinformation including leading to offline street violence and killings
32. Cultural Sensitive Harms (e.g. Cheating Tools, Dating Tools, Immoral Entertainment)
33. Scams and Deceptions
34. Copyright Infringement (much easier online)
35. IPR Infringement
36. Spam Emails, Phishing

---

[61] Facebook-Cambridge Analytica scandal - BBC News
[63] BlackMatter Strikes Iowa Farmers Cooperative, Demands $5.9M Ransom | Threatpost

19. Unlicensed operators (numerous in most countries due to Internet) 20. Media Gateway Frauds 21. SIPVicious[62] Malicious Apps 22. VoiP or Traffic Pumping & Apps	and Spyware 37. Botnets/Cyber Sabotage 38. Internet censorship and surveillance 39. Virus and Trojans 40. Ransomeware/Cyber Extortion 41. Likes and Views Risks 42. Rogue Apps Stores 43. Financial Scams/Mobile Money scams[64] 44. Incitement of Hatred 45. Hacking 46. Illegal Downloads 47. Encryption (as FBI says much criminality is hidden online) 48. Online corruption 49. SIM Bank Frauds 50. Internet Gateway Bypasses

Table 5 – Online Harms are literally numerous (the first four are those Facebook has already suggested needs new Online rules)

---

[62] SIPVicious | Penetration Testing Tools (kali.org)

[64] Uganda banks, MTN, Airtel hacked by mobile money fraudsters — Quartz Africa (qz.com)

Figure 29 (a pictorial version of Table 5) – Online Harms are literally numerous (the top or first four are those Facebook has already suggested needs new Online rules)

Table 5 shows that the online harms that need regulation are literally numerous to be able to address all. I have covered most of the online harms in the previous chapter.

All of these online harms of Table 5 and Figure 29 are real today. If you believe these are not real in your country today – think again! Of the 50 or so categories captured in Table 5, at least 50% of those would be happening in your country on a weekly basis. Consider the following:

- *DDOS Attack in Liberia[65]- Cyber Sabotage (2016):* Liberia is one of the poorest countries in the world, yet in 2016 was subject to a massive distributed denial of service (DDOS) attack. The attack used a massive network of hijacked computers to overwhelm the poor country with botnets directing massive amounts of data towards the country at more than 600 gigabits per second. All these data was directed towards Liberia's key mobile company Lonestar/MTN. This literally crashed Liberia's Internet with people in the country not being able to access servers of key Internet companies like Twitter, Facebook or Google. This DDOS attack was orchestrated by a Briton called Daniel Kaye who has since been jailed[66]. This was a key example of cyber sabotage.

- *Cybercrime Damages Reach USD 6 Trillion in 2021[67]:* Cybersecurity Ventures expected cybercrime damages to reach USD $6 Trillion in 2021. To put this number in context, the GDP of the biggest economy in the world – the USA – was circa USD $20 Trillion for 2020. Ransomware attacks, like Liberia's in 2016 above, are just becoming prolific and more expensive to recover from. Data is the key top target for hackers. The USD $6 Trillion cybercrime cost prediction "includes damage and destruction of data, stolen money, lost productivity, theft of intellectual property, theft of personal and financial data, embezzlement, fraud, post-attack disruption to the normal course of business, forensic investigation, restoration and deletion of hacked data and systems, and reputational harm"[68]. No country on earth is immune from cybercrime – and the biggest companies in your country – the biggest banks, the biggest telecom

---

[65] Hack attacks cut internet access in Liberia - BBC News

[66] Briton who knocked Liberia offline with cyber attack jailed - BBC News

[67] Cybercrime is Fastest Growing Crime in US (natlawreview.com) - https://www.natlawreview.com/article/c-suites-cybercrime-damages-expected-to-reach-6-trillion-2021

[68] Cybercrime damages expected to cost the world $6 trillion by 2021 | CSO Online

operators, the biggest Government Departments, etc. – are all targets for cybercrime. In 2019 alone, the Indonesian National Cyber and Crypto Agency reported 290 million cases of cyberattacks causing losses of USD $34.2 billion for the country[69]. Do not be both negligent. Cybercrime is happening near you.

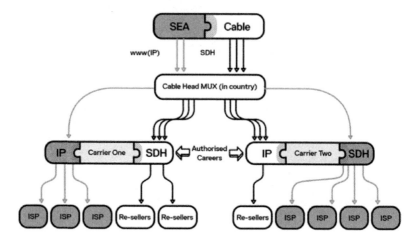

Figure 30 – Expected Physical Deployment of Two Carriers in a Country

Source: Illustrated from Graham Butler (www.bitek.com)

- *Digital Data Traffic Bypass, Illegal Operators and National Security:* I work with partners in many countries across the world, and we can prove to many authorities that, not only most traffic coming into your country is digital data traffic, but that some 70% of it and growing bypasses your country cable (SDH[70]) or Sea (IP) headends and authorised Internet Gateways (IGWs). Figure 30 depicts the ideal hierarchical expected physical deployment structure expected in your country of both IP and SDH data coming into your country. Guess what? If we (some of my partners and my team) map out the digital traffic flows in and out of your country, I can guarantee you would see more of a spaghetti map, full of digital

---

[69] Cybersecurity Protection in Indonesia - Policy Brief CIPS (cips-indonesia.org)

[70] Synchronous Digital Hierarchy refers to a transmission standard originally conceived for optical fibre transmission, but also used for copper too, typically at multiples of 155Mbps.

traffic bypassing this ideal hierarchical structure and replete with illegal digital operators (multiples of them), using SIM Banks to illegally makes monies in your country at the expense of your licensed operators. With digital traffic going in and out of your country clandestinely, this presents massive national security concerns that all Governments should be worried about.

- *Beware of Insider Attacks and Breaches[71]:* Research suggest that insider threats account for anywhere between 60 to 75% of security breaches. Rogue employees with access to key applications and data storage systems and basic human errors contribute to this high percentage of security breaches in both the public and private sectors. Figure 31 is an example of the scale of data breaches that can happen (and have happened) online.

- *Mobile Money Hacks in Africa[72]:* In October 2020, a major mobile money hack compromised Uganda's mobile money network and literally plunged the country's telecoms and banking sectors into crisis. The breach happened through which mainly affected bank to mobile wallet transfers. Pegasus Technologies' financial and billing platform used by the operators and banks was breached. The hackers used circa 2000 mobile SIM cards to get access into the mobile money payment system, which the hackers used to instruct the banks to transfer millions of dollars to the telecom companies, and the monies into the 2000 mobile SIM cards. The key Ugandan operators MTN and Airtel had to suspend mobile money transfers between them to date due to what they called "unprecedented technical challenges". Using another African country by way of illustrating the risks of a mobile payment systems [where consumers have turned to it in their millions], EcoCash's mobile payments system came to a complete halt[73] for 2 days in early July 2018. It literally crippled Zimbabwe and exposed the risks of dependency on a single monopoly in Zimbabwe and the vulnerability of going

---

[71] Insider Threats Account for Nearly 75 Percent of Security Breach Incidents (securityintelligence.com)

[72] Uganda banks, MTN, Airtel hacked by mobile money fraudsters — Quartz Africa (qz.com)

[73] https://qz.com/africa/1321152/zimbabwes-ecocash-mobile-money-crash-has-people-worried/ (last accessed August 2021)

cashless. Shoppers were literally stranded in supermarkets and other shops for over two days. I must stress that EcoCash system crash was not a hack. Mobile Operator Econet said the unexpected crash occurred due to a scheduled system upgrade, which they were not able to fix for two whole days.

-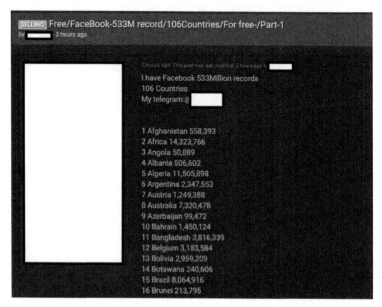

Figure 31 – 533 Million Peoples Facebook Records from 106 Countries being offered Online (Source[74])

- *Can Governments ignore such massive data breaches?* A hacker gained access to 100 million Capital One credit card applications and accounts[75]. The hacker Paige Thompson was accused of illegal access (via a misconfigured web application firewall) to Capital One's server gaining access to 140,000 Social Security numbers, 1 million Canadian insurance numbers and 80000 bank account numbers.

---

[74] 533 Million Facebook Users' Phone Numbers and Personal Data Leaked Online (thehackernews.com)

[75] Capital One data breach: A hacker gained access to 100 million credit card applications and accounts - CNN

What about the leak of personal data of 533 Million Facebook users leaked online[76] (see Figure 31)? This happened in 2019, and it included phone numbers, full names, locations, email addresses and biographical information. In context, this is greater than the population of the EU, and hackers could use this data to impersonate people and commit untold numbers of frauds. Even Facebook's CEO Mark Zuckerberg's phone number was leaked. The leak involved 106 countries and your country is probably one of them. Facebook found and fixed the vulnerability.

All I have tried to illustrate with these several scenarios above is to remind the reader – whether you are a Digital Economy Policy maker in a developed country like the USA or UK – or a developing economy like Indonesia or Liberia, your country faces major online vulnerabilities.

Do not be complacent and negligent – if some of the biggest financial institutions in the world such as Capital One and some of the biggest companies in the world such as Facebook can suffer online hacks, so can it happen in your country.

---

[76] Personal Data Of 533 Million Facebook Users Leaks Online (forbes.com)

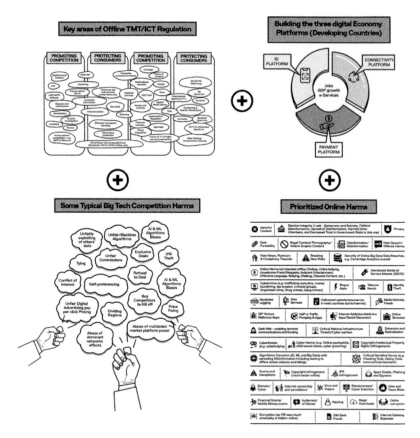

Figure 32 – Summary Problem Statement for Digital Economy Policy makers

3.10 What then is the Digital Economy Problem Statement?

A key reason for this chapter (and book) is to provide as best as possible a definition of the combined *offline* (as in offline TMT/ICT) and *online* (IVC) set of challenges. This attempts to define the *problem statement* of the overall policy and regulatory challenges that face Digital Economy Policy makers and regulators.

Well I believe at this juncture, the problem statement can be simply defined as the sum total of the following:

- The current extant *offline* TMT/ICT Regulation Challenges +
- the new Big Tech Regulation Challenges +
- the prioritised *online* Regulation Challenges (for your country) +
- the building of the three digital economy platforms for your country [required mostly for developing countries].

Pictorially, I try and capture this in Figure 32 which summarises what the new Digital Economy statement covers.

As the reader can see, the problem statement is a sum union of the challenges shown in Figures 25, 26 and Table 5. Collectively, the overall challenges for Digital Economy policy makers, regulators and network operators are truly humongous and non-trivial. Understanding these all would be critical for your country. Countries need to assess – realistically – the Digital Economy challenges they both face and can do something about. Then proceed to develop the necessary national laws and regulations to both deliver good outcomes and minimise bad harms for their consumers and citizens. There really is no excuse but to start **now**.

One last thing – regulators must be forced to report annually and defend in front of competent internationally-pedigree Parliamentary, Senate or Presidential Committees on all the above. I see too many countries with some of the best statutes and regulations on the books – but without any reporting with respect to these statutes, regulators and Government agencies get away with murder not doing what they have been mandated to do.

Once again - do not be complacent and negligent – the Digital Economy you are seeking or working towards in your country has consequences. If Figure 32 does *not* tell you that, I have utterly failed.

3.11 Beware of Regulating Away your next Online Giant

I could not conclude this chapter without this salient cautionary warning. I have noted several times that to regulate is to *control*. I hope you did not read - to regulate is to *stifle*!

Facebook, Google, Twitter, Netflix and many more household Big Tech/Online Businesses grew to what they are today because of favourable regulatory environments. Let me explain by briefly introducing two important set of US and EU laws/statutes:

- Section 230 US Federal Communications Act
- Article 12—14 of the EU E-Commerce Directive.

Section 230 of the 1996 US Federal Communications Act

Section 230 is sometimes dubbed the most important law for online speech[77]. It is a section of Title 47 of the US code enacted in 1996 known as Communications Decency Act – the long version name of 47 US Code 2030 is *Protection for private blocking and screening of offensive material*[78]. The law stipulates that an "interactive computer service" cannot be treated as the publisher or speaker of third-party content. Specifically, it stipulates:

> No provider or user of an interactive computer service shall be treated as the publisher or speaker of any information provided by another information content provider.

Do not be fooled with these seemingly benign set of words: Section 230 protects any US online website from lawsuits and violations of US Federal law if any user using the website posts illegal material on it. This means online intermediaries that host and republish speech (read of the likes of Facebook, YouTube, Twitter and Instagram) are protected against a whole

---

[77] Section 230: everything you need to know about the law protecting internet speech - The Verge

[78] 47 U.S. Code § 230 - Protection for private blocking and screening of offensive material | U.S. Code | US Law | LII / Legal Information Institute (cornell.edu)

range of US laws that may otherwise be used to hold them responsible for what 3rd parties do and say on their platforms. These "interactive computer service" providers also include Internet Service Providers (ISPs) like all the major mobile operators in your country as well as new innovative online businesses being set up in US garages. There are some exceptions for violations against copyright, sex work-related material, Intellectual Property Rights (IPR) and other federal crimes. The key to take away with Section 230 is that protects online innovation and online free speech.

Articles 12-14 of the 2000 EU Commerce Directive

The EU's e-Commerce Directive [79] has three Articles that are truly foundational to the Online Sector in the EU. A Directive is a legal act of the EU.

This section draws from this UK House of Lords publication which articulates the three directives excellently [80]. The e-Commerce directive excludes liability for 'Information Society Service Providers' where they are acting with respect to any content as:

- **"Mere conduits" Access Providers (Article 12)** "which enable the transmission of information automatically and transiently, or provide access to a communication network. To qualify for this limitation, an intermediary must not (1) initiate the transmission, (2) select the receiver of information or the actual information in the transmission, or (3) modify it. The information transmitted must take place for the sole purpose of carrying out the transmission only, and not be stored for a period longer than reasonably necessary for the purposes of the transmission. Telecommunications operators such as mobile networks perform this function".

---

[79] Electronic Commerce Directive 2000 - Wikipedia

[80] House of Lords - Regulating in a digital world - Select Committee on Communications (parliament.uk)

- **Caching providers (Article 13)** "which store transmitted information automatically and temporarily "for the sole purpose of making more efficient the information's onward transmission to other recipients of the service upon their request". The intermediary must not modify the information. Internet service providers, such as BT, Sky Broadband and Virgin Media, perform this function".

- **Hosting providers (Article 14)** "which store data specifically selected and uploaded by a user of the service, and intended to be stored ("hosted") for an unlimited amount of time. Hosting providers can benefit from the liability exemption only when they are "not aware of facts or circumstances from which the illegal activity or information is apparent" (when it concerns civil claims for damages) or when they "do not have actual knowledge of illegal activity or information." This can apply to some but not all activities of social media companies, search engines and other online platforms".

The 'Information Society Service Providers' include internet service providers and most online platforms like E-Bay, Facebook, Instagram, WhatsApp and more.

3.11.3 Why are these two sets of laws relevant to innovation?

The answer to this question is simple. The US Section 230 legal and policy framework allows for YouTube users to upload their own videos, it allows Facebook, Instagram and Twitter to offer more than one third of humanity to be on their social networks. Without Section 230, E-Bay, Craigslist and Amazon would not be able to offer millions of user reviews. It would be virtually be impossible for these players to prevent illegal (or even legal but harmful) content to appear on their platforms.

Similarly, Articles 12 to 14 of the EU's e-Commerce Directive allows for these same companies to operate unchallenged by legal liabilities in the EU.
If Section 230 in the USA and Articles 12-14 of the e-Commerce Directive in the EU did not exist, I would easily venture that that the mega-digital

platforms (Facebook, Twitter, Instagram, TikTok, YouTube, etc.) would be nowhere near the sizes they have attained. Indeed, some of them could not even exist at all, because it may not have been worth founding them. These laws are the most influential laws in the USA and EU to allow the Online Sector and Internet value chain to emerge, as well as protect them.

Therefore outside Europe and USA, e.g. in South East Asia, Africa, Caribbean and Latin America – if laws are introduced that stifle such innovation – do not be surprised at the consequences either of a still-birth Digital Economy. Do not say you have not been warned. A word to the wise is enough!

3.12 Summary

This concludes the definition of the set of challenges that Digital Economy policy makers and regulators face as they strive to create digital economies in their countries. It is one definition problem statement – mine. Other authors may define the challenges differently.

I have chosen to define the Digital Economy problem statement as the sum total of the combined (i) *offline* (as in offline TMT/ICT) set of policy and regulatory challenges we have today, (ii) the new Big Tech ones and (iii) the numerous *online* set of harms that come with the Internet value chain and (iv) the necessary pillar platforms of the Digital Economy.

Together, I hope they provide the *problem statement* of the overall policy and regulatory challenges that face Digital Economy Policy makers and regulators. However, as I note too, beware of regulating away your next online giants too.

I clearly assume the current ICT policy makers and regulators would have to morph into the Digital Economy ones. Their challenges are both daunting, but also in my humble opinion exhilarating. Digitalising economies has consequences, but would also be quite a journey.

Part III — Towards the Future of Data Economy Policy Making & Regulation: *some brief suggestions, recommendations and ways forward on key challenges*

Chapter 4 Headline: Digital Economy Policy makers, regulators and network operators should consider prioritizing the eleven broad thematic areas for the reasons provided therein.

Chapter 5 Headline: Some suggestions, recommendations and ways forward on the eleven prioritized areas are provided. "Sometimes the smallest step in the right direction ends up being the biggest step... Tiptoe if you must, but take a step". This chapter helps you tiptoe.

Chapter 6 Headline: "This is one I prepared earlier". Taking one of the eleven prioritized areas and doing a "deep dive" delve into it – OTT Regulation. An exemplar for what you the reader and your team would do to any or all of the other ten areas that I do not do a deep dive into.

Chapter 4

Selected Priority Digital Economy Areas

The first step to success is knowing your priorities— Aspesh

You are entering Part III of this book. I hope I achieve the core top three goals that I set out to realise in this book (see the Preface) with the prior Parts I and II.

The first step to Digital Economy success would be knowing your priorities. In this chapter, I select some thematic challenging areas that clearly emerge from the three previous chapters. As a Digital Economy Policy Maker, you would need to identify your digital economy priorities in your country to succeed.

This chapter highlights the prioritised thematic areas I have chosen and why.

Selecting Thematic Areas

In my preface I note a supplementary goal to the three broad main goals of this manuscript – that of taking some of the new opportunities, risks and harms areas of the Digital Economy problem statement, defining them a bit further and making some brief recommendations on *what*, *where* and *how* Digital Economy Policy Makers can start addressing them. In other words, this manuscript also attempts to proffer some ideas about what policy makers and regulators do about some of these new IVC-inspired challenges, not forgetting the old ICT/TMT challenges. This is the subject of the three chapters of this Part III of this book.

However, how did I select the thematic areas of this (what I consider) supplementary Part III of this book? The answer is simple. Even you the reader would have noticed some recurring thematic challenging areas from the two previous parts of the book and from all the 'mini-case studies' I cover.

I provide my list of priority areas following and justify briefly [and sequentially] why they emerge. You may disagree and would have preferred to see some slightly different themes to the ones I select – that is fine too.

I have put together some of the thematic areas in some hopefully logical groupings for brevity.

4.2 Offline TMT/ICT Policy and Regulation to achieve availability, affordability and awareness still remains top priority

The UN General Assembly (UNGA) "declared Internet access a human right[1]" in 2016 by, albeit through a *non-binding Resolution*. Now here is the truism. The *offline* TMT/ICT sector arguably has as big a role if not bigger in making this a reality in your country than the *online* IVC sector activities that may be going on. Just think about it. The Internet-only players and ISPs in your country are unlikely to be building the fibre backbone in your country, or building 4G broadband sites.

I believe I am crystal in the definition of the Digital Economy problem statement in Chapter 3 for policy makers and regulators that offline TMT/ICT policy making and regulation (see Figure 27) still takes top priority to realise their digital economy goals too.

In addition, the UN's 2030 Agenda for Sustainable Development features 17 Sustainable Development Goals (SDGs)[2] which were unanimously adopted by world leaders at a historic UN summit in September 2015. Coming from Africa, the SDGs are very laudable and well-meaning, but

---

[1] OHCHR | Home
[2] THE 17 GOALS | Sustainable Development (un.org)

read hopelessly optimistic: (1) No Poverty, (2) Zero Hunger, (3) Good Health and Well-Being, (4) Quality Education, (5) Gender Equality, (6) Clean Water and Sanitation, (7) Affordable and Clean Energy, (8) Decent Work and Economic Growth, (9) Industry, Innovation and Infrastructure, (10) Reduced Inequalities, (11) Sustainable Cities and Communities, (12) Responsible Consumption and Production, (13) Climate Action, (14) Life Below Water, (15) Life on Land, (16) Peace Justice and Strong Institutions and (17) Partnerships for the Goals. However, it is just factual that ICTs are the key enablers that will accelerate the realization of these 17 SDGs. In other words, Internet/web access is just a prerequisite for many of these SDGs.

Furthermore, SDG 9 speaks to Industry, Innovation and Infrastructure. The TMT/ICT sector, via its mobile/cellular sub-sector, is investing hundreds of billions of USD to drive broadband adoption.

I must note that the non-binding UNGA resolution declaring Internet access a human right does not address governmental responsibility to provide access to all at all. The challenges of "universal access" [or availability] on the *supply side* by building widespread fibre, FWA and mobile/cellular networks still remains preeminent – just as is the case with *demand side* education, awareness and the Internet-skilling of the population. Infrastructure policy, regulation and their implementation to achieve universal availability, affordability and awareness still remain a largely offline TMT/ICT challenge. By infrastructure I include fibre ducts, fibre poles and their overhead fibre lines, sites, towers and their 2G/3G/4G/5G/FWA passive and active electronics on them, submarine Internet cables, national terrestrial and last mile to homes/offices networks, etc.

Offline TMT/ICT Policy and Regulation to achieve availability, affordability and awareness still remains top priority.

4.3 Digital Economy Platforms Policy & Regulation

My second priority theme is digital platforms. As I note in the previous chapter, particularly for developing economies, there must be a concerted effort to put in place the three core foundational platforms of any digital economy: (i) an ID platform, (ii) a payments platform and (iii) the connectivity platform. Developed economies largely have this covered since, e.g. only circa 6% are unbanked in Europe and North America whilst the unbanked in Asia Pacific, South/Central America and Middle East/Africa are 24%, 38% and 50% respectively[3]. Developed markets have identified all of their citizens and are also largely covered by infrastructure networks to practically all of their populations.

Offline ICT/TMT policy and regulation covers the connectivity platform for sure as I cover earlier. I believe the same applies to the other two platforms too in most countries. However, here is a problem I frequently see in many developing market countries I visit or that I know about.

The problem is countries may have created Digital Economy ministries, but the responsibility for these three platforms still falls under different ministries. In Nigeria, the Ministry of Communications and Digital Economy (MCDE) as of October 2021 oversees the connectivity and ID platforms, but not payments – and there are several equivalent "identity" cards still, not a unique one. In South Africa, the Ministry/Department of Home Affairs (DOH) is responsible for the ID platform; the Ministry of Communications and Digital Technologies (MCDT) oversees the connectivity platform; and the payments platform is under the Ministry of Finance. In India, one ministry oversees connectivity and ID platform (the Aadhaar platform), but another oversees payment gateway platforms. The efforts across these key digital economy platforms need to be well coordinated – and these platforms need to be individually evolved.

Considering payment platforms in particular, they are part of the Enabling Technologies & Services segment of the IVC (see Figure 1). As I cover in Chapter 3 for developing countries with millions of unbanked, mobile financial services provide the only large-scale payments platforms. Mobile financial services is catch-all term for financial services provided over a mobile network, e.g. from mobile money services (including transfers and payments) to banking-type services (including deposits and borrowing).

---

[3] World's Most Unbanked Countries 2021 | Global Finance Magazine (gfmag.com)

4.4 The Future of Content, Broadcasting & Media Policy and Regulation

My third pick priority theme is Content. The Internet value chain is led by the Content Rights Segment (cf. Figure 1). One of the biggest key differences between offline and online value chains is the ubiquity of content online. Many countries working on their digital economies just do not seem to realise this basic fact – the future of their content industry is truly key, and it has clear links to broadcasting and media policies. Content-led industries including media, broadcasting, radio, news, TV, videos, content apps, etc. are responsible for so many jobs in developed markets – multiple times the numbers of jobs in telecoms or technology sectors. I stress this in Nwana (2014). Remember too that media can range from the biggest TV stations in your country, to the biggest newspaper chain all the way to a singular online blogger/publisher. They are all in the content business, and the Internet provides an incredible publishing platform as I cover in Chapter 2 with the long tail theory.

There is more to the future of content and media as I show with the Netflix effect in the Thailand case study (of the previous chapter). It covers how Netflix is significantly changing the content and broadcasting value chains in Thailand. Netflix – as an OTT service - is replacing the erstwhile monopoly Thai home video and DVD markets and the traditional film value chain. As the fixed line infrastructure to stream content to homes improves using fibre or FWA, so would the traditional content value chains in your country change markedly. I note in the last chapter how the asymmetric regulation across traditional broadcasting and new media (like OTTs) is a clear concern.

However, one area I would like to emphasise is local language content on online platforms in your country. Do not let your local content and languages to die because they are 'overrun' by foreign content.

Even in a developed Europe (cf. Chapter 2), Augusto Pretta (IT Media Consulting[4]) points out the need for three things:

(i) more concentrated investments in original and local content

(ii) partnerships between EU broadcasters and pay-TV operators and

(iii) regulations on European content quota and non-linear services (VOD) obligations.

So even developed Europe is concerned about *cultural concerns* (e.g. Hollywoodization/Americanisation) that are looming even larger than ever with the Content Rights segment of the IVC. I note that it would be the case that other regions of the world and other major content rights producing countries such India (Bollywood) and Nigeria (Nollywood) may have to adopt similar Content Rights strategies.

What about a Swahili[5] equivalent TikTok app/service for East Africa? Or a social and community service is Hausa, Yoruba or Igbo – all widely spoken and written in Nigeria? Local content would be at the core of both preserving national identities, national languages as well as much digital economy innovations.

4.5 Online/Internet Policy & Regulation and the true cost of "free" models

My fourth pick priority theme is Online Regulation. I think I make the case for Online Policy and Regulation in depth in Chapter 3. There is a school of thought that may be Online Regulation can be delayed in many countries. I argue in Chapter 3 that it is indispensable now because the harms are not only so numerous – but the disproportionate nature (as in the potential harm to society) of their societal negative impacts truly make Online Policy and regulation a priority.

---

[4] *Ibid.*

[5] Swahili is an language widely spoken in East Africa – and is a lingua franca of the East African Community (EAC) spoken by 60 millions to 150 million people.

Would you want to see online videos and instructions which tell teenagers how to kill themselves leading to suicides like has happened in the UK and elsewhere? On allow for online hate speeches which incite offline street violence like happened in Myanmar? Or allow for botnets to impact elections? Should children be exposed to some of the most gruesome and/or harmful content? I hope I make the case cogently for online regulation in the last chapter.

There are five core priority online harm areas that truly concern me as you may have picked up from the previous chapters:

(i) *Online protection of children*: the UK is addressing this with its UK Children's Code. I cover in Chapter 2 how the Irish is doing ditto with its "Children's Fundamentals" code – a guide to protecting children's personal data[6] which proposes 14 key principles. Children really need to be left to be children, and I am afraid the IVC is getting in the way.

For example, children bullied on Instagram go home from school suffering all through the rest of the day and night from the consequences of such bullying which is likely to be increasing during the day and/or night, just for them to return to school the next day to more bullying. Online bullying follows children all day long. In general the evidence seems to suggest that children know they feel harmed using platforms like Instagram or Facebook but they also confess they cannot stop using it – the addiction problem. They want the next click, the next like – almost a dopamine rush. These are really major harms to our children. Social media should not be making children feel bad because of body image issues such as body dysmorphia. This is a mental health condition when one cannot stop thinking about what they perceive as defects or flaws in their appearance. Platforms such as Instagram and Snapchat have beauty and augmented-reality facial/body features and filters. Indeed I hear youngsters talking about their [doctored] 'Instagram face'. So children effectively "perfect" their images online and compare themselves to other similarly doctored images of their

---

[6] The "Children's Fundamentals" – A guide to protecting children's personal data | 18/03/2021 | Data Protection Commission

friends – or worst still, of doctored images of well-known celebrities. Then these young girls (typically) end up feeling bad when their real appearance does not match the online versions of themselves. This could lead to anxiety harms amongst the young, social isolation, depression, eating disorders and even to seeking out cosmetic surgery. These are real consequential harms to children.

(ii) *Harmful content, election integrity, privacy and data portability*: these are the four areas that have been offered up by Facebook as worthy of regulation now. I cover privacy and data portability later.

Harmful content is obvious. I have seen and studied inappropriate (direct) or implied ads to children between 13 to 17 say - ads that promote anorexia/weight loss, or ads that promote drugs, ads that promote finding partners online. The risks and harms here are huge. Ad approval systems may need to be regulated, particularly those targeting children. Eating disorders are serious harms to children. Recall also the alleged Facebook internal research I report in Chapter 3 that found that 13% of British children and 6% of US children trace suicide desires to Instagram[7]. To a regulator, such findings should be flashing red lights and not ones a company like Instagram should be keeping silent on – no matter the contexts. It should have been disclosed to the right authorities external to the organisation.

Election integrity has emerged as a key concern. Politicians in your country are also likely to be very concerned about election integrity and democracy. In October 2021, a Facebook whistleblower[8] made herself known and spoke to the US Senate about the harms of the Facebook platform. Frances Haugen, a former Facebook employee who had secretly stashed away thousands of internal Facebook documents told the US Senate that Facebook "weakens democracy" and that "they have put immense profits before people". She told CBS' *60 Minutes* program that she had seen an internal Facebook report wherein major European political parties

[7] Facebook Knows Instagram Is Toxic for Teen Girls, Company Documents Show - WSJ
[8] Frances Haugen: Facebook weakens democracy, says ex-employee - BBC News

"... feel strongly that the change to the algorithm has forced them to skew negative in their communications on Facebook ... leading them into more extreme policy positions." (Source CBS[9])

Recall in Chapter 2's case study on Facebook, I note how Facebook CEO Mark Zuckerberg announced a major change in its Facebook core rankings algorithm called EdgeRank[10] in 2018.

Is it not incredible to learn that major European political parties allegedly complained a year later in 2019 that they have been compelled to skew negative in their communications on Facebook, leading them to adopting more extreme positions? Essentially, European political parties are allegedly complaining that the Facebook platform is impacting how they run their countries. This is truly big and severe harm if true.

(iii) *Fake News on Social Networks and Online Safety*: this is a particular bug bear with politicians across several continents of the globe from Africa, to South East Asia, to Europe and the Americas. The German Government enacted a new law in 2017 called the Network Enforcement Act[11] aimed at combatting fake news on social networks particularly Facebook's, leading to the law being dubbed the Facebook Act.

(iv) *Online Safety* in the UK, the Government has introduced an Online Safety Bill[12] in May 2021 which aims to provide "global leadership with our groundbreaking laws to usher in a new age of accountability for tech and bring fairness and accountability to the online world.". Through the Bill when it eventually becomes an Act, telecoms and broadcast regulator Ofcom would be designated to enforce the new Online Internet services regime through the preparation and implementation of codes of practice. The current Bill is novel in the sense that it tries to regulate various Internet

---

[9] Report: European political parties complained Facebook is forcing them to take more extreme policy positions - CBS News

[10] EdgeRank - http://edgerank.net/ (last accessed August 2021)

[11] Network Enforcement Act - Wikipedia

[12] Draft Online Safety Bill - GOV.UK (www.gov.uk)

services covering: (i) addressing illegal and harmful online content by imposing a *duty of care* concerning such content, in particular, terrorist content, racist abuse and fraud; (ii) protecting children from child sexual exploitation and abuse (CSEA) content; (iii) protecting users' rights to freedom of expression and privacy; and (iv) promoting media literacy. The bill speaks of "user-to-user services" which is a synonym for user-generated content on social media like Twitter and Facebook and even "search services" such as on Google.

The EC's response would be addressed with its Digital Services Act (DSA)[13]. As I cover in Chapter 3, it proposes to address both illegal and harmful content.

(v) *"Free", Virality, Disinformation & Misinformation with Digital Platforms*: I have a particular bug bear with this one. Just think about it. If factual news on Twitter takes 6x longer than fake news to be seen by 1500 people on Twitter as published in the journal *Science*[14], then surely it goes without saying that these digital platforms can make multiple times the advertising revenues off fake news than off factual news. I think this is such an implicit problem that comes with the "free" to Internet users, i.e. that comes with advertising models and digital platforms like Twitter, Facebook and others. This is because the conflict of interest and ethical issues with these platforms that come with them being "free" at the point of use are immense.

The evidence is mounting that these digital platforms maximise engagement by using engagement-based rankings which in turn use AI/ML. A clear emerging causality of maximising engagement is problematic use (i.e. addiction) – a clear harm. The *amplification algorithms* at play here are also very worrying and [potentially] very harmful. It appears clear that the maximisation of engagement via amplification also means the maximising of virality of posts via

---

[13] The Digital Services Act: ensuring a safe and accountable online environment | European Commission (europa.eu)

[14] *Science*, DOI: 10.1126/science.aao4960 & Fake news travels six times faster than the truth on Twitter | New Scientist

reshares of posts, likes, etc. And as we have seen, the more viral posts are more likely to be those that misinform/disinform than those that are factual. This also means more viral hate speech. And in turn more virality means more profits.

I am not sure a profit maximising company should own such an ethical challenge, and this for me is arguably one of the strongest reasons for outside regulation of the viral model along with disinformation, misinformation with these digital platforms. These companies should be saved from themselves on such challenges. How does a company like Facebook or Twitter balance posts reshares vs. the impacts of hate speech, misinformation or violent posts being reshared? This is very important because according to Facebook whistle-blower Frances Haugen's evidence to the US Congress, in some countries, reshares make some make up 35% of the content that people see. Do you really trust these companies to make their platforms deliberately less viral (less reshares) when more virality equals profits with ads targeted on age, gender and location-based bases?

As I am concluding this book, the UK Government's online safety bill is in progress. It will give my previous employer and esteemed regulator [Ofcom] when it becomes an Act the power to fine companies up to 10% of qualifying revenue for breaches of the law. The Ofcom CEO Dame Melanie Dawes said that it was time to hold social media giants to much greater account.

> Too often, companies appear to have prioritised growth over the safety of their users. By designing their services to maximise reach, they may have inadvertently promoted harmful content: bullying or harassment, hate speech, self-harm. They may not be quick enough to tackle terrorism or sexual abuse... If these companies are regulated at all, it is only by outrage. The time has come for strong, external oversight...

> We will hold companies to account on how they use algorithms, address complaints and ensure a safe experience for children. The biggest services must also explain how they protect journalistic and democratic content. Today, these

decisions are being made behind companies' doors, with no visibility or accountability. Source[15]:

What Dame Melanie Dawes notes above is quite apt to me.

I am not pretending every single country would be able to do much about online regulation, but they should be able to understand and prioritise what online harms really matter to them and take the priority steps to address them. The EU's 27 countries is banding together to face off these mega platforms. Your country may want to learn from the EU and band likewise with other countries too.

4.6 Big Tech Policy & Regulation

My fifth priority theme is Big Tech regulation. Chapter 3 makes the case for this in depth. I note in Chapter 3 that the US Congress is pursuing several different Bills to control Big Tech, and as of June 2021 Congress unveiled 5 bipartisan Bills that mark the biggest steps yet in regulating Big Tech[16].

4.7 Cybercrime/Cyber-harms and Cybersecurity Policy & Regulation

My sixth pick priority theme is Cybercrime and Cybersecurity. These are two different issues but clearly related. Chapters 2 and 3 are replete with all kinds of cyber-harms and cybercrimes, necessitating every country to have a clear set of policies and implemented programs to manage them.

Your country would almost certainly require separate Cybercrime and Cybersecurity legislations. The latter, i.e. cybersecurity legislations, typically comprise

---

[15] Ofcom chief: time for 'strong external oversight' of social media – Digital TV Europe

[16] US lawmakers introduce bills targeting Big Tech - BBC News

directives that safeguard information technology and computer systems with the purpose of forcing companies and organizations to protect their systems and information from cyberattacks like viruses, worms, Trojan horses, phishing, denial of service/distributed denial of service (DOS/DDOS) attacks, unauthorized access (stealing intellectual property or confidential information) and control system attacks. There are numerous measures available to prevent cyberattack

(Source: Wikipedia[17]).

A piece of cybercrime legislation on the other hand typically covers unlawful acts or criminal activities where a computer or an electronic communication network is used either as a tool, a target or both. This will cover areas such as forgeries, frauds, thefts, defamation of people and more we see in earlier chapters.

Cybercrime may harm peoples' financial health or their security. The classic categories for cybercrimes are (i) financial, e.g. stealing financial information or monies (ii) hacking (iii) cyber-terrorism (iv) cyberextortion (v) cybersex trafficking (vi) drug trafficking (vii) cyberwarfare (viii) online harassment, etc.

4.8 Artificial Intelligence, Big Data Policy & Regulation

My seventh pick priority theme is AI and Big Data. Recall that Facebook has since admitted its AI and Machine Learning-based ranking algorithms helped to "incite offline violence" in Myanmar[18] with the Rohingya Muslim crisis. Similarly too from Chapter 3, recall that Facebook's EdgeRank algorithm allegedly promotes or promoted extremist groups with "Groups You Should Join" recommendations increasing their membership! I note in Chapter 2 an internal Facebook presentation that noted "64% of all extremist group joins are due to our recommendation tools", thanks to the AI models behind such "Groups You Should Join" and Facebook's "Discover" platform features.

---

[17] Cybercrime - Wikipedia

[18] Facebook admits it was used to 'incite offline violence' in Myanmar - BBC News

Any technology with such [real] offline costs to society need to be regulated – and this is clearly the case with AI and Machine Learning. We need more Trustworthy AI and ML.

It is not only about Facebook's AI. AI/ML features as a concern in practically all the segments of the Internet value chain. I note the following that emerges (from previous chapters) about AI, ML and Big Data:

- In the Content Rights segment in Chapter 2, I note how Content Rights expert Augusto Pretta clearly highlights how consolidations across the IVC allows for the greater role of Big Data and Artificial Intelligence in the identification and servicing of subscribers (i.e. shifting from a B2B strategy to a direct to consumer offering). They do this in order compete with emerging future content behemoths like Netflix and Amazon by using Big Data and AI to create data and content packages directly to consumers (typically, triple and quad plays bundles across voice, data, fixed, mobile Internet access and video/TV).

- In the Online Services Segment, the role of AI, Machine Learning, as we see Facebook greatly employs AI and Machine Learning (ML) techniques in its News Feed algorithm which does the core rankings called EdgeRank[19] (which controls organic reach vs. paid-for reach), though it uses other non-ML algorithms too. I also covered Twitter's ranking algorithm too which uses AI/ML – wherein in fake news travels faster than factual news.

- In the Enabling Technologies and Services segment, I cover the role of AI, ML and Big Data algorithms with Google Ads, Google Search, Google Analytics and with Amazon's massive use of Big Data too, allegedly preferring its own products in their "Buy Now" box over others. AI and ML are being considered in the UK for online age identification.

- In the User Interface segment, thousands of Apps use AI, Big Data and ML algorithms

All the above are just from Chapter 2. In Chapter 3 there many references too to AI, ML and Big Data. The AI, ML and Big Data themes emerge

---

[19] EdgeRank - http://edgerank.net/ (last accessed August 2021)

greatly with Big Tech and Online Regulation – and clearly require policy scrutiny.

Big data is already with us – and is the other side of the coin to AI. You may ask where it comes from and why does it matter? Consider the following from Techjury.net[20]:

- There were 4.66 billion active Internet users around the world in January 2021.

- Experts predict search engines' searches will amount to about 2 trillion for the whole of 2021. This equates to 6 billion searches a day.

- 2.5 quintillion[21] data bytes of data was created daily in 2020 (Source, Domo[22]).

- On average, every human created at least 1.7 MB of data per second in 2020 (Source: Domo[23])

- Facebook generated 4 petabytes of data every day in 2020, i.e. 4 million gigabytes.

- Machine-generated data accounted for over 40% of Internet data in 2020, with 60% human generated.

- Storage data growth statistics show that public and private cloud infrastructure grew from 4.4 zettabytes[24] (ZB) in 2019 to 44ZB in 2020, expected to be 200+ZB by 2025.

The sheer volume, variety and velocity of the data being stored and analysed in simply mindboggling as the last bullet shows.

This is why my favourite definition of "Big data" is the following: big data technologies describe a new generation of technologies and architectures,

---

[20] https://techjury.net/blog/how-much-data-is-created-every-day/#gref

[21] A quintillion is 1 followed by 18 zeroes.

[22] Press Release - Domo Releases Annual "Data Never Sleeps" Infographic | Domo

[23] *Ibid.*

[24] A zettabyte is 1 followed by 21 zeroes.

designed to economically extract *value* from very large *volumes* of a wide *variety* of data, by enabling high-*velocity* capture, discovery, and/or analysis[25].

AI and Big Data have now evolved to be two sides of the same coin. This is because AI – which has been around since the 1950s – has come into its element as it is increasingly used to extract value from high-velocity big data. Today, with (i) huge amounts of data (Big Data), (ii) advanced algorithms, (iii) oodles of storage and (iv) high end computing power – AI has been put on steroids.

4.9 Privacy (Liberty) & Data Protection vs. Innovation Policy & Regulation

My eighth pick priority theme is Privacy and Data Protection and its tension with Innovation and likely societal harms. As the previous section's big data statistics show, the wide adoption and broad range of Online usage has ushered vast collection and analysis of information about individuals' preferences, behaviours and attributes including purchasing intentions, hobbies, gender and location. This is partly what leads to the billions of data-points being collected and used by OTT players like Facebook and Google, and gathered and aggregated across multiple sources (online as well as offline) by data providers (infomediaries).

The data is analysed to develop and deliver innovative and personalised services as well as targeted advertising, creating value for service providers and for consumers themselves.

However with all these data collected, two core issues arise immediately: privacy and data protection.

- *Privacy*: consumers and citizens' privacy must be respected online, or else all trust is lost. The right to privacy is enshrined in many international and national laws/declarations.

---

[25] https://journalofbigdata.springeropen.com/articles/10.1186/s40537-016-0059-y

- Article 12 of the UN's 1948 Universal Declaration of Human Rights (UDHR) speaks to the right of protection to any individual, his/her family or home against "arbitrary interference", "nor any attacks upon his honour and reputation. Everyone has the right to the protection of the law against such interference or attacks"[26].

- Article 17 of the UN's International Covenant on Civil and Political Rights enshrines similar rights like the UDHR's Article 12 above[27].

- Article 7 of the EU's Charter of Fundamental Rights stipulates "- "Everyone has the right to respect for his or her private and family life, home and correspondence"[28].

- Etc.

- *Data Protection*: there is an obvious link from privacy to Data Protection. For example, under the Article 8 of the EU Fundamental set of Freedoms stipulates

  > everyone has the right to the protection of personal data concerning him or her. Such data must be processed fairly for specified purposes and on the basis of the consent of the person concerned or some other legitimate basis laid down by law. Everyone has the right of access to data which has been collected concerning him or her, and the right to have it rectified.[29].

So privacy and data protection are fundamental rights, irrespective of whether individuals are offline or online. Our privacy and data protection rights need to be codified in laws for the online world too.

Also in this book, I cover in several to many places the tension between personal privacy (liberty) vs. Innovation as enabled by Section 230 (in the USA) and Articles 12-14 (in the EU). I also cover in many mini-case studies the tensions between personal liberty vs. risks to wider society. Does your individual right to privacy trump the rights of society to be kept safe, if you are planning a bomb attack online?

---

[26] Universal Declaration of Human Rights | United Nations

[27] OHCHR | International Covenant on Civil and Political Rights

[28] text_en.pdf (europa.eu) - https://www.europarl.europa.eu/charter/pdf/text_en.pdf

[29] *Ibid*.

4.10 Electronic Commerce Laws, Policy & Regulation

My ninth pick theme is electronic commerce. Online to most people means Search, Social Media and e-Commerce. E-Commerce, or Electronic Commerce, is the online industry of buying and selling goods, services or products via the Internet.

Figure 3 [in Chapter 1] depicting the IVC shows that the Online Services segment was valued at 47% of the IVC. I note there too that the size of this segment was expected to have almost doubled by 2020 as forecasted from 2015 (as again can be seen in Figure 3) growing to 52% of the IVC. E-Commerce is one of the biggest of the five clusters of the Online Services segment; and it consists inclusive of (i) E-retail including major B2C brands like EBay, Alibaba and Amazon, and other dedicated B2B exchanges (ii) E-travel including Expedia, Uber, Airbnb, etc. Covid19 lockdowns would have increased this projected 52% to perhaps much higher.

I note in Chapter 2 that Amazon dominates the e-Commerce Online Services category of the IVC as no other company does, with circa 50% of this category globally [excluding China of course]. What is not in doubt is the growing and rapid shift from offline retail to online retail.

Clearly, there must be laws to underpin e-commerce in your country, as such a law applies to contracts concluded electronically between a buyer and a seller online. E-Commerce policy, law and regulations encompasses all the legalities and processes associated with the e-commerce industry.

The laws could cover (i) consumer data, (ii) disclosure of information (iii) advertising electronically (iv) contract termination, etc. E-Commerce merchants in your country would typically need to be registered, and perhaps even overseas businesses that offer products and services in your country through enabling your consumers to have access.

E-Commerce laws, policies and regulations that apply may be numerous and complex – but they are be needed if your country does not have them.

4.11 OTT Policy & Regulation

My tenth pick theme is OTT Regulation in general. I note that all the services in the Online Services segment of the Internet Value Chain (IVC) are all Over the Top (OTT) services. In its 2016 Report on OTT, the Body of European Regulators for Electronic Communications (BEREC) defines OTT as "content, a service or an application that is provided to the end user over the public Internet"[30]. All the categories of the Online Services segment of the IVC contain content (e.g. UGC content), services (e.g. Google or Wikipedia) or applications (e.g. gaming apps) are all OTTs. All these OTT categories come with incredible positive externalities but as we have seen in Chapters 2 and 3, there are significant negative externalities too.

Yet there are significant calls for just one of the sub-categories of this segment to be regulated, i.e. social media category players like Facebook and WhatsApp principally. Selective regulation for certain categories and not others – without very clear reasons to do so – is questionable, unfair and would arguably fail.

4.12 Capacity Building and Training on Digital Economy

My eleventh and last pick theme is Capacity Building and Training. Of course, it is strictly speaking not really a theme that requires policy making and regulating, but nonetheless I have included it as something that Digital Economy policy makers and regulators must have top of mind. It is at the heart of why I wrote this book.

Never has capacity building and training be more evident and required – I hope this much at least is clear from what you have read so far of this book. Writing this book is one way I hope I have contributed to Capacity Building and Training in this key area of the Digital Economy. The speed

---

[30] BEREC Report on the Public Consultation on the "Report on OTT services" (europa.eu)

of evolution of the Digital Economy is much faster than Policy makers, regulators and network operators' ability to react.

4.12 Summary on Thematic Areas

I believe the above eleven priority areas are some truly key areas that require close scrutiny, but certainly not the only ones.

Chapter 5

Towards Future Policy & Regulations for Selected Digital Economy Areas

Sometimes the smallest step in the right direction ends up being the biggest step... Tiptoe if you must, but take a step

— *Naeem Callaway*

Key to what I do in this Part III section of the book is to do what Naeem Callaway's quote above says – to assist Digital Economy Policy makers and regulators with some small steps in the right direction.

As Callaway says in her brilliant quote above, tiptoe into some of these areas if you must, but do take the steps because your Digital Economies need them.

I therefore take every thematic priority area of the previous chapter and providing some suggestions, ways forward and recommendations on how to start "tiptoeing" into them. This is for Digital Economy Policy makers and regulators.

For easier readability, comprehension and standardisation – I make my contributions towards addressing the thematic challenges above through a table summarising the following: (i) the current offline context (ii) the Online trends (iii) the typical current regulatory context in a country (iv) the key issues and challenging that need controlling and (v) some starter-for-ten recommendations from me.

5.1 Offline TMT/ICT Policy & Regulation

Current TMT/ICT and Digital Economy Realisation Context

- The UN General Assembly (UNGA) "declared Internet access a human right[31]" in 2016 by, albeit through a *non-binding Resolution*. I note this when I overview my thematic choices in Chapter 4 that the *offline* TMT/ICT sector arguably has the bigger role in making this a reality.

- Only the offline TMT/ICT sector would help realise the widescale *supply side* infrastructure rollout of the national middle terrestrial fibre, the last mile to homes and offices with fibre, FWA, 4G/5G mobile or Wi-Fi. This is the availability/access challenge.

- Issues of *affordability* (prices of services, cost of devices, etc) and *awareness* (e.g. demand side education and skilling) are both *offline* TMT/ICT policy and regulatory challenges too.

- *Key Takeaway here*: offline ICT/TMT policy making and regulation remains key. If anything, the Digital Economy even puts more emphasis on *rigorous implementation* by policy makers and regulators on the offline TMT/ICT sector. I insist on rigorous implementation because in many developing countries, implementation of good competition policy, spectrum policy and public policy still leave much to be desired. For example, the failure of the promises of universal service funds (USFs) just cannot continue – and such lackadaisical policy, regulation and implementation as we see with USFs would ensure the digital economy your country seeks would be very much delayed. Another example would be the release of 700MHz and 800MHz through the digital switchover process (DSO) very much delayed in many developing countries. This is an offline TMT/ICT challenge which is this need to release and assign much needed low frequency spectrum for 4G and 5G.

---

[31] OHCHR | Home

TMT/ICT Sector Trends

- As I cover in Chapter 1, the various TMT value chains are being impacted in different ways by the Internet value chain. The TMT/ICT and IVC value chains are not mutually exclusive as I explain in Chapter 3.

- Most countries are now engaged in building their digital economies too – which they need to build on the back of the offline TMT/ICT sector.

Typical Current Regulatory Context on TMT/ICT Sector

- In most countries, the process of offline TMT/ICT policy making and regulation is well advanced, typically along the four key bucket areas of promoting competition, protecting consumers, allocating/managing public assets like spectrum/numbers and public policy. See Figure 27.

Issues & Challenges with realizing TMT/ICT Sector Outcomes

- They remain many and varied which I cover in depth in Nwana (2014) I would not repeat them here as it is the purpose of the entire 2014 book I wrote. For the purposes of this section, I only mention two key ones:

  (i) Poor or lackadaisical regulation and rigorous implementation by regulators in *many developing countries mainly* in order to realise the key outcomes (see Chapter 3) of (i) competitive TMT markets (ii) protected and empowered consumers/citizens (iii) efficiently allocated scare resources like spectrum and (iv) good public policy outcomes like universal available networks.

  (ii) Now they now have to deal too with online IVC challenges which means the limited resources would now be spread thinly over offline and now online issues.

251

- Recalibrate and improve TMT/ICT sector regulation and more *rigorous* implementation including issues like USF reforms. Use the impetus that the digital economy needs offline TMT/ICT implementation to succeed to put more emphasis on this offline area.
- Nwana (2014) details many other recommendations in this area.

5.2 Digital Economy Platforms Policy and Regulation

Current Typical *offline* Digital Economy Platforms Context

- I note when I overview my thematic choices in Chapter 4 that there are three core platforms of any digital economy (see Figure 25): the Identity (ID), the Connectivity and the Payment platforms.
- I note that developed countries already have widespread versions of all three platforms – and hence are ready, indeed already engaged with the digital economy.
- However, for developing markets with significant percentages of unbanked, significant percentages of unconnected and with weak ID systems, they are mostly not ready for the digital economy they strive for.
- *Key Takeaway here*: these platforms need to be developed in developing countries quickly.

Digital Economy Platforms Trends

- Developed countries are fine with their IDs like passports/driving licenses/national IDs; with near ubiquitous debit/credit cards/mobile banking; and with widespread networks.
- Developing countries, by and large, have a long way to go to achieving them.

Typical Current Regulatory Context on Digital Platforms

- For developing economies who desperately need these platforms, the story is mixed.

- India for example has solved the Identity Platform problem with Aadhaar. India also has its National Payment Corporation which has launched its unified payments interface (UPI) system with 29 banks using a smartphone app. However, India is still 20% unbanked (same number as China's) and with 34% Internet penetration as of January 2021[32]. Even India still has a long way to go on their payments and connectivity platforms. However Africa would have to rely on mobile financial services (MFS) like Kenya's m-PESA for mobile payments, and even Brazil has sub-50% banking penetration.

- Sub-Saharan Africa (SSA's) situation is obviously much worse than India's. Take Nigeria – the largest economy in Africa. Figure 26 shows it is 60% unbanked even though it has 70% penetration, true broadband penetration in Nigeria is much lower. Nigeria's national identification efforts are still fledgling in 2021. Nigeria needs a concerted effort to develop these much-need widespread platforms. Widespread connectivity in many SSA countries is still beset by availability, affordability and accessibility challenges. Universal Service Funds (USFs) set up to achieve universal access for voice have mostly failed to achieve this – yet alone achieving universal access to broadband.

Issues & Challenges with realizing Digital Economy Platforms

- The issues and challenges in realizing these platforms in developing countries are many and varied:

  (i) The biggest one I perceive is lack of appreciation and awareness that these platforms are the true pillars to any digital economy. Without them, Ministers and Presidents pronouncing on their countries striving to be Digital X (e.g. Digital Nepal or Digital Malawi)– and basically spouting nothing.

  (ii) The lack of appreciation and awareness has led to little policy,

---

[32] https://www.gfmag.com/global-data/economic-data/worlds-most-unbanked-countries

253

regulatory and implementation efforts to realise these platforms. This has to change for many developing countries.

(iii) Access to electricity is a major one in Sub Saharan Africa (SSA) – 600M Africans are in darkness every night in SSA.

(iv) Universal Availability to broadband – this is even much harder given that many countries are struggling with universal availability to voice services only today.

(v) Universal Access to broadband – it is one thing for the network to be available; it is another to have access.

(vi) Affordability: Access (Reach) without affordability is futile. Affordability without reach is sterile.

(vii) USFs (mostly in Africa) have largely failed apart from a few countries like Namibia and Uganda.

(viii) Literacy is obviously a factor in SSA too.

The Future of Digital Platforms Policy & Regulation - Some Suggested Recommendations for Developing Economies *only*

- Digital Economy policy makers, regulators and network operators [for developing countries] must understand the key importance of the pillar Digital Economy platforms.

- Policy, regulation and proper implementation towards a truly national ID platform – like India has done

- Policy, regulation and proper implementation towards a truly national payments platform like India is trying to do – even if it means a MFS one or a Mobile Money one. The platform may be *de facto* like M-PESA in Kenya or *de jure*.

- USFs Policy and Implementation would need to be revamped. Their mandates should be updated to include broadband (as the mandates of most still refer to voice services). They should do more Measurement and Evaluation using geographical information system (GIS)-based techno-economic modelling database as is being used by Uganda's Rural Communications Development Fund (RCDF)[33].

- Nwana (2014) details many other recommendations in this area.

---

[33] https://www.ucc.co.ug/rcdf/

5.3 The Future of Content, Broadcasting and Media Policy & Regulation

Current Typical *offline* Content, Broadcasting and Media Contexts

- Recall from Figure 4 (Chapter 1) that the offline contexts cover TV programming and broadcasting; sound recording and music publishing; news and information service; motion, TV and video; arts; advertising and media presentation; radio broadcasting; publishing of books and newspapers; printing and recorded media; publishing of computer gaming and software.

- Recall from Figure 23 (on Netflix in Thailand) the classic film/audio-visual value chain covers production (by major studios and independent film makers) to cinemas, to home video/discs/TV to the audience.

- Nwana (2014) detailed many key challenges with this offline context already (just reflect for your country's context) including: the future of Govt-owned broadcasters; the public service broadcasting challenge (e.g. of MCOT in Thailand; SABC South Africa; NTA Nigeria); the public service news challenge; the financing challenge; the newspapers/press challenge; the widespread availability challenge; the affordability challenge; the political/institutional challenge; the skills/knowledge challenge; the digital switchover of TV (DSO) challenge and the regulatory challenge to achieve all the above.

- The poor state and coverage of terrestrial TV broadcasting has pushed up the demand satellite TV broadcasting across many developing countries.

- *Key Takeaway here*: even before the arrival of online IVC opportunities, the offline contexts have numerous challenges, particularly in developing countries.

Online IP Streaming Platform Encroachment Trends (developing markets)

- The Thailand Netflix case study of Chapter 3 shows the *substitution* effect that quickly emerges with widespread emergence of IP-based *fixed* infrastructure - to compete with outdated analogue terrestrial TV and still-to-be-developed widespread digital terrestrial TV platforms.

- Netflix entry in Thailand is significantly disrupting erstwhile films and broadcasting value chains, replacing the home video/DVD markets; controlling the production, distribution and presentation of content broadcasted in Thailand; changing TV watching behaviours with more binge-watching

- The OTT IP Streaming platform (of the likes of Netflix, Amazon Prime, etc.) with its AVOD, SVOD, TVOD and hybrid of these offerings dictate upstream original content production – and even more so when the other distribution platforms (e.g. digital terrestrial and satellite) provide much weaker demand for the original content in your country.

- As countries neglect their duty towards plurality of non-IP streaming platforms (e.g. other broadcasting and media platforms), they should not be surprised if and when advertising revenues migrate to OTT players.

- User Generated Content (UGC) consumption (long form or short form) is growing exponentially on other streaming platforms like YouTube, TikTok, etc. enabling different segmentation of audiences than in the linear world.

- *Key Takeaway here*: OTT alternatives would disrupt old linear model content, broadcasting and media value chains. Growing but finite advertising budgets would move to OTT.

Typical Current Regulatory Context on Content

- Typical offline content regulation duties, e.g. the UK's, tend to protect (i) against Crime (ii) against Harms and Offence (iii) Children (iv) Religion (v) Impartiality (vi) Fairness (vii) Privacy and (viii) plurality of content, distribution platforms and channels. These are all to provide as much choice and diversity to citizens. These are at the core of content regulation.

- Telecoms regulators in many countries typically do not regulate Content, broadcasting and media because they are neither converged regulators nor do some governments truly want to lose control over content/media regulation.

- And even if the regulator is converged, they would not typically have

- duties and powers to do much about cross-border Online streamed content for example.

- Like with the Thai-Netflix case study of Chapter 3, regulator NBTC only regulates licensees that are *local* – cross-border streaming players are not Thai-registered businesses and license holders from NBTC. The Ministry of Digital Economy and Society in Thailand has legal authority over computer-related offences and harms that spans online content.

- *Key Takeaway here*: Asymmetric regulation is with us, i.e. different rules for the same content across different platforms (e.g. across satellite broadcast, terrestrial broadcast, cinema and online/Internet platforms). There are some very good reasons to have such differential regulation across broadcast platforms, VOD platforms from the likes of Netflix, and Online non-VOD services from the likes of YouTube, e.g. got reasons around democratic debate or protection of children. So it is sometimes justified that broadcast platforms are subject to stricter *statutory* rules and regulation, whilst VoD platforms may be *self-regulating*, with virtually *no regulation* on online non-VoD platforms. For how long would this be tenable in your country?

Issues & Challenges that need controlling, i.e. that require policy and regulation

- Linear (broadcast) TV platforms are clearly – in my humble opinion – even more needed. Not only for platform plurality, but because national platforms are best placed to promote national content, and to promote widespread availability of genres like news and local sports.

- Cultural concerns and cultural imperialism [34] (Hollywoodization/Americanisation) are real in many countries.

- The regulatory challenges of the offline context already highlighted in Nwana (2014) still remain in many developing countries including: the future of Govt-owned broadcasters; the public service broadcasting challenge (e.g. of MCOT in Thailand; SABC South Africa; NTA Nigeria); the public service news challenge; the financing challenge; the

---

[34] Cultural Imperialism: Hollywoodization – communicationtechnology101 (wordpress.com)

newspapers/press challenge; the widespread availability challenge; the affordability challenge; the political/institutional challenge; the skills/knowledge challenge; the digital switchover of TV (DSO) challenge.

- Asymmetric regulation across platform (and across offline and online) and service types (linear TV, VOD and online non-VOD) is becoming more and more indefensible and untenable.

- Protection of Children and the Vulnerable in particular is even more paramount but also the broader protection of adults too as consumers of media.

- Protection of consumers and citizens as individuals – their privacy online should be protected.

- Lastly for me after some of the lessons I have learnt writing this book, protection of democratic debate. This is usually referred to in the UK as *impartiality* obligations. As the USA 2020 pre and post elections have taught us, we lose mass broadcast platforms that promote impartial and factual news and debate at society's peril!

The Future of Content Regulation - Some Suggested Recommendations

- Digital Economy policy makers, regulators and network operators must understand the Content, Broadcasting and Media issues and challenges above. My own contribution in this manuscript has been to articulate them as clearly as I can, not pretending they are exhaustive.

- It is logical from the above that enhanced regulatory protection of children and the vulnerable in particular – with the onslaught of online content harms – is necessary now.

- There almost certainly would be a mix of statutory, co-regulatory and self-regulatory regimes to protect consumers and citizens across players in your country. I strongly recommend this this carefully thought through.

- Like Augusto Pretta advises, Digital Economy policy makers, regulators and network operators need to promote (i) more concentrated investments in original and local content (ii) partnerships between national broadcasters and pay-TV operators and (iii) regulations on [country] content quota and non-linear services (VOD) obligations.

The latter is to address the cultural and Hollywoodization-type concerns.

- Lastly, careful and step-by-step policy and regulatory making to achieve the outcomes and minimise the harms of the "Issues and Challenges" section above.

5.4 Online/Internet Policy & Regulation

Current Online Regulation Context – how has it come to this?

- Recall in Chapter 3, I note what Sir Tim Berner-Lee, founder of the World Wide Web[35] has since noted: " The changes we've managed to bring have created a better and more connected world. But for all the good we've achieved, the web has evolved into an engine of inequity and division; swayed by powerful forces who use it for their own agendas". You must admit this is truly powerful.

- Facebook CEO Mark Zuckerberg says of Online Regulation – it is "not whether there should be or not". In 2019, he proposed the four areas of (i) harmful content (ii) election integrity (iii) privacy and (iv) data portability.

- Earlier in this chapter, I outline my personal online harms priorities wherein the risks are so disproportionately high. I prioritised the Online protection of children, cf. UK Teenager Molly Russell, 14, killing herself in 2017 after seeing graphic images of self-harm and suicide on Instagram (source BBC)[36]. I prioritise the four areas Facebook CEO highlights particularly Election integrity and the role of algorithms. I prioritise Fake News on Social Media as well as general Online Safety. Lastly, I prioritise the online costs of "free", virality, disinformation with digital platforms because of the massive conflict of interests that emerges from maximising engagement. Essentially virality is not cost

---

[35] Sir Tim Berners-Lee, 'One Small Step for the Web…', *Medium* (29 September 2018): https://medium.com/@timberners_lee/one-small-step-for-the-web-87f92217d085 [accessed September 2021]

[36] Molly Russell: Social media users 'at risk' over self-harm inquest delay - BBC News - https://www.bbc.co.uk/news/uk-england-london-55986728 (last accessed August 2021)

free to society with disinformation/hate speech being more viral than factual news.

- *Key Takeaway here*: Although Online is not quite a lawless 'Wild West', it hosts a large volume of harms that would not be tolerated offline (as shown in Figure 29), and the harms are quite disproportionately high. Supervision of digital services has largely been ineffective with largely no means of cooperation and information sharing. There are hardly any national digital services "coordinator" as the EC Digital Services Act (DSA) Bill is aiming for.

Online/Internet Harms Trends

- They risks and harms are literally numerous, see Tables 3 and 5 and Figure 29.
- The implications of the some of the harms are truly egregious and would continue to be so, e.g. offline teenage deaths, or offline violence like in Myanmar with the Rohingya Mulsims, or the streaming of New Zealand terrorist attack of 51 people at mosques on Facebook.

Typical Current Regulatory Context on Online/Internet Harms

- In most countries, Online/Internet regulation is not yet controlled or regulated comprehensively. Even in Europe, the EC has only just proposed its Digital Services Act (DSA) in December 2020 to address online transparency, user safety and consumer protection.
- Some developed countries are beginning to address this. For example, the UK included the regulation of several online harms in its Digital Economy Act of 2017[37]. This UK Act tackles (i) restricting access to online pornography (ii) protection of IPR in connection with electronic communications (iii) to allow for information sharing with some key agencies (iv) allows for provisions for the regulation of direct marketing, e.g. targeting children (v) allows for provisions for Internet filters (vi) allows for provisions about preventing or restricting the use of communication devices in connection with drug dealing offences (vii) allows for provisions to regulate and restrict "criminal content, (viii)

---

[37] Digital Economy Act 2017 (legislation.gov.uk)

code of practice for providers of online social media platforms, etc. I also briefly cover earlier the UK's Online Safety Bill and the areas it would cover including (i) addressing illegal and harmful online content by imposing a duty of care concerning such content, in particular, terrorist content, racist abuse and fraud; (ii) protecting children from child sexual exploitation and abuse (CSEA) content; (iii) protecting users' rights to freedom of expression and privacy; and (iv) promoting media literacy.

- Therefore. New Online powers were given to regulators Ofcom (for telecoms, media and technology) and the Information Commissioner's Office[38] (ICO) (for Data Protection).

- I note early in this chapter the German Network Enforcement Act to tackle fake news on social media as well as the proposed UK Online Safety Bill which would address several online harms.

- The Data Protection and Privacy regulators – if your country has already established one – may already have powers and duties which they can use to develop codes of conduct or regulations addressing some of the prioritised online risks/harms. This is how the UK's ICO was able to evolve the UK's age-appropriate design code for online apps, particularly those aimed at children (see Chapter 2). Recall the UK ICO calls for "a better Internet for children".

Issues & Challenges with addressing Online/Internet Harms

- There are several including
  (i) There are just a numerous number of these harms as seen in Tables 3/5 and Figure 29.
  (ii) I list what the UK has covered in its Digital Economy Act of 2017 above as well as the proposed UK Online Services Bill. I cover both of these (i.e. the Digital Economy Act 2017 and the Online Safety Bill 2021) because it shows the list of online harms and risks that the UK has chosen to prioritise and has enacted/is enacting more duties and powers to regulators to deal with.

---

[38] Home | ICO - https://ico.org.uk/

(iii) There are significant definitional issues that are non-trivial to address, e.g. what is "pornographic material"? what is "extreme pornographic material"? What is "criminal content"? What do the Internet filters filter? What is "democratic importance" or "journalistic content" with the Online Safety Bill?

(iv) Bluntly, the UK's ICO and Ofcom may be able to evolve and produce regulations" for age-appropriate design code for online apps" and Online Safety codes of conduct/practice respectively – which online companies like TikTok, Facebook, YouTube and Instagram would abide by. Would these same companies react similarly to similar codes developed in your country? I believe depending on how significant and strategic the market is to these companies, they would, but not for others.

(v) Do not regulate away some of the potential big Internet companies that may emerge from your country as I explain in Chapter 3.

The Future Online/Internet Policy & Regulation - Some Suggested Recommendations

- Start with understanding and prioritizing the Online risks and harms that matter to your country.

- Like for the UK example, enact the laws that address the online risks and harms that are priority to your country.

- Empower the appropriate regulators, e.g. converged telecoms regulator, the data protection regulator or the content regulator, or a combination of all of them.

- If your country is not as strategic to the Big Tech and online players, your country may want to work with other countries in your region to gain better leverage.

- Socio-cultural aspects would loom large with definitional challenges with the new Online laws like what is "pornographic material"

- Any new laws like the UK's Online Safety Bill, the German Network Enforcement Act or the EC's Digital Services Act (DSA) need to delicately balance *Safety* on the one hand and *Freedom of Expression* on the other.

- As the EC's DSA proposes, it would make sense to have a national level 'Digital Service Coordinator' who would have wide ranging enforcement and supervisory powers, as well as coordination role to address online safety harms. This is because, in reality, there would be an ecosystem of actors providing such oversight: from self-regulation, to consumer watchdog organisations to data protection/privacy agencies, from university researchers to independent auditors; from big data scientists to statutory telecoms/broadcast/content regulators. I believe all these actors would need a national coordinator who would need to supervise, coordinate and report on online safety issues to Government, parliament, senate or whatever appropriate body.

5.5 Big Tech Policy & Regulation

Current Big Tech Context

- For this section, I assume Big Tech covers FANGAM and maybe more, i.e. Facebook, Amazon, Netflix, Google (Alphabet), Apple and Microsoft and BATX for China.

- Big Tech may soon dominate many other services out there beyond communications (e.g. WhatsApp, Instagram, etc.). Big Tech would dominate books (Amazon), media (Facebook), food and grocery delivery, flight bookings, tourism, publishing, mobile banking, digital advertising, retail, wholesale, digital printing, etc. – and even privatized transnational currencies and payment systems (e.g. Facebook's Diem proposal[39]).

- As I note in Chapter 3, we absolutely need good competition outcomes from Big Tech including more choices, fair trading, trust, transparency and contestability across all these services. I hope it is clear by now that regulating Big Tech is proving most non-trivial.

- *Key Takeaway here*: the concentration and dominance of Big Tech firms

---

[39] Diem (digital currency) - Wikipedia

in key 'relevant' markets (e.g. digital advertising, App Stores, Mobile operating systems, social media, search, streaming video, e-Commerce, etc.) is clear to see. The 'abuse of their dominance' as seen in many jurisdictions across the world and covered in many of the case studies in this book also speak for themselves.

Big Tech Harms Trends

- The market concentrations and market shares of Big Tech like FANGAM appear either stable or growing, and they are already mostly very high already, e.g. see Figure 13a and 13b.
- They defend and string out (over years) many of the anti-trust/competition cases against them – and they are arguably already too big to fully regulate.
- There are numerous and proven harms (see Figures 18-22) that Big Tech comes with, particularly harms to the vulnerable and impressionable in society like children, teenagers and the old – harms whose consequences fall on the rest of society.
- Their gatekeeping roles leading to significant conflicts of interests are also clear – and they are not transitory. They will persist.
- The "black box" nature of their algorithms using sophisticated AI, Machine Learning and Big Data analyses and techniques presents clear harms.
- Etc. (see Chapter 3 Big Tech section).

Typical Current Big Tech Regulatory Context

- Big Tech (by and large until latterly) have not been regulated leading to an almost "Wild West" situation which is becoming increasing unsustainable.
- Several to many developed countries/regions like Australia, South Korea, France, Italy, the EU, the UK, etc. are grappling with controlling the competition harms of FANGAM, using competition/anti-trust laws to check on both (i) market power and (ii) abuse of dominance by Big Tech by carrying out investigations and fining them if they are found to have committed anti-trust violations

like is happening or has happened in the EU, US and China.

- Some countries/regions like the EU, China, Australia, USA and the UK are looking at some *ex ante* regulation of Big Tech.
- Big Tech and other large Online content businesses like TikTok, YouTube, WeChat are already subject to Privacy (e.g. data breaches) and Data Protection regulations – and increasingly subject to more online content regulations.
- Current anti-trust laws that were developed for the *offline* world do not appear to be that effective with the *online* IVC challenges.
- Behavioural remedies are arguably failing because of complex conflict of interests.
- Merger controls are arguably not constraining enough.

Issues & Challenges with regulating Big Tech

- There are several at least (not exhaustive):
    - (i) These Big Tech are already mostly too big and too powerful to fully regulate, typically companies with Trillion dollar valuations. There are less than ten Trillion dollar economies in the world for context.
    - (ii) In the West, anti-trust or anti-competitive investigations of Big Tech are awfully expensive and can run to almost a decade to conclude. As I note in Chapter 3's Google Shopping case, one of the lead complainants [Foundem] filed its complaint about Google as far back as 2009! Google was finally fined in 2017. Google started appealing the fine in 2020. Contrast with China's Government fining Alibaba the equivalent of $USD 2.8 Billion (4% of 2019 revenues) for antitrust violations[40] for having found Alibaba to be behaving monopolistically. This was in April 2021. Recall I note in Chapter 3 that Alibaba accepted the penalty "with sincerity and will ensure our compliance with determination[41]".
    - (iii) Only big economies or region (e.g. South Korea, Australia,

---

[40] China fines Alibaba $2.8 billion for behaving like a monopoly - CNN
[41] *Ibid.*

UK, France, USA, China, the EU, etc.) appear to be able to truly check on the market power and dominance abuse of these Big Tech companies.

(iv) The policy and regulatory tools are hardly in place to regulate fully regulate Big Tech anyway – they are still very much in progress. This was in April 2021.

The Future of Big Tech Policy & Regulation - and few draft recommendations

- For smaller economies (say sub USD 100 Billion GDP), taking on Big Tech feels futile with anti-trust cases. Let the EU, France, China, South Korea, USA, etc. deal with them.

- In Chapter 3, I detail what these big economies/regions are doing: EU (with its Digital Markets Act (DMA) and Digital Services Act (DSA) Proposals of December 2020), UK (with its pro-Competitive digital markets consultation of July 2021, Australia (with its concluded Inquiry into digital platforms, social media platforms, search engines, content aggregation platforms and more), etc

- I note in Chapter 3 too that the likely most significant regulation of Big Tech appear to be emerging from FANGAM's their home market – the USA. Congress unveiled 5 bipartisan Bills that mark the biggest steps yet in regulating Big Tech[42].

- *Local Registrations:* Big Digital platforms *may* have to be subject to be locally registered as South Korea has legislated for (August 2021). This is so that a local representative of the Big Tech firm may be responsible for consumer protection and respond to investigations and inquiries. This would require amendments to some Digital Economy laws. South Korea also requires filling details of annual traffic usage for example with the regulator.

- *Cooperation with local legally-authorised agencies*: like in the UK, the Digital Economy Act of 2017as regards   mandates Big Tech/content firms provide relevant data and information, e.g. for criminal investigations.

- *Strengthen competition law tools and consumer protection/privacy/data*

---

[42] US lawmakers introduce bills targeting Big Tech - BBC News

protection statutes: these appear to be inadequate today for Big Tech.

- *Countries may want combine their anti-competition efforts Big Tech:* e.g. as the EC does for the EU 27, formerly 28 with the UK. The Caribbean countries for example may empower the Caricom Competition Commission[43] and pool together resources more efficiently. African countries would need to pool their competition resources similarly to deal with Big Tech,. For example, the Comesa Competition Commission [44] covering 19 African member states commenced regulation of mergers in January 2013. It would have to improve its track record to deal with Big Tech.

---

[43] Caricom Competition Commission

[44] COMESA COMPETITION COMMISSION

LEGAL

- Cybercrime legislation
- Cybersecurity regulation
- Containment/curbing of spam legislation

TECHNICAL MEASURES

- CERT/CIRT/CSIRT
- Standards Implementation Framework
- Standardization Body
- Technical mechanisms and capabilities deployed to address Spam
- Use of cloud for cybersecurity purpose
- Child Online Protection mechanisms

ORGANIZATIONAL MEASURES

- National Cybersecurity Strategy
- Responsible Agency
- Cybersecurity Metrics

CAPACITY BUILDING MEASURES

- Public awareness campaigns
- Framework for the certification and accreditation of cybersecurity professionals
- Professional training courses in cybersecurity
- Educational programs or academic curricular in cybersecurity
- Cybersecurity R & D programs
- Incentive mechanisms

COOPERATION MEASURES

- Bilateral agreements
- Multilateral agreements
- Participation in international fora/associations
- Public-Private Partnerships
- Inter-agency/intra-agency partnerships
- Best Practices

Figure 33 – ITU Global Cybersecurity Index (GCI) 5 Commitment Pillars
Source of Picture: Dr Martin Koyabe, MWK Consult based on ITU's GCI 2020[45]

---

[45] Global Cybersecurity Index (itu.int)

5.6 Cybercrime & Cybersecurity Policy & Regulation

Current Cybercrime and Cybersecurity Contexts

- I note when I overview my thematic choices in Chapter 4 that Cybercrime and Cybersecurity cover different challenges and your country would likely require two separate pieces of legislation covering both these areas.

- Cybercrime broadly covers the use of ICT and/or the Internet to steal valuable assets from rightful owners. It also covers using ICT/Internet to carry out actions to carry out actions that would be considered criminal if it were done by a human.

- Cybersecurity concerns policies, processes and technologies that would help reduce or prevent the negative impacts that can result if hostile or malevolent actors deliberately carry out cyberattacks or cyberthreats.

- Cybersecurity harms are just so numerous as we see in Chapters 2 and 3, as so are cybercrimes/cyber-harms that I hardly need to overview them here again.

Cybercrime and Cybersecurity Trends

- Cyber-threats are on the rise in all countries with increasing connectivity. These threats covers the 3Ds of Disruption, Distortion and Deterioration. *Disruption* would happen with fragile connectivity. *Distortion* happens due to loss of trust in information integrity. *Deterioration* happens when controls are eroded either through technology, regulation or other. These threats are on the rise with attacks on critical national infrastructure, ransomware attacks, insider attacks (i.e. disruptions); fake news or subverted blockchains (i.e. distortions); and exposing private data, privacy breaches, data poisoning, etc., i.e. deterioration. Such categories of 3D attacks and more are on the rise. Cybersecurity laws leading to policies, processes and technologies are needed to counteract these cyber-attacks.

- Cybercrimes categories include (i) financial, e.g. stealing financial information or monies (ii) hacking (iii) cyber-terrorism (iv) cyberextortion (v) cybersex trafficking (vi) drug trafficking (vii) cyberwarfare (viii) online harassment, etc. These crimes are all on the rise as I cover in earlier chapters.

- As an example, a recent 2021 Interpol Report as I conclude this book identifies top 5 cyberthreats in Africa as follows[46]:

  (i) **"Online scams**: fake emails or text messages claiming to be from a legitimate source are used to trick individuals into revealing personal or financial information;

  (ii) **Digital extortion**: victims are tricked into sharing sexually compromising images which are used for blackmail;

  (iii) **Business email compromise**: criminals hack into email systems to gain information about corporate payment systems, then deceive company employees into transferring money into their bank account;

  (iv) **Ransomware**: cybercriminals block the computer systems of hospitals and public institutions, then demand money to restore functionality;

  (v) **Botnets**: networks of compromised machines are used as a tool to automate large-scale cyberattacks"

- Cyberthreats are therefore very real.

Typical Cybercrime and Cybersecurity Regulatory Context

- Most countries realise they need a National Cybersecurity Strategy (NCS).

- The ITU publishes an annual Global Cybersecurity Index[47] (GCI) – a "trusted reference that measures the commitment of countries to cybersecurity at a global level – to raise awareness of the importance and different dimensions of the issue...., each country's level of development or engagement is assessed along five pillars – (i) Legal Measures, (ii) Technical Measures, (iii) Organizational Measures, (iv) Capacity Development, and (v) Cooperation – and then aggregated into an overall score"[48].

- Figure 33 shows the 5 core pillars of the ITU's GCI. I believe they are self-explanatory. The legal measures cover cybercrime legislation, cybersecurity regulation and containment/curbing of spam legislation.

---

[46] INTERPOL report identifies top cyberthreats in Africa - https://www.interpol.int/en/News-and-Events/News/2021/INTERPOL-report-identifies-top-cyberthreats-in-Africa

[47] Global Cybersecurity Index (itu.int)

[48] *Ibid.*

Technical measures covers CERT, CIRT and CSIRT and more. I do not overview the rest because I believe Figure 33's picture of the pillars speaks more than a thousand words from me.

- According to the GCI (2020) scores all developed world countries demonstrate a high commitment to cybersecurity, i.e. to all five pillars. The Caribbean and Latin American countries "have developed complex commitments and engage in cybersecurity programmes and initiatives". African countries, by and large, have just started to initiate commitments in cybersecurity as of 2020.

Issues & Challenges with realising National Cybercrime and Cybersecurity Outcomes

- They remain many and varied (non-exhaustive)
    - (i) Political Will is a MUST, and so is national leadership says Cybersecurity expert Dr Martin Koyabe of MWL Consult[49].
    - (ii) Legislation and regulation needs both the political and national leadership.
    - (iii) Funding challenges for national CERTs, CIRTs and CSIRTs are usually challenges for developing countries as they need significant operational and capital expenditure costs.
    - (iv) Balancing of citizens privacy and national security is usually a challenge
    - (v) Educating, training and skilling cybersecurity and cybercrime professionals – and retaining them within the agencies – is difficult for developing countries. Cultural challenges sometimes get in the way too as I found on a cybersecurity project in Afghanistan before the August 2021 re-take over by the Taliban.

---

[49] MWK CONSULT LTD · 20-22 Wenlock Road, London, N1 7GU (opengovuk.com)

The Future of Cybercrime and Cybersecurity Policy & Regulation - Some Suggested Recommendations for Developing Economies *only*
•

- Political will and national leadership must be sought to drive Cybersecurity and Cybercrime leadership.
- Funding must be ringfenced for the long term along with a firm commitment to capacity building and training of staff of CSIRTs, CERTs or CIRTs.

5.7 Artificial Intelligence & Machine Learning Policy & Regulation

My thematic choice of AI and ML as key to the Digital Economy is clear in Section 4.8. A few definitions to start with as I am yet to formally define AI and ML. Artificial Intelligence (AI) is a branch of computer science that simulate intelligent behaviours using computers and machines. Machine Learning (ML) is that sub-part of AI that deals with algorithms that learn from new observations by creating new rules by themselves. Perhaps a better definition of machine learning is a "state when a software program is able to change its algorithms through data, without any human intervention while making predictions to get to the desired result."[50].

AI and ML are at the core of some emerging Digital Economy harms. For example in Chapter 3, I note that Facebook's Mark Zuckerberg allegedly fully acknowledges the problem of AI-based ranking models favouring controversy, misinformation and extremism as depicted in Figure 24. Recall that the more a post approaches the Facebook prohibited content policy line, the greater the user engagement. The algorithms that maximise engagement reward more inflammatory, controversial and/or extremist content. This has

---

[50] https://hackernoon.com/what-is-machine-learning-how-does-it-work-13615bd20a89

real world consequences. Therefore the harms[51] that AI and ML are enabling are not only real offline, but also ethically very difficult.

Lest you think that such AI/ML harms only apply to Big Tech companies, you will be wrong. Consider the following:

- AI and Machine-Learning based Facial Recognition software *wrongly* matched 2000 as possible criminals in the Cardiff, Wales in 2018[52]. Civil Liberty groups were incensed, rightly citing lack of regulation and human rights concerns:

> It is a far more powerful policing tool than traditional CCTV - as the cameras take a biometric map, creating a numerical code of the faces of each person who passes the camera. These biometric maps are uniquely identifiable to the individual.
>
> "It is just like taking people's DNA or fingerprints, without their knowledge or their consent," said Megan Goulding, a lawyer from the civil liberties group Liberty which is supporting Mr Bridges.
>
> However, unlike DNA or fingerprints, there is no specific regulation governing how police use facial recognition or manage the data gathered. Liberty argues that even if there were regulations, facial recognition breaches human rights and should not be used.
>
> (Source: BBC[53])

- "Artificial Intelligence has a problem with Gender and Racial Bias...[54]". These are the words of MIT graduate student Joy Buolamwini who has founded an organisation called the Algorithmic Justice League[55]. Her research found that some facial analysis software [from IBM, Microsoft and Amazon] could not detect her *dark-skinned* face until she put on a white mask, because the systems were trained on predominantly light-skinned men.

> The companies I evaluated had error rates of no more than 1% for lighter-skinned men. For darker-skinned women, the errors soared to 35%. AI systems from leading companies have failed to correctly classify the faces of Oprah Winfrey,

---

[51] E.g. joining Facebook terrorism groups or Amazon 'Buy Now' anti-competitive harms, etc.

[52] 2,000 wrongly matched with possible criminals at Champions League - BBC News

[53] Police facial recognition surveillance court case starts - BBC News

[54] Artificial Intelligence Has a Racial and Gender Bias Problem | Time

[55] Research - The Algorithmic Justice League (ajl.org)

Michelle Obama, and Serena Williams. When technology denigrates even these iconic women, it is time to re-examine how these systems are built and who they truly serve.

Joy Buolamwini[56]

MICHELLE OBAMA

OPRAH WINFREY

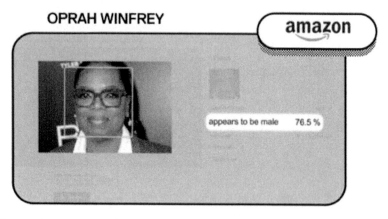

Image 5 – AI & Machine Learning Software getting it badly wrong
(Source Joy Buolamwini[57])

According to her [Joy Buolamwini] research, Oprah Winfrey "appears to male 76.5%" using Amazon and Michelle Obama was "a young man

---

[56] Artificial Intelligence Has a Racial and Gender Bias Problem | Time
[57] Ibid.

wearing a black shirt, confidence: 0.7999446" according a Microsoft facial recognition system. China's Face++ system simply classified tennis legend Serena Williams as male. She is making recommendations on how to get such systems to address such obvious biases and discriminations in them.

The terminology Trustworthy AI[58] has emerged to start addressing such challenges with AI and ML systems.

And do not think that AI/ML is just a growing problem for US and Chinese Big Tech firms. The mobile/cellular operators in your country, the banks, the mobile money providers, etc. are all generating massive amounts of data every day and they are (or would be) employing AI/ML algorithms.

AI and ML are being increasingly democratized, and therefore would be used in your country – along with all its potential benefits *and harms*!

Current Typical *offline* Contexts

- Offline AI/ML did precede the Internet value chain, and had some applications in the offline TMT/ICT sector in areas like voice to text features, e-mail spam filters, process automation, automated insights in industries such as financial services, work force scheduling of tens of thousands of engineers, predictive maintenance, failure detection, prediction of network traffic and demand, etc. I have personally been involved in the use of AI and ML in some of such areas and more.
- Such traditional "offline" use of AI and ML have hardly raised significant widespread policy and regulatory concerns. It is the online use of AI along with high velocity Big Data that is proving truly problematic.

---

[58] https://ec.europa.eu/futurium/en/ai-alliance-consultation/guidelines

Online AI & ML Trends

- The major new trends come with its uses across the Internet Value Chain - in ranking algorithms across Twitter, Facebook, Ebay in the Online Services segment of the IVC; in Big Data algorithms with Google Ads, Google Search and Google Analytics. Amazon, etc., in the Enabling Technologies & Services segment and in the User Interfaces segment too.

- However, the real big changer from my perspective is the combination of the following coming together at the same time
  - (i) Huge amounts of data being collected (Big Data)
  - (ii) Advanced AI and ML algorithms
  - (iii) Oodles of cheap storage in massive data centres
  - (iv) And high end computing power

  AI has essentially been put on steroids because of this combination of drivers.

Typical Current Regulatory Context on AI & ML

- Up until the past five years (circa 2016), regulating Tech and AI/ML was not that much a priority. The calls have just become louder due to examples I outline in this manuscript and more.

- *Key Takeaway here*: Big Tech and other firms using AI/ML have largely been *self-regulating*, with virtually no statutory regulation or code of conduct of AI and ML algorithms.

AI & ML Issues & Challenges that need controlling, i.e. that require policy and regulation or Code of Conduct

There are many and they largely overlap with Big Data concerns too. In this section, along with my own views, I draw from some brilliant work being done by Dr Nozha Boujemaa[59]:

- Offline harms "instigated" online by AI/ML algorithms (e.g.. hate

---

[59] https://ec.europa.eu/info/sites/default/files/about_the_european_commission/contact/presentations/tef2018_nozhaboujemaa_ai.pdf

speech)

- Online misinformation travelling 6x faster than factual news, thanks to AI/ML algorithms (e.g.. Twitter)

- *Dominant platforms* (e.g. Google and Amazon) *prescribing* [by directing large amounts of traffic) because of their

    (i)   Rankings mechanisms using AI/ML (e.g. with Search engines)

    (ii) Recommendation mechanisms like Buy Boxes using AI/ML (e.g. Amazon)

    (iii) For the latter, how does one *ethically balance* Personalisation vs. Supplier Welfare here? i.e. more accurate product or service recommendation to me as user vs. the Seller like Amazon or Google maximising their profits?

- *The Concern of AI Blackbox Opacity* in the *use* of sensitive data and its processing

    (i)   Consent? Is it respected, and do ticking boxes online like with GDPR suffice?

    (ii) "Free" advertising business models – does this mean free to part away with most sensitive data of people?

    (iii) Credit scoring, recruitment, image identification, age identification, etc. - how fair is it?

- *New Discriminations Concerns*: are you comfortable that some web designers who know how Google Ads and Facebook algorithms work – can use it for their benefits and for the benefits of their clients?

- *Concerns with Explaining decisions and Tractability of [AI/ML] Algorithms:*

    (i)   Decision responsibility – who is to blame if it goes wrong?

    (ii) Reasoning mechanisms – can this be made explicit instead of being black box?

    (iii) How do I trust a AI and ML prediction then?

- *Unintentional or Intentional Discrimination Harms*

    (i)   Inbuilt AI Bias (due to data set) vs. deliberate "corruption" vs. Business Gain/Society Costs

    (ii) AI Data Bias: poorly selected, incomplete, incorrect, old, representative and/or malicious

(iii) Algorithm Bias: poorly designed, historical bias, incorrect, correlation vs. causation concerns

The Future of AI & ML Policy & Regulation - Some Suggested Recommendations

The above harms and concerns are so significant that many international organisations are evolving policies, Acts and ethical guidelines for AI/ML. These organisations include the EC's AI-HLG (High Level Group), the OECD, UNESCO, the World Economic Forum (WEF) and more.

The EC has proposed an Artificial Intelligence Act Bill[60] in April 2021 still to be voted upon at the European Parliament. It focuses on 2 areas: *excellence in AI* and *trustworthy AI*. The idea of the European approach to AI is both to ensure that people's safety and fundamental rights are protected whilst any AI improvements are based on rules that safeguard the functioning of markets and the public sector. The EC AI Act includes fines of up to 6% of a company's annual revenues for noncompliance — fines that are higher than the historic penalties of up to 4% of global turnover that can be levied under the GDPR. This is very high to me.

I particularly want to point out to these ethical principles and guidelines from the EU AL-HLG which I believe are sensible for most countries building their digital economies[61].

The 4 ethical AI principles they recommend include:

(i)   Respect for human autonomy

(ii) Prevention of harm

(iii) Fairness

(iv) Explicability

Their 7 core AI requirements include:

i.   Human agency and oversight

---

[60] EUR-Lex - 52021PC0206 - EN - EUR-Lex (europa.eu) - https://eur-lex.europa.eu/legal-content/EN/TXT/?qid=1623335154975&uri=CELEX%3A52021PC0206

[61] https://ec.europa.eu/futurium/en/ai-alliance-consultation/guidelines

ii.   Technical robustness and safety

iii.   Privacy and Data Governance

iv.   Transparency

v.   Diversity, non-discrimination and fairness

vi.   Societal and environmental wellbeing

vii.   Accountability

Therefore my recommendations to start with for AI/ML are simple and the following:

- Digital economies – no matter how small – would hit harms and challenges with AI/ML. This is because there are innovators in your country would rightly exploit democratised AI/ML algorithms with Big Data they have access to in your country.

- Policy maker and regulators should be aware of the benefits and harms of AI/ML as I have hopefully covered in this chapter – in some more detail.

- Adopting the EC's 4 ethical principles and 7 core AI guidelines appear to me to be a very good start which policy maker and regulators in your country.

- In general, the EC's excellence in AI and trustworthy AI dual set of goals appear a very sensible place to start – though there are similar other guidelines and principles proposed by the OECD, the WEF and UNESCO. I recommend what ever your country does, you should start by thinking about collaboration with these organisations.

- Going as far as proposing an AI Act or a Law like the *developed* EC has proposed in April 2021 may be premature for many *developing* countries who may adopt a *watching brief* position, and just propose and adopt ethical and design guidelines like the EC's. A law may follow much later if necessary. This would make sense of the perceived risks of AI today in your country are low.

- For developed countries they may judge the risks with AI to be high for competition and harms to their citizens, they may choose to work towards a Law like the proposed EC's.

5.8 Privacy & Data Protection Policy & Regulation

Current Typical Online Privacy and Data Protection Contexts – *why* it is important

- I note when I overview my thematic choices in Chapter 4 that [Data] Privacy and Data Protection present different challenges and your country would likely require two or more separate pieces of legislation covering both these areas.

- The core reason we cover Privacy and Data Protection is very basic and simple. Privacy and data protection are fundamental rights, irrespective of whether individuals are offline or online. In Chapter 4, I cover the UN, EU and other declarations that enshrine these rights. Their offline privacy and data protection rights need to be codified in laws for the online world too. Without privacy being respected, all trust online is lost.

- As Internet users grow – 4.66 Billion active Internet users around the world in January 2021[62] - their online privacy needs to be protected. Similarly, the 1.7 MB of data per second[63] (in 2020) that every human created needs to be protected.

- Companies have concerns too. They are digitising their customer and supply chain interactions, how they do customer support and more. They vastly collect and analyse of information about individuals' preferences, behaviours and attributes including purchasing intentions, hobbies, gender and location.

- Data sovereignty: Can they legitimately export these data on your nationals outside your country? How do they collect and manage these data on your country's citizens?

- Data breaches: If their vast data sets are breached, who do they report too? What rights, if any, do your citizens have to see and/or correct data held about them? What security controls do companies put around sensitive data?

- Liberty: Privacy and protecting personal data is intimately linked to the

---

[62] • Internet users in the world 2021 | Statista

[63] 18_domo_data-never-sleeps-6+verticals

liberty.

Brief Online Privacy and Data Protection Trends

- Covid19 vastly increased companies' collection and analyses of peoples' data across all countries. McKinsey and Co.'s October 2020 research[64] found the following: 27 times factor increase customer demand for online purchasing/services; 24 times factor increase in the migration of assets and data into the cloud; 43 times factor increase in remote working and/or collaboration; etc.

- Such trends not only note the exponential gathering growth in the gathering of data, but also the exponential growth in the risks that come with mishandling such quantum of data.

- In Chapter 3 (Figure 31), I note how 533 Million Peoples Facebook Records from 106 Countries were being offered online[65]. U. S. approved a $5B Facebook settlement over such privacy issues[66]. In September 2017, Equifax announced a data breach which had exposed the personal information of 147 million people and was fined at least US $425M to help people affected by the breach[67].

- Such data breaches are becoming more and more common. Amazon was hit in July 2021 with a USD $886.6M fine by the smallest of all of EU member states – Luxembourg[68]. The fine was issued by Luxembourg's National Commission for Data Protection, which claimed Amazon's processing of personal data did not comply with EU law. In September 2021, Ireland's Data Protection Commission issued WhatsApp's second-largest ever GDPR fine of €225m[69].

- Clearly, the privacy and data protection trends are arguably not

[64] COVID-19 digital transformation & technology | McKinsey

[65] 533 Million Facebook Users' Phone Numbers and Personal Data Leaked Online (thehackernews.com)

[66] Facebook fine: FTC fines company $5 billion for privacy violations (usatoday.com)

[67] Equifax Data Breach Settlement | Federal Trade Commission (ftc.gov) (last accessed August 2021)

[68] Amazon hit with $886m fine for alleged data law breach - BBC News - https://www.bbc.co.uk/news/business-58024116

[69] WhatsApp issued second-largest GDPR fine of €225m - BBC News

encouraging.

Typical Current Regulatory Online Privacy and Data Protection Context

- Law firm DLA Piper based in London maintains an up-to-date map on Data Protection Laws across the world[70]. As of October 2021, it shows "heavy" regulation and enforcement across the North Americas (USA plus Canada), Western Europe, China and Australia. Latin America is rated of "moderate" and/or "limited" regulation/enforcement just like Russia and all the Russian States. India, Pakistan, Kazakhstan, Iran and the Small Pacific States are rated "limited" regulation/enforcement. Africa largely shows up as having limited or no data protection regulations.

- In general, most developed countries and regions (e.g. the, USA, Canada, Australia and EU) have very strong Online Privacy and Data Protection laws and frameworks, e.g. the EU's well-known General Data Protection Regulations (GDPR). The GDPR in Europe replaced the 1995 Data Protection Directive. As I note in Chapter 4, EU Privacy rights are enshrined in the EU's Charter of Fundamental Rights.

- In developing countries, the story is more checkered. Consider Africa – the African Charter on Human and Peoples' Rights (1981)[71] contains no rights to privacy. Partly for this reason, of the 54 countries in Africa, only 15 had Data Protection Agencies as of 2019/20 though about 50% of them had National Data Protection Laws – but as DLA Piper suggests, very little to no regulation/enforcement. However, there are some proposed regional "model laws" on Data Protection, e.g. the Southern African Development Community (SADC) model law[72].

---

[70] DLA Piper Global Data Protection Laws of the World - World Map (dlapiperdataprotection.com) (last accessed October 2021)

[71] African Charter on Human and Peoples' Rights | African Union (au.int)

[72] Data Protection: Southern African Development Community (SADC) Model Law | Legal research | DataGuidance

Issues & Challenges with Online Privacy and Data Protection Laws (developing countries only)

- They remain many and varied:
    - (i) Lack of privacy regulations (in Africa in particular) as I note earlier
    - (ii) Lack of harmonisation across regional data protection frameworks, like with EU's GDPR.
    - (iii) Challenges of having to deal with several key IVC-related legislation and regulations as such countries have to deal with privacy, data protection in addition to others such as cybersecurity, cybercrime and E-commerce.
    - (iv) Being "compelled" to largely adopt data protection regulations from other regions because they are *de facto* preconditions to trade, e.g. some African countries adopting the very "heavy" GDPR-type regulations from the EU as they need to trade with EU countries.
    - (v) There are hardly any national Data Protection Agencies to enforce anything in developing markets like Africa.
    - (vi) Challenges of non-functioning agencies when they do exist due to poor skills in the composition of such agencies, lack of independence.
    - (vii) Lack of funding.

NB: Privacy is *not* the same as Security. And what is the link to Data Protection?

- Security and privacy are often used almost as if they are interchangeable. However, it is important to understand that security is not the same as privacy.
- Though privacy and security are intricately linked, one often follows the other. As the GSMA notes, it is possible to have poor privacy and good security practices. On the other hand, it is difficult to have good privacy

without security.

- The GSMA [73] rightly emphasises that good privacy is about the appropriate collection and use of information, being transparent with individuals, and respecting the rights and choices of individuals.

- Good security, however, is about ensuring data is secure both in transit and at rest (when stored), ensuring the confidentiality, integrity and availability of data.

- Security is a means to an end. The true objective of security is the protection of privacy – and by implication *Data Protection.*

- However, technology cannot be relied on solely to ensure good privacy or good security practices —achieving both requires a good and accountable compliance programme!

- We need all the above to establish and maintain *trust* in the Digital World - an invaluable currency of the Digital Economy.

The Future of Privacy & Data Protection Policy & Regulation - Some Suggested Recommendations for Developing Economies *only*

- Political will and national leadership must be sought to drive Data Privacy and Data Protection Legislations. Your citizens going online deserve these rights protected online.

- Seek to harmonise any Privacy and Data protection regulations regionally if not continent wide. Start with regional "model" regulations if one exists.

- Funding must be ringfenced for the long term along with a firm commitment to capacity building and training of staff of DPAs once they are set up.

- Pre-empt and address the challenges identified above.

---

[73] GSMA | Data privacy and security - #BetterFuture - https://www.gsma.com/betterfuture/resources/data-privacy-and-security

5.9 Electronic Commerce Laws, Policy & Regulation

- E-Commerce, or Electronic Commerce, is the online industry version of buying and selling goods, services or products via the Internet. E-Commerce is one of the biggest of the five clusters of the Online Services segment; and it includes (i) E-retail including major B2C brands like EBay, Alibaba and Amazon, and other dedicated B2B exchanges (ii) E-travel including Expedia, Uber, Airbnb, etc.

- E-Commerce is practically synonymous to E-Business, meaning it covers the exchange of data pertaining to the financing, billing and payment of e-business transactions.

- Just consider the typical aspects of E-Commerce and it would be clear to you laws are needed to underpin them: online marketing; online advertising; online sales; delivery of online-bought products; delivery of online-purchased services; online billing; online payments; handling of customer data including his/her address; return shipping of products bought online; etc.

- The contexts could be Business to Business (B2B), Business to Consumer (B2C), Consumer to Business (C2B) and Consumer to Consumer (C2C).

- The core reason we need E-Commerce Laws and Policies is that your country would need – if not already – legal recognition of both E-Commerce and most/all of its aspects and contexts.

- *Issues covered by E-Commerce Laws*: Imagine you receiving a defective or wrong product? Imagine the seller refuses to replace wrongly-delivered product? Imagine seller refuses or delays refunding monies paid online? Imagine unreasonable delays in delivering your product? What about the risks of your personal information used for online transactions being shared? What about warranty and guarantee of online-purchased products and services? These are not imaginations. These issues would almost certainly happen. What laws in your country would protect consumers from such harms?

- It is typically several laws to address all these E-Commerce issues. For example, your Consumer Protection law could ensure that customers receive what was promised by the seller and are not cheated or subjected to unfair trade practices, whilst an E-Commerce law may cover the other aspects.

Brief E-Commerce Trends

- The acceleration of E-Commerce throughout the world, particularly over the lockdowns of 2020/2021, is evidently visible as consumers did their shopping online mostly often out of necessity.

- McKinsey and Co.'s October 2020 research[74] found the following: 27 times factor increase customer demand for online purchasing/services..

- *Real E-Commerce Opportunity across most of the world:* However, this latter general McKinsey statistic hides a true E-Commerce opportunity in most countries. Economist Christoph Ungerer (2021) reveals that the biggest e-retailer in the world Amazon runs online stores and warehouses in only 16 countries[75] (i.e. 9% of the countries globally), making it very costly and not convenient for consumers to do international shipping of goods. Interestingly, he notes this 9 countries represent 74% of global GDP – and he proceeds to ask the question, 'what about the 91% of countries'? Ungerer notes online markets are still "shallow" in most parts of the world even though e-commerce is a key opportunity for economic development, creating jobs in sectors such as local tech companies, payment service providers, logistic companies, marketing businesses and more.

Typical Current E-Commerce Laws Context

- UNCTAD tracks and publishes a summary of the adoption of E-Commerce legislation worldwide[76]. I note earlier that typically laws in a country that address E-commerce. Not surprising then that UNCTAD tracks the state of e-commerce laws across its 194 member states

---

[74] COVID-19 digital transformation & technology | McKinsey

[75] The emerging markets e-commerce opportunity (brookings.edu) - https://www.brookings.edu/blog/future-development/2021/03/26/the-emerging-markets-e-commerce-opportunity/

[76] Summary of Adoption of E-Commerce Legislation Worldwide | UNCTAD

covering e-transactions, consumer protection, data protection/privacy and cybercrime adoption. Overall, UNCTAD finds that a healthy 82% of countries already have E-transaction laws. 56%, 66% and 80% of UNCTAD member countries have Consumer Protection laws, Privacy Laws and Cybercrime laws respectively[77]. This website is up to date on which, if any, of these 4 E-Commerce-related laws each of the 194 countries have enacted.

Issues & Challenges with E-Commerce Laws (developing countries only)

- There are several:
    (i) End-2-end E-Commerce legislation typically involves several pieces of laws as I note earlier covering E-Transactions, Consumer Protection, Privacy and Cybercrime laws.

    (ii) Many developing countries typically have 2 or a max of 3 of these laws enacted. Across 47 Least Developed Countries (LDCs), 64%, 40%, 45% and 66% have enacted E-Transactions, Consumer Protection, Privacy and Cybercrime laws respectively[78].

    (iii) Being "compelled" to largely adopt data protection regulations from other regions because they are *de facto* preconditions to trade, e.g. some African countries adopting the very "heavy" GDPR-type regulations from the EU as they need to trade with EU countries.

    (iv) Challenges of non-functioning agencies when they exist, poor skills in the composition of such agencies, lack of independence.

    (v) Lack of funding.

---

[77] Ibid. (as reported on website, 20th October 2021).

[78] *Ibid.*

- As Ungerer notes "a still shallow national online market may be of limited appeal for the e-commerce giants. But it can nonetheless leave plenty of room for the growth of low-cost local startups" [79].

- Seek to harmonise any E-Commerce-related laws and regulations regionally if not continent wide. Start with regional "model" regulations if one exists.

- Funding must be ringfenced for the long term along with a firm commitment to capacity building and training of staff of agencies and courts to enforce these laws once E-Commerce kicks off in your country.

5.10   Over the Top (OTT) Policy and Regulation

I have the devoted the entire next and last chapter to OTT Policy and Regulation. I draw in this section from my Cenerva colleague Chris Taylor's excellent 2018 short report on OTT (Taylor, 2018).

Current Over the Top (OTT) Context

- For the purposes of this section, I prefer to reuse the same definition of OTT I use in earlier in Chapter 4 as "content, a service or an application that is provided to the end user over the public Internet" [80]. I note in the prior chapter too that all categories of the Online Services segment are either content (e.g. UGC content on Facebook), services (e.g. Google Search or Wikipedia) or applications (e.g. gaming apps). This means they are all OTTs.

- The impacts of OTTs are significant and far reaching. OTT

---

[79] The emerging markets e-commerce opportunity (brookings.edu) -
https://www.brookings.edu/blog/future-development/2021/03/26/the-emerging-markets-e-commerce-opportunity/

[80] BEREC Report on the Public Consultation on the "Report on OTT services" (europa.eu)

communications services like Zoom, Microsoft Teams, Facebook, WhatsApp, and Skype are now in common use every day all over the world. For many people, they are the default method of communication, replacing in-person meetings, phone calls, SMS and e-mail.

- WhatsApp and Facebook Messenger are replacing mobile as the *de facto* voice and messaging tools in many parts of the world.

- As I cover in earlier chapters, Netflix's mega-budget streaming productions are released on the same day across the world thereby satisfying demand for binge viewing. This affects the revenues of traditional media and telecoms companies, who must transform their business models to compete.

- All these OTT categories come with incredible positive externalities but as we have seen in Chapters 2 and 3, but there are significant negative externalities too. The consumer and citizen benefits they bring in terms of price, convenience, choice, innovation and entertainment are unarguable.

Brief OTT Trends – the rise and rise of OTTs

- Do I really need to explain anymore the rise and rise of the OTTs? Demand for OTTs has grown exponentially in the since circa 2010. Think where we were then and where we are now in our use of social media, messaging services, audio-visual streaming and Voice over IP (VoIP) telephony.

- As Taylor (2018) notes, between 2011 and 2017, active subscriber numbers for the four biggest online messaging services (Facebook Messenger, WhatsApp, WeChat and Viber) grew by a factor of 18, and subscribers to the four largest social media platforms (Facebook, Instagram, Twitter, LinkedIn) trebled. He also notes that "at the same time, consolidation led to increased scale and scope for some of the industry's largest players; Microsoft acquired Skype for $8.5bn in 2011 and Facebook bought WhatsApp for $16bn in 2014".

- The drivers for this phenomenal growth has been both demand-side and supply-side. On the supply side, handset manufacturers have offered better and cheaper handsets (c.f. the User Interface segment of the IVC) whilst network/cellular operators have offered faster, better and higher capacity networks with which to access online services (cf. via the Connectivity segment of the IVC). OTTs like WhatsApp and Netflix have delivered services similar to those offered by network operators and terrestrial broadcasters like Verizon and CNN, but at lower prices.

- The innovation that come with OTT providers have also been immense with increasingly innovative applications and content.

Typical OTT Policy and Regulatory Concerns

- Taylor (2018) rightfully notes that rise and rise of OTTs raises important policy questions, like:

    (i) Should OTT consumers be protected in the same way as phone users - e.g. with guaranteed availability and quality, and always-on emergency call access?

    (ii) Should OTT providers be required to contribute to the costs of network development as consumer demand for bandwidth grows?

    (iii) Should OTTs contribute to the costs of universal service?

    (iv) Should OTTs pay licence fees and/or local taxes in the markets where they operate?

    (v) Can and should services be regulated across borders?

- Taylor's 2018 short report addresses these issues and more.

Issues & Challenges with OTT Policy and Regulation Making

- There are several key ones:

    (i) There are many OTT myths out there gaining more and more currency that need to be busted.

    (ii) OTTs are incredibly misunderstood. OTTs are not homogeneous; they are rather heterogenous. They have to be defined carefully before appropriate policy and regulations can be developed and enacted in your country.

    (iii) There is a legitimate debate over whether/how OTTs should be regulated. Either 'levelling up' (e.g. licensing OTTs in the same way mobile operators are licensed) or 'levelling down' (e.g. the operators are liberalized more by taking away some of the onerous licensing constraints moving them in the direction of the unlicensed OTTs).

(iv) Related issues such as "net neutrality" in particular are at the heart too of any policy making and regulations of OTTs. Net neutrality at its core is about the non-discrimination rules that forbids operators of IP networks to discriminate against third-party applications, content or services. If one takes a very strong approach to net neutrality – i.e. no discrimination or the minimum amount of discrimination – one ends up at one set of policy and regulatory positions on OTT. If one takes a weaker position on net neutrality, one ends up in a different set of positions. This happened in the USA as the FCC flip-flopped on net neutrality in 2015 and 2017 respectively. In 2015, the FCC under Democratic President Barack Obama agreed to reclassify broadband as public utility under Title II of the US Communications Act[81]. This strong net neutrality position (called the US FCC 2015 Net Neutrality Order) suggested aspects like (i) no throttling or blocking of broadband services and (ii) no paid prioritisation of broadband services. Guess what? The Big Tech OTT players like Facebook and Google supported it whilst the big US operators like AT&T and Verizon opposed it. Then in 2017 under Republican President Donald Trump, the FCC voted to repeal the 2015 net neutrality order returning to the previous "light touch" regulatory framework for OTTs[82]. Obviously, the Operators love this. The final repeal of the 2015 Order became law in June 2018. My point here is net neutrality rules truly impact and influence the regulation of OTTs.

(v) OTTs have also ushered in the need for Online Content regulation because of the incredible quantum of (a) illegal online content (b) legal but harmful online content (c) Hate speech (d) Privacy issues € harms to children, etc. However, as I

---

[81] Feds to cable industry: Embrace broadband competition, or else - CNET (last accessed October 2021)

[82] FCC reverses Open Internet Order governing net neutrality (cnbc.com) (last accessed October 2021)

note earlier, these are Online Content regulation concerns – not OTT regulation ones. Many regulators and policy makers I train confuse the two.

The Future of OTT Policy and Regulation - Some Suggested Recommendations

I have an entire Chapter next devoted to OTT Policy and Regulation.

- Whilst not preempting the next and last chapter, there is no easy blueprint or 'one size fits all' policy or regulatory response to OTTs. European ECC and US FCC initiatives show that there are levers - including removal of regulation or forbearance - available to regulators.

- As a starting point for analysis in any market, I believe well-established principles of regulation should apply. In particular (Taylor, 2018):

  (i)   Regulators should forbear from intervention unless it is needed. This means the benefits of regulation must outweigh the costs.

  (ii) Any remedies should be targeted at identified market failures or consumer protection needs.

  (iii) Regulation should be applied in a non-discriminatory way

I completely agree with my colleague Chris Taylor as the reader will realise from the next chapter.

5.11 Capacity Building & Training on Digital Economy Policy & Regulation

I hope this entire insignificant manuscript and this Chapter (to a large degree) has demonstrated more than anything I can add here why Capacity Building and Training Digital Economy is truly important. The rate of evolution of the new Digital economy far outstrips the ability for even the best resourced policy makers and regulators to cope, yet alone the much less resourced ones.

I believe such capacity building across the new IVC and the Digital Economy is severely lacking – a core reason I penned this manuscript. I hope the reader agrees, and why – in my own small way – I hope I have ameliorated this position. The reader can always contact my organisation www.cenerva.com if they want Policy and Regulatory Training.

5.12 Summary on Ways Forward

I start this chapter with what I consider a brilliant quote from Callaway: "sometimes the smallest step in the right direction ends up being the biggest step… tiptoe if you must, but take a step".

I hope I have introduced enough across these eleven thematic areas to allow for you the reader who may have felt lost before this chapter to (at least) start "tiptoeing" into Digital Economy policy making and regulation.

Chapter 6

OTT Regulation 101

Regulating Over the Top (OTT) Services requires clear acknowledgement and understanding of the reality of the encroached Internet Value Chain into Telecoms[83]

I wrote the above in 2019 as the title of my contribution when I was invited to speak on regulating OTTs by the ITU in October 2019 in Geneva. I do not demur from a word of it two years hence. This is a chapter on regulating OTTs in a book about the Internet Value Chain, so I thought it apt to start this chapter with it.

The last Chapter (Chapter 5) draws from Callaway's brilliant quote which starts it, i.e. to "tiptoe if you must [into some of these Digital Economy areas], but take a step", in order to help digital economy policy makers, regulators and network operators to take their first steps into these thematic areas. This chapter does much more than "tip-toeing"; it takes one of the digital economy areas and does a much deeper dive into it – demonstrating how the other thematic areas could be further developed too.

The Cambridge English Dictionary defines regulation as "an official rule or the act of controlling something". More specifically, the key purposes of regulation [of any sector or area including OTTs] remain:

    i.   to seek to achieve those desirable and justified objectives for consumers and citizens – those that do not arise naturally from the market and

---

[83] Nwana (2019), Internet Security Primer-research-190701 (itu.int) - https://www.itu.int/dms_pub/itu-d/oth/07/1a/D071A0000070001PDFE.pdf

ii.   regulate where there is 'market failure'[84] and where the result brings net benefit.

OTTs have unquestionably benefited consumers, citizens, industry, SMEs and economies around the world. At the same time, they have created an unregulated sector which overlaps significantly with, and in some cases is a substitute for, regulated electronic communications, broadcasting and media.

Therefore, there have been clear calls from many stakeholder groups to "control" or regulate OTTs, yet – drawing from the purposes of regulation I present earlier - the many proponents calling for the regulation of OTTs typically neither point to any market failure nor to any evidence of consumers and citizens being unhappy with their OTT services. A claim like network perators lose revenues – whether accurate or not – would not count as a good reason to regulate against significant consumer and citizen benefits of OTT services when tested against the above key purposes of regulation. Some operators claim OTTs pay little or no taxes, or that they benefit from their network investments which they do not pay for (the "free rider problem").

Therefore, this 101 chapter on OTTs [and their regulation] expounds much more on OTT Policy Making and Regulation. This OTT regulation 101 chapter attempts to address the following questions:

- Why choose to expound more on OTT Regulation of all the thematic Digital Economy areas of this book?
- What is behind the rise and rise of OTTs?
- The rise and rise of OTTs have inevitably led to many myths. What are some of these myths?
- What is the relationship between OTTs and Net Neutrality?
- What then are the typical key open OTTs policy and regulatory questions?

---

[84] Market failure typically leads to high prices, low choice, low quality of service (QoS), low innovation, high barriers to entry, etc.

- On the basis that one cannot regulate what one cannot define, what is an appropriate definition for OTTs that would facilitate policy making and their regulation?
- Should OTTs be taxed, and if so how?
- What are some main recommendations on OTT policy making and regulation for Digital Economy policy makers? I propose a 10-point framework.

I acknowledge at this juncture that this chapter draws from Nwana (2019), Talyor (2018) and even more so from Stork, Nwana *et al.* (2020). I am indebted to these colleagues for significantly helping improve my education on OTTs.

6.1 Why expound on OTT Regulation than other themes?

I have prioritised and defined the sub-problem statements of eleven broad digital economy challenging thematic areas in the last chapter. Yet I have chosen to expand on only one of them as a full chapter in this volume – OTT Policy and Regulation. Why? This is a fair question. The reasons are the following:

(i) This book is most about defining the Digital Economy problem statement using the IVC as a tool, with only a *supplementary* goal of identifying, prioritising and further defining these thematic areas. I did not set out to fully elaborate on every digital economy thematic challenge I selected, not least because it would make this book much longer that it is already, but more so because I am frankly not qualified to do justice to all eleven broad areas. I made an exception for just one thematic area that I have been actively engaged in over the last several years, partly for the following reasons.

(ii) OTTs are by far the biggest and most numerous 'side effects' of the IVC. Looking at Figure 1 or perhaps better looking at Figure 3, this is evident as the Online Services segment was 47% of the value of the IVC in 2016. All the services in this segment are OTT services using the OTT definition I introduce in Chapter 4 as "content, a service or an application that is provided to the end user over the public Internet"[85]. I (re)emphasise that all categories of the Online Services segment are either content (e.g. UGC content on Facebook), services (e.g. Google Search or Wikipedia) or applications (e.g. gaming apps). This means they are all OTTs. Yet, there are many OTT myths out there gaining more and more currency that need to be busted, making OTTs incredibly misunderstood. OTTs are not homogeneous; they are rather heterogenous. They have to be defined carefully before appropriate policy and regulations can be developed and enacted in your country. This is a key driver of this chapter.

(iii) Policy makers and regulators are typically bombarded with calls "to do something" about OTTs. Some of these calls are legitimate and others frankly nonsensical. However, policy makers, and regulators are also typically confused as to what they are being asked to do. I hope I help teas some of the intertwined issues in this book. By "doing something", are the complainants referring to several inter-twined issues:

a. Platform competition issues: this is all about Big Tech competition concerns from the digital mega-platforms regulation (cf. Chapters 3 and Figure 28 in particular) like tying, conflicts of interest, refusal to deal and many more? These are Big Tech Platforms regulation challenges.

b. Online content harms: like fake news, disinformation and much worse? This is the Online Regulation challenge.

c. Concerns with AI and ML amplification algorithms: we see this with Twitter, Facebook and more This is the AI and Big Data algorithms challenge.

d. Citizens online rights being violated and data breaches: this is a data protection and privacy problem.

e. Concerns about streaming platforms like Netflix 'over-running' their broadcast and media sectors? This is a future of content, broadcasting and media regulation challenge.

---

[85] BEREC Report on the Public Consultation on the "Report on OTT services" (europa.eu)

f.   Concerns about falling operators/carriers revenues, OTTs "free-riding", OTTs not being locally registered, OTTs "not being taxed", "unlevel playing field", etc? These latter complaints fall more squarely under the OTT Policy and Regulation challenge.

My substantial point above is that, when Digital Economy policy makers and regulators are called upon to do something about OTTs, there are a "multitude of sins" or harms as seen above that the complainants could be refereeing to, and I usually find they are never clearly teased out. A key contribution of me adding this chapter is that of making this simple but fundamental point, in addition to providing some – hopefully – more evidenced approach and recommendations on "what you do" about OTTs.

6.2 What is behind the rise and rise of OTTs?

Well, I hope it is clear and evident that the primary answer to this question is the IVC. Without the IVC, the Online Services segment of the IVC which 'hosts' all the OTTs would not exist.

However as Taylor (2018) illustrates in Figure 34, there are several noteworthy demand and supply side drivers to the rise and rise of OTTs. On the supply side, handset manufacturers and network operators offer faster, better and cheaper handsets and networks with which to access online services. OTTs like WhatsApp, Skype and Netflix deliver services similar to those offered by network operators, but at much lower prices in many cases.

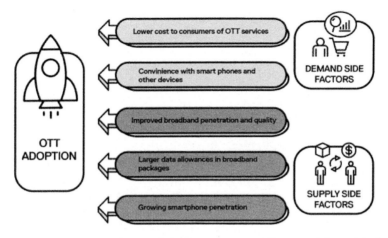

Figure 34 – Drivers of OTT Adoption (Source, Illustrated from Taylor 2018)

Taylor (2018) rightly cites the case of international calls across national borders. He gives this specific example: in December 2017, a call made from a UK phone roaming in the United Arab Emirates costed up to £3 per minute, and that it also costed £1.25 per minute to receive a call, 35p per minute to send an SMS, and £6 per Megabyte to use data. I use this historic example to emphasise the fact that it was (and still is) rational for consumers to avoid such eye-watering charges by using OTT communications services like Skype and WhatsApp on free broadband Wi-Fi networks. I do not know what the costs of my international non-OTT calls to most countries are, but I know for sure that my OTT calls are generally free once a broadband connection is established, particularly on Wi-Fi.

So on the demand side as shown in Figure 34, the rise and rise of OTTs has been driven by low cost to consumers of OTT services along with the *convenience* of smartphones and other devices such as IPads and more. Recall the Iphone effect since it was introduced in 2007 by Steve Jobs. On the supply side, growing smartphone penetration is obviously key to more OTT adoption along with improved broadband network penetration/quality along. With better and more expansive networks (4G and Wi-Fi mostly), operators are providing ever and ever larger data allowances in their broadband packages.

Another key driver not explicit (but implicit) in Figure 34 is the *innovation* that comes with OTTs. OTT providers increasingly develop innovative applications and content. The innovation dividends that come with OTTs are just humongous. This is because OTTs are entirely software-based and delivered using the Internet Protocol (IP) suite. Developers of OTT services face fewer restrictions than developers of bespoke services for communications networks like 2G or 3G networks. These OTT developers do not design their applications for use with dedicated hardware, such as specific 2G or 3G handsets only, set-top boxes or have to be compliant with specific signalling protocols such as CDMA. No!

Instead, the software-based products and services approach enables services on the IVC to be delivered without prior authorisation or permitted access that was formerly required from mobile network/cellular operators, in order to carry OTT services to their consumers. The IVC ensures that the Connectivity segment just increasingly concentrates on providing the communications 'bits pipes', not caring whether it is 4G, satellite, fibre or Wi-Fi. This is a game changer for innovation – OTTs not being a slave to their underlying 'bit pipes'. The operators may and do not like this, but it is very good for citizens and consumers. So as big operators complain about OTTs, as a Digital Economy policy maker, you should be broadly sceptical but attentive to understanding their underlying concerns.

The fact is that the rise and rise of OTTs has transformed the functionality and ease of use offered by telecoms traditional services. Just compare a Zoom or Microsoft Teams call that many of us are now taking for granted during the pandemic to the previous conference calls you used to get with your fixed or mobile communications provider. They previous conference calls were frankly "clunky" and were booked through central telecoms services, and would only support several attendees. Would you return to your old Telco-provided conferencing services anytime soon? Would you swap the apps on your smartphone for the earlier clunky ones the mobile operators abysmally used to try and provide us?

Before you start trying to regulate and/or tax OTTs in your country, forbear and reflect on the innovation dividends they are likely already providing in your country in addition to their proven citizen benefits. If you do not believe me see Figures 35 and 36.

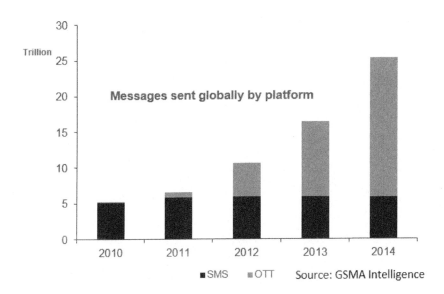

Figure 35 – Messages sent globally by platform

Figure 35 shows that the OTT messages of the IVC Online Services' two categories of Social/Community and Communications (see Figure 1) overtook 2G/3G SMS messages as far back as 2013. The 'explosion' you see in 2014 with OTTs is likely as a result of Facebook's acquisition of WhatsApp for USD $19 B in February 2014[86].

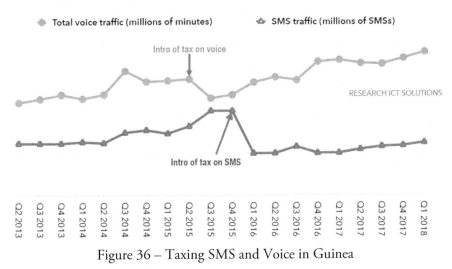

Figure 36 – Taxing SMS and Voice in Guinea

---

[86] Facebook buys WhatsApp for $19bn - BBC News

Figure 36 should be very educative and salutary to any digital economy policy maker about blunt taxes on SMS and 2G/3G voice revenues, because SMS use was reducing as shown in Figure 34, and presumably the same was happening with traditional 2G/3G voice. This all happened in the Central African country of Guinea.

As you would have gathered already by now, I love it when the data just speaks for itself. The Guinean Government decided to increase the taxes on 2G/3Gvoice in Q2 2015 with an immediate drop the following quarter in the use of 2G/3G voice. Well as if this was not bad enough, two quarters later in Q4 2015, the Guinean Government decided to increase the taxes on SMS too. Pretty dumb given what had already happened with the tax on voice. The result was clear – it killed SMS in the country of Guinea presumably most messaging moving onto OTT platforms like WhatsApp.

My key message of this section yet again, forbear with any rash ICT taxes. In this case (as in Figure 35), they only helped to drive the rise and rise of OTTs.

6.3 Briefly busting some OTT Myths

The rise and rise of the OTTs which I explain in the previous section has led to many explicit and implied myths in the OTT debate which truly need busting.

Figure 37 from Stork, Nwana et al. (2020) summarises the myths vs. the facts in the OTT debate. However, before I even get to summarise and bust the myths briefly only, I start by busting some implied myths which I suspect the reader would now agree with – or be completely frustrated with - as I have hammered them long enough.

First, all the "Online Services" in the Internet value chain of Figure 1 are all OTT services. This blows away the first usually implied myth: *OTT is not equal to social media apps!* E-Retail, streaming, gaming, search and cloud services apps (and more) all also run over-the-top. Secondly, the Internet value chain shows OTTs sitting in a totally different segment (Online Services) whilst operators sit in the Connectivity segment. Therefore the idea that policy makers, regulators and network operators should treat OTTs and Operators similarly is another myth: the different segments should be looked at by Digital Economy policy makers.

Myths		FACTS		DATA
	OTTs cause falling tax receipts	1	MNO revenues are increasing and so is VAT from airtime	
		2	OTT applications stimulate broadband adoption and thus economic growth and tax receipts	
	OTTs cause lower revenues for MNOs	3	Voice traffic is still growing and OTTS drive data revenues	
		4	Network investment in the last 15 years has been in faster data networks	
	OTTs aren't subject to the same regulations as MNOs	5	MNOs and OTTs are in different parts of the global Internet value chain	
		6	ICT regulators' jurisdiction is limited to national boundaries	VOICE
	OTTs don't pay taxes	7	OTTs pay taxes wherever the company is incorporated	
		8	ICT sector is often taxed excessively	
	OTTs don't pay for the infrastructure they use	9	Each segment of the Internet Value chain comes with its own risks, opportunities, regulatory obligations and investment requirements	

© RIS 2019

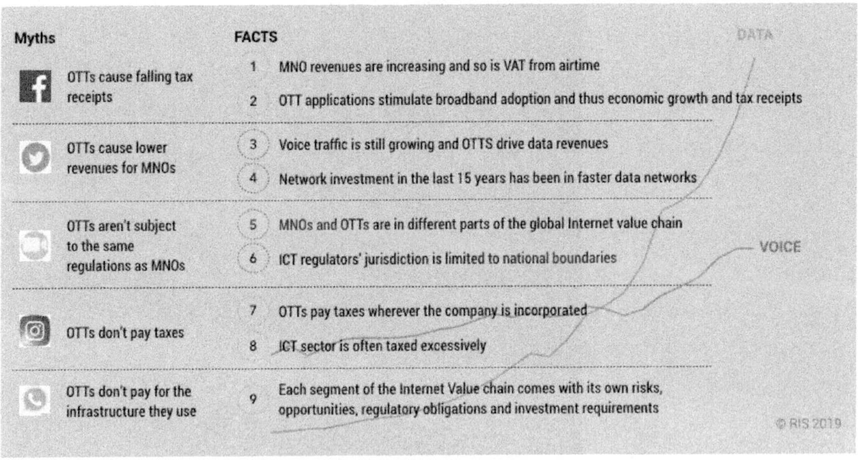

Figure 37: Myths vs. Facts in the OTT Debate
Source: Stork, Nwana, Esselaar & Koyabe (2020)

Now returning to Figure 37, our paper Stork, Nwana *et al.* (2020) comprehensively debunks the five myths on the left of the Figure with qualitative and quantitative data/arguments on the right. The facts on the right of Figure 37 speak for themselves, but our 2020 paper has loads of real data and evidence to back them all up. The report unapologetically draws and derives much of its lessons and key messages in Figure 37 from data and case studies from many African countries, but its essential tenets apply elsewhere beyond Africa. I strongly advise Digital Economy policy makers interested in OTTs to read this paper[87].

---

[87] CTO-OTT-Final-Report-for-Publication-Web_Online-22-May-2020 -
https://cto.int/wp-content/uploads/2020/05/CTO-OTT-REPORT-2020.pdf

6.4 What is the relationship between OTTs and Net Neutrality?

In the last chapter as I expound on OTT Regulation digital economy thematic challenge, I introduce the concept of Net Neutrality and I explain briefly in there why it is germane to OTT policy making and regulation. I explain that at its core, net neutrality is about the non-discrimination rules that forbids operators of IP networks to discriminate against third-party applications, content or services. Blocking or deprioritising OTT traffic may fall foul of net neutrality rules - if you have them. If you do not have them, you need to understand them before you try regulating OTTs.

Telcos [network operators] have finite bandwidth on their networks and they manage the rise and rise of OTT traffic by applying traffic management policies and operations in their networks. This allows operators to prioritise certain traffic, particularly at busy times, in order to prevent congestion. However, even such basic traffic management is contentious and controversial. Some argue against it on "net neutrality" grounds – stating that all Internet content should be equally available. This *strong approach to net neutrality* maintains that if regulators and policy makers allow operators to use traffic management prioritise services or content, they would use it unfairly to benefit their own traffic/content to thew detriment of third-party traffic, and which would in turn lead to unfairly anticompetitive outcomes. This strong view would also pre-empt any paid prioritisation of third-party OTT traffic.

The *weak approach to net neutrality* – if I could term it as such maintains that as bandwidth demands grow, operators need to intervene to ensure network operations and traffic flows are efficient. Ergo, OTT traffic discrimination rules must be allowed.

There are already net neutrality rules are already in place in a number of jurisdictions. For example:

- In Europe, the net neutrality rules are set out in the European Union's Regulation 2015/2120 [88] which established that networks could implement traffic management policies as long as these were proportionate, non-discriminatory and transparent; and that traffic management could not be based on "commercial considerations".

- As I note in the last chapter, USA's FCC flip-flopped on net neutrality rules between 2015 and 2017. In 2015, the FCC under Democratic President Barack Obama agreed to reclassify broadband as public utility under Title II of the US Communications Act[89]. This Open Internet Order[90] protected net neutrality by prohibiting preferential treatment to any user or content provider. This meant that networks could *not* prioritise (or de-prioritise) any internet traffic. i.e. (i) no throttling or blocking of broadband services and (ii) no paid prioritisation of broadband services. Not surprisingly, Big Tech OTT players like Facebook and Google supported it whilst the big US operators like AT&T and Verizon opposed it. Then in 2017 under Republican President Donald Trump, the FCC voted to repeal the 2015 net neutrality order returning to the previous "light touch" or weak approach to net neutrality[91]. The operators rejoiced. The final repeal of the 2015 Order became law in June 2018.

- In Brazil, ISPs are not allowed to discriminate between types or uses of OTT traffic, or even to charge differently for types of internet content. These net neutrality requirements are enshrined in the "Marco Civil" Law of 2014.[92]

What is my key point? If one takes a very strong approach to net neutrality – i.e. no discrimination or the minimum amount of discrimination – one

---

[88] http://eur-lex.europa.eu/legal-content/EN/TXT/PDF/?uri=CELEX:32015R2120&from=en

[89] Feds to cable industry: Embrace broadband competition, or else - CNET (last accessed October 2021)

[90] https://www.fcc.gov/document/fcc-releases-open-internet-order

[91] FCC reverses Open Internet Order governing net neutrality (cnbc.com) (last accessed October 2021)

[92] For discussion of the Marco Civil Law see https://www.economist.com/news/americas/21599781-brazils-magna-carta-web-net-closes

ends up at one set of policy and regulatory positions on OTT. If one takes a weaker position on net neutrality, one ends up in a different set of positions. Your country needs to decide where on this net neutrality continuum it stands.

6.5 What then are the typical key open OTT Regulatory issues?

So what then are the key open Policy and Regulatory issues that you are likely to engage in order to address OTTs in your country or region? There are many.

- *Clear Definition of OTTs*: OTTs need to be clearly defined, and sensibly-defined too. One cannot regulate what one cannot define. Much confusion arises because OTTs do not have a common definition. Much confusion as you have hopefully understood this far also arises because there is much lack of understanding of the Internet value chain wherein OTTs sit in a totally different segment (Online Services) as opposed to [mobile/cellular] operators who sit in the Connectivity segment.

- *Should OTT definition be a matter of national sovereignty?* A key ITU OTT Report recommendation notes, rather unhelpfully in my opinion, that the "definition of OTTs is a matter of national sovereignty and may vary among Member States" (ITU 2019). No – it should not be. Two neigbouring countries having two different definitions on OTT is not clever – particularly, when there is likely to be cross-border delivery of OTT services like E-Commerce or Streaming services. I strongly recommend multi-country, i.e. regional, common consensus on OTT definition.

- *Clear Position on Net Neutrality*: I hope I have now made the case above clearly on the links between net neutrality and OTT Policy and regulation.

- *Should positions on net neutrality be a matter of national sovereignty?* I suspect you can guess from my earlier position on ITU's recommendation on OTT definition what my position on this would be. Yes, your country should consider its position on net neutrality, but I strongly recommend in the Digital Economy world that your country and your neighbours try and adopt a common consensus position on net neutrality too, i.e. regional multi-country net neutrality positions are preferred.

- *Consumer protection with OTT Services*: for example, should narrowband voice OTT consumers (e.g. WhatsApp calls) be protected in the same way as non-OTT phone users are - e.g. with guaranteed availability and quality, and always-on emergency call access?

- *Contribution to Terrestrial Network Costs*: should OTT providers be required to contribute to the costs of network development as consumer demand for bandwidth grows?

- *Contributions to Universal Service Funds (USFs):* should OTTs contribute to the costs of universal service? I have been asked this question as well as the next many times in my presentations on OTTs.

- *Payments of license fees*: should OTTs pay licence fees and/or local taxes in the markets in which they operate?

- *Cross-border policy and regulation of OTT services:* can and should services be regulated across borders?

- *Should OTTs not be regulated at all?* This is another typical question I get. The short answer is No – there are issues with OTTs that need regulating.

This non-exhaustive list of OTT issues would be addressed in the rest of the chapter. I hope by the close of this chapter, the reader would be much informed on how to address questions such as the above and more in your jurisdictions and regions.

6.6 OTT Definitions and towards a consensus definition

I have emphasized many times already so far in this book that one cannot regulate what one cannot clearly define, as one falls into the risks of inconsistencies and unfairness at the very least. For example, why single out Social Media in Figure 1 (one of many classes of Online Services) for special tax treatment, and not Online Gaming or Search? There may be some very good reasons (e.g. online social media harms) to justify such singling out – but this has to be clearly defined. And in any case, not all OTT services are the same. And not all definitions would be good enough to form the basis to regulate (or control) OTTs.

6.6.1 Two Brief Definitions of OTT

Complete independence of a regulator neither is desirable nor is it really necessary. A regulator

Contrast ITUs definition vs. BEREC's definition of OTTs.

- *ITU's OTT Definition of 2019*: ITU (2019) defines OTT as

  an application accessed and delivered over the public Internet that may be a direct technical/functional substitute for traditional international telecommunication services.

  Admittedly, it is an international telecoms focused working definition of OTT.

- *BEREC's 2016 OTT Definition*: BEREC stands for the Body of European Regulators for Electronic Communications. BEREC defines OTT content, a service or an application that is provided to the end user over the public Internet.

  BEREC's definition proceeds to be more precise on its definition along with examples of "content", "service" and "application" as follows:

  - OTT-0: electronic communication services (ECS) that are able to terminate on fixed-line or mobile networks such as Skype-out calls.

  - OTT-1s: are not electronic communication services (ECS) but potentially competing with them, e.g. WhatsApp.

  - OTT-2: encapsulates all other OTT services that are not captured by OTT-0 and OTT-1 (e-commerce, video and music streaming etc).

6.6.2 Comparing and contrasting the two definitions

Whilst the ITU's working definition of OTT is meaningful, BEREC's definition and sub-distinctions are incredibly more helpful (to regulators), clearer and more precise. It is more regulatory-focused definition along with some further helpful sub-distinctions.

Let me elaborate more on BEREC's (2016) *regulatory* focused definition.

(i) an OTT-0 ECS is an electronic communication services (ECS) that is able to terminate on fixed-line or mobile networks. A Skype out call which terminates on a mobile or fixed network is potentially subject to *ex-ante* regulations like telco termination and roaming ones. This is because an OTT-0 service arguably is a substitute with other competing ECS services such as PSTN voice to PSTN voice or mobile to mobile. Therefore, OTT-0s are arguably subject to *ex ante* regulation.

(ii) An OTT-1 ECS is *not* an electronic communication services, but they *potentially* compete with other traditional ECS services, e.g. WhatsApp. A WhatsApp call, may arguably not be seen as competing with traditional voice calls, or less so – and hence may be subject to lighter controls or wholesale regulation – if any. Therefore OTT-1s may or may not be subject to *ex ante* telecoms regulations.

(iii) An OTT-2 ECS encapsulates all other OTT services in the Online Services segment of the IVC that are not captured by OTT-0s and OTT-1s (e.g. e-commerce, video and music streaming etc). So OTT-2s include streaming content services such as Netflix, broadcasting public and commercial content such as BBC and CNN respectively, YouTube UGC content and online newspapers/magazines content.

Clearly these do not compete with traditional ECS services and would arguably not be subject to ex-ante telecoms regulations. However, OTT-2s may be subject though to *ex-ante* broadcasting rules.

And after such a clearer and more precise (hopefully) OTT definition[93] – and a clear understanding and acknowledgement of the new Internet value chain – only then can policy makers, regulators and network operators proceed to local and/or regional policies and regulations.

6.7 A more fine-tuned OTT definition, Policy and Regulation

Esselaar & Stork (2019) argues that even the much better BEREC definition is mainly pertinent to telecommunication regulation and less relevant to other types of OTTs, such as those in the broadcasting and streaming sectors. They argue that a good OTT definition should be based on a taxonomy that *"separates out issues that need be addressed by different regulators"*. They note that Call termination is, for example, addressed by a telecoms regulator while streaming services may be subject to broadcasting standards and regulation. I believe this is very helpful addition indeed. Issues to do with OTTs are typically regulated by several regulators within a country.

Esselaar & Stork (2019) propose a definition for four categories of OTTs: OTT-ECS, OTT-Com; OTT-Content and OTT-Other as shown in Table 6. Their more elaborate definition follows:

> OTTs can be content, a service or an application that is provided to the end user over the public Internet. OTTs can be distinguished between those that are electronic communication services (OTT-ECS), those that potentially compete with electronic communication services (OTT-Com), those that potentially compete with broadcasting services (OTT-Content) and those that neither compete with electronic communication services nor broadcasting services (OTT-Other).

---

[93] That is OTTs/Social Media sit in a different segment/layer of the value chain (the Internet value chain)
than Connectivity (cf. Figure 1).

	OTT-ECS	OTT-Com	OTT-Content	OTT-Other
Competing with ECS?	Yes	Potentially	No	No
Competing with national broadcasting services?	No	No	Potentially	No
Description	OTT voice and text with the ability to make calls to fixed or mobile telephone networks (eg Skype Out)	Applications that allow voice calls and instant messaging provided to the end user over the public Internet	Content provided to the end user over the public Internet	E-commerce and online services provided to the end user over the public Internet
Potentially Responsible Ex Ante regulatory bodies (if regulation is pursued)	Telecom Regulator	Telecom Regulator	Broadcasting Regulators	None
Potential regulatory impact	Termination and roaming regulation	Lighter voice and SMS wholesale regulation	VAT collection from foreign streaming services	None

Table 6 – Esselaar & Stork Fine-Tuned OTT Definition

Sources: Esselaar & Stork (2019), Stork, Nwana *et al.* (2020)

What Esselaar & Stork's Table 6 and their fine-tuned definition clear depict is that OTT applications typically fall into more than one subset.

They note Skype, for example, is an OTT-ECS because voice and text can terminate on Public Switched Telephone Network (PSTN) and mobile networks for a fee. They also note it is also an OTT-Com because it also offers free services between Skype users. Facebook provides access to lots of UGC content (OTT-Content) while also allowing instant messaging and voice calls via its integrated Messenger feature (OTT-Com).

Therefore they rightly note that OTT applications can be subject to various regulatory regimes at the same time. From a policy and regulatory perspective, this is most germane. Table 6 could or should prove – along with their earlier definition – very powerful tools to drive policy and regulation of OTTs in your country/region.

You can quickly observe that OTT-ECS services clearly fall under the purview of the telecoms regulator (for reasons like call termination and roaming regulations, and maybe the use of local numbers too); whilst an OTT-Com service *may* fall under the Telecom regulator or not at all depending on whether SMS wholesale regulation is a relevant market in your country. An OTT Content service like Netflix should *not* really be subject to a telecoms-only regulator, and a broadcast (content) regulator is arguably more appropriate. For OTT-Content, the Government may choose to collect Value Added Services (VAT) taxes from foreign streaming providers like Netflix.

With a good fine-tuned definition of OTTs, a brilliant tool like Table 6 and the Internet value chain, I hope you can now predict my views on the open questions I listed earlier. See if you agree or disagree.

- *Clear Definition of OTTs*: OTTs need to be clearly defined, and sensibly-defined too. One cannot regulate what one cannot define. The good BEREC definition has been significantly enhanced in my view by Esselaar & Stork's (2019).
- *Should OTT definition be a matter of national sovereignty?* Clearly No – it should not be! I strongly recommend multi-country, i.e. regional, common consensus on OTT definition as I note earlier.
- *Clear Position on Net Neutrality*: This is absolutely needed.
- *Should positions on net neutrality be a matter of national sovereignty?* No. Multi-country and/or regional net neutrality positions are recommended.
- *Consumer protection with OTT Services*: for example, should narrowband voice OTT consumers (e.g. WhatsApp calls) be protected in the same way as non-OTT phone users - e.g. with guaranteed availability and quality, and always-on emergency call

access? Well Table 6 depicts that WhatsApp is an OTT-Com service that may or may not be regulated by the telecoms regulator. If OTT-Coms are not regulated, the requirement for WhatsApp emergency call 24/7 access arguably falls away. There also would not be any QoS/QoE regulations imposed on OTT-Com services.

- *Contribution to Terrestrial Network Costs*: should OTT providers be required to contribute to the costs of network development as consumer demand for bandwidth grows? What the Internet value chain tells us is that OTTs sit in their own lane (i.e. the Online Services segment) whilst the connectivity services providers sit in their own (Connectivity). Each segment of the value chain has its own business model, risks and opportunities as well as regulatory frameworks. Calls for intervention to regulate OTTs or to limit their use are usually premised on the assumption that OTTs are part of the Connectivity segment of the value chain. No- they are not! They are part of the Online Services segment with its own business models, risks and opportunities and legislation. The Internet value chain (see Figures 1 and 3) shows that this premise is false. Why only pick on social media apps too? Why not pick on E-Commerce, gaming or cloud services players to contribute to networks costs too? OTT players like Facebook or Google build data centres, submarine cables, etc.

- *Contributions to Universal Service Funds (USFs)*: should OTTs contribute to the costs of universal service? I have been asked this question as well as the next many times in my presentations on OTTs. This question is usually premised on a view that OTTs are causing overall mobile revenues and or USF revenues/profits to fall. As we show comprehensively in Stork, Nwana *et al.* (2020) using much African data, this is not the case. Operators' revenues have been generally increasing steadily as summarised in Figure 37. Like I note for contributions to the costs of terrestrial networks above, OTTs sit in a different segment of the IVC and should not be subject to the same regulatory license fees and contributions as those in the Connectivity segment.

- *Payments of license fees*: should OTTs pay licence fees and/or local taxes in the markets where they operate? OTTs are typically not licensed in every country, and license fees go with licensing for (i) market access and/or (ii) access to scarce resources like spectrum and numbers and/or (iii) authorization to provide services. Mobile/cellular operators therefore have many more "rights" that come with being licensed operators including interconnection rights, the ability to obtain telephone numbers and most importantly, allocations of spectrum. For these rights also come obligations. OTT providers typically are unlicensed players and free of the requirement to pay fees. They typically neither have no rights to interconnect nor access to telephone numbers nor access the spectrum.

- *Cross-border policy and regulation of OTT services:* can and should services be regulated across borders? By definition many OTT services in the Online Services segment of the IVC would happen cross-border. I note in the Chapter 5 that Economist Christoph Ungerer (2021) reveals that the biggest e-retailer in the world Amazon runs online stores and warehouses in only 16 countries[94] (i.e. 9% of the countries globally representing 74% of global GDP). Most really useful OTT services would be cross border. Live with it! Get used to it! This is exactly why I argue strongly for regional common consensus positions on OTTs definition and net neutrality. In this ways online cross-border services start becoming more seamless.

- *Should OTTs not be regulated at all?* This book has been clear on the fact that there are several issues and challenges that come with OTT players, particularly the Big Tech ones. Calls for OTT regulations covers a "multitude of sins" as I explain earlier. With the latter who double up as OTT players too (think Google, Facebook, Amazon, Microsoft and Amazon), *competition issues* are plenty that need regulation. *Online content* regulation issues abound too: issues, such as cyber bullying, cyber threats, critical national infrastructure attacks, disinformation, fake news, election-meddling, terrorism, pornography, harmful content, hate speech, data privacy and data protection are being looked at closely. Some OTT players, such as Facebook, are already demanding regulation

---

[94] The emerging markets e-commerce opportunity (brookings.edu) - https://www.brookings.edu/blog/future-development/2021/03/26/the-emerging-markets-e-commerce-opportunity/

anyway. Facebook, for example, identified four areas for regulation: privacy, data portability, election integrity, and harmful content[95]. So the issue is not whether unlicensed OTTs should not be regulated. Unlicensed does not mean unregulated!

6.8 OTTs and Taxes – Look before you leap

One key area which Governments have been selectively using to "control" OTTs is via taxing them. I use the word "selectively" to be more politically correct that "discriminatorily". As Stork, Nwana *et al.* (2020) note. since many successful OTTs are outside of the jurisdiction of most countries, some governments have resorted to end-user taxation as a regulatory tool We note in this paper [Stork, Nwana *et al.*, 2020] how Uganda implemented a "social media tax", which charges the end-user a daily fee if they access Facebook, WhatsApp, FaceTime and other OTTs.

The justification for this is that data usage produces externalities that are not captured in the original transaction. Therefore, bizarrely, the tax is imposed to reduce usage. As I note and "dismiss" earlier, some MNOs want OTTs to pay for the infrastructure they use. I highlight some of the purported and/or ridiculous reasons below as I briefly review several countries that have tried OTT taxes.

Essentially in several countries, these calls to Regulatory and Tax authorities "to do something about OTTs" have led to real negative outcomes (see Stork, Nwana *et al.* 2020):

- Uganda: a social media tax of 200 UGX (Ugandan Shillings) per day ($US 0.05) levied in July 2018 led to an estimated number of Internet users dropping by nearly 30% between March and September 2018. Plus it is clearly a very regressive tax, with significant more drop in Internet users in poorer regions. It was

---

[95] Zuckerberg, M. 30/03/2019. The Internet needs new rules. Let's start in these four areas. Washington Post. https://www.washingtonpost.com/opinions/mark-zuckerberg-the-internet-needs-new-rules-lets-start-in-these-four-areas/2019/03/29/9e6f0504-521a-11e9-a3f7-78b7525a8d5f_story.html

also a most disproportionate tax because 200 UGX per day over thirty days a month is 6000 UGX. At the time the tax was introduced, this (6000 UGX) represented 75% of the monthly Average Revenue Per User (ARPU). Just incredible! Some will justifiably call it "Just nuts"!

- Benin: In September 2018, Benin introduced a new OTT tax (CFA 5 or USD 0.8 cents per Mbyte and 5% tax on airtime) for the purpose of *"protecting investment in network infrastructure"* and pushing OTT players to pay regulatory fees/taxes. The regulator claimed CFA 30 Billion turnover (circa US $50M) was lost between 2016 and 2018 due to *"the invasion of OTTs"*. Benin citizens protested and the Government repealed the tax within weeks. Esselaar & Stork (2019) estimate that these withdrawn taxes would have resulted conservatively in forgone GDP growth of USD 260 million and forgone taxes of USD 40 million. The tax was also regressive.

- Zambia: in August 2018, the Government introduced a 30 Ngwee per day excise duty tariff on Internet phone calls, the purpose being to *"protect traditional phone calls"* and *"jobs in companies such as Zamtel, Airtel and MTN"*. Zambians rightly protested and the tax is yet to be implemented.

- Colombia: in 2016 the Government imposed VAT on foreign suppliers of digital services (i.e. OTT content), Foreign Service Providers (FSPs). FSPs are required to register in Colombia and pay VAT bimonthly. It turns out that it is *not* that easy to implement as practically all foreign online services layer players (see Figure 1) are arguably caught by the new tax. The tax has not been implemented, arguably as it is not only controversial but unimplementable. As of January 2021, this system had not been implemented. In addition to the implementation of VAT on foreign digital services, a national excise tax was implemented as part of the same tax-reform package

These above brief examples demonstrate why a rush to regulate OTTs may not also meet the test of the key purposes of regulation, and that their implementation may not be trivial to do and enforce anyway. These examples also clearly speak to "Look before you Leap" with OTTs, as no clear (regulatory) Impact Assessments were carried out prior to these taxes being imposed. These should be standard best practice.

Table 7 is a summary of OTT regulatory developments across Africa, Latin America and Asia as compiled by Esselaar & Stork (2019).

	Date	Description
Angola	09/06/2016	Overview of challenges facing the sector. Regulator will monitor developments.
Burundi	05/12/2018	Presentation by Mr. Constaque Hakizimana, technical director of ARCT. Conclusion was to investigate the regulatory framework around OTTs, specifically to address tax evasion, data privacy, unequal playing field with MNOs.
	05/12/2018	Regulator held a workshop on the impact of OTTs.
DR Congo	14/06/2018	Data prices were increased by the regulator based on 2 factors: 1) MNOs were apparently in a price war, and 2) the impact of OTTs was reducing operator revenue.
Cote d'Ivoire	01/12/2016	Analysis of the impact of OTTs in Cote d'Ivoire. Aim of document was to encourage debate, especially in light of the fact that OTTs must be governed globally.
Ghana	5 May 2016	National Communications Authority (NCA) is reviewing the situation and will in due course take decisions for an enabling environment that will benefit all stakeholders.
Guinea	30 Sep 2017	Recommended 4 strategies to regulate OTTs.
	30 Sep 2017	Presentation on the OTT Strategic Report by Guinea to the African Council of Regulators.
Indonesia	1 Aug 2017	Draft regulations for international OTT providers. Foreign OTT providers would need to establish a permanent presence in Indonesia or formally partner with local network providers. It has subsequently been withdrawn.
	1 Apr 2018	Indonesia's Minister of Trade proposed digital taxes on e-books, digital music, and other e-commerce

	Date	Description
		services. No tax has been implemented yet.
Kenya	9 Jan 2019	Request for consultancy services for the study of OTTs in Kenya.
	21 Sep 2018	Excise duty on mobile money transfer services increased from 10% to 12%.
Liberia	no date	The Liberia Telecommunications Authority (LTA) will also consider the demand and supply-side substitution effects posed by OTT services when looking at competition assessment
	25 Feb 2019	Government introduced a price floor for voice and data and a voice and data surcharge of US$0.008 and US$0.0065 per MB.
Malaysia	2020	Effective from 1 Jan 2020, all foreign digital suppliers with revenues exceeding USD120,000 must register with Malaysian authorities and remit a 6% sales tax. A consumer is considered Malaysian if they use a credit or debit card that is registered in Malaysia, if the business has an IP address registered in Malaysia and/or resides in Malaysia.
Morocco	4 Nov 2016	The National Telecommunications Regulatory Agency (ANRT) is following the question of OTTs with interest.
Mozambique	1 Dec 2016	Review of the telecom market for 2016. Mobile revenues overall increased (Figure 6 of the report). On-net call increased as well.
Niger	2020	Government proposed a new internet tax of 0.05 CFA per MB for 2020. The tax was subsequently withdrawn.
Nigeria	4 Mar 2016	The Nigerian Communications Commission (NCC) has no plans to regulate OTTs and encourages operators to explore more efficient business models to take advantage of the move to data.
	3 Oct 2019	Proposed 9% communication service tax to be levied on electronic communication services, like voice calls, SMS, MMS, surfing data from both telecommunication services providers and Internet

318

	Date	Description
		service providers, as well as pay-per-view TV stations. Tax has not been implemented.
	5 Aug 2019	Government may appoint banks as agents to deduct 5% VAT on all local online purchases with a bank card. VAT on foreign suppliers has not been implemented yet.
	18 Feb 2018	Meeting between the Association for Respiratory Technology and Physiology (ARTP) and Facebook. ARTP repeated the claim that mobile operators are losing revenues due to OTTs.
Senegal	30 Apr 2017	Expression of Interest (EOI) for an analysis of the impact of OTTs on the Senegal ICT ecosystem. No information as to whether this was actually conducted or if findings were made public.
	30 Jun 2018	The last paragraph of Article 27 of the Code provides: "The regulatory authority may authorise or impose any traffic management measure that it considers useful for, inter alia, maintaining competition in the electronic communications sector and ensuring fair treatment of similar services." The imprecise wording has people worried that this might be used by operators to block OTTs.
Singapore	1 Jan 2020	All foreign digital businesses must pay GST of 7% as long as they have an annual turnover exceeding SGD$1 million and local services to Singaporean customers of SGD$100,000.
	15 Jan 2019	Included a discussion on impact of OTTs on the broadcasting sector.
South Africa	22 Sep 2017	OTTs are not a substitute for traditional voice and do not have an impact on whether there is effective competition in the voice market. Future market analysis should take OTTs into account.
Thailand	26 Aug 2019	The director-general of the Revenue Department said Thailand is expected to introduce VAT on electronic businesses, effective from 1 Jan 2020. No formal regulations have yet been passed.

	Date	Description
Tanzania	27 Aug 2018	Consultancy services to establish OTT service tariffs. No information on whether study was conducted or if findings were made public.
Zambia	2019	Excise duty of 17.5 percent on airtime and is backdated to 1 January 2011. ISPs are thus required to back pay excise duties.
Zimbabwe	30 Jun 2016	Consultation document that discusses whether OTT services should be regulated, asking stakeholders to respond to 21 questions.
Sources	Based on Esselaar and Stork (2019)	

Table 7: OTT regulatory developments in Africa, Latin America and Asia

Source: Stork, Nwana, Esselaar & Koyabe (2020)

Where OTTs truly need to be taxed, I strongly recommend the five best practice principles[96] of an efficient tax system are abided by as shown in Table 8. Stork, Nwana *et al.* (2020) assess how the OTT tax regimes across several countries abide by these best practice principles.

Principle	Description
Broad-based	A broad base of taxation means that a lower tax rate is required to raise the same revenue, while sector-specific taxes distort incentives and require higher levels of taxation to get the same revenue.
Take into account externalities	Excise duties should be imposed on activities with negative externalities where the objective is to lower consumption, such as alcohol or tobacco, and should not be imposed on sectors with positive externalities, such as telecoms.

---

[96] See GSMA. (2016b). Digitalisation and mobile sector taxation in Europe: The experience in Hungary. Retrieved from https://www.gsma.com/mobilefordevelopment/wp-content/uploads/2016/03/GSMA_Digitalisation_and_mobile_sector_taxation_experience_in _Hungary.pdf

Principle	Description
Simple and enforceable	Taxes should be clear, easy to understand, and predictable, thereby reducing investor uncertainty and ensuring better compliance.
Incentives for competition & investment should be unaffected	Higher taxes for one sector in comparison to the rest of the economy could reduce investment in that sector.
Progressive not regressive	The tax rate should increase as the taxable amount increases. Specific value taxes on small amounts should be avoided because they make the poor pay more.
Source	Esselaar & Stork, 2018a, based on GSMA, 2016

Table 8: Best-practice principles for taxation

Source: Stork, Nwana, Esselaar & Koyabe (2020)

6.9 Recommendations: OTTs Emerging Framework & Checklist

On the bases of all of the previous sections and more, I propose the following emerging framework and checklist when considering OTT Interventions in your countries or regions. It is unapologetically aimed at Digital Economy *Regulators, ICT Policy Makers and Tax Authorities* when considering any OTT Interventions. All these checklist recommendations may require stakeholder trainings.

The 10-point framework is the following.

1. **Understand & Acknowledge the new Internet Value Chain**

2. **Take a clear view on Net Neutrality & Traffic Management**

3. **OTTs must be clearly defined**

4. **Countries/Regions must take a view on Competition Issues, Big Tech Regulation and Online Content Regulation**

5. **Continue to Employ traditional and best practice Regulatory & Tax principles**

6. **Recognise and Collaborate with existing and relevant Institutions to OTTs in your country**

7. **Evidenced-based OTT interventions including stakeholder consultations should be mandatory**

8. **Always carry out Economic, Social and Regulatory Impact Analyses**

9. **Implement OTT Light touch controls that foster innovation**

10. **Collaboration amongst IVC Oversight Institutions**

Table 8: A 10 point Emerging OTT Framework & Checklist

I briefly elaborate on each of these ten recommendations following.

6.9.1 Understand & acknowledge the new Internet value chain

The Internet value chain of Figure 1 is our clear new reality in our erstwhile TMT/ICT sector. There is no more denying this. OTTs are just one symptom of such much needed rethinking. Along with the positive externalities of the new value chain comes numerous negative ones too.

Digital Economy/ICT Regulators, ICT Policy Makers and Tax Authorities collectively must acknowledge and understand the Internet Value Chain and how it impacts the ICT and Mobile sectors in your country, particularly in Developing and Emerging Market countries. This is because in some of these markets like Myanmar or Zambia, the Internet literally equals the Mobile Internet (and equals Facebook). Countries need to understand the implications of this value chain: both good and bad, the implications on interconnection, bypass, cybersecurity, etc. The early chapters of this book cover this.

This new reality must be acknowledged and understood. Telecoms Regulatory Master Class (TRMC)Training on the Internet value chain (and its implications) is a strong recommendation here. As seen in this chapter, you can only intervene and/or regulate and/or tax OTTs after a good understanding and acknowledgement of the IVC. This is why I start the chapter with a quote stressing this.

6.9.2 Regions/Countries to take clear Position on Net Neutrality & Traffic Management

Telcos have sought to manage growing demands for finite bandwidth by applying traffic management policies and operations in their networks. However, traffic management is contentious; some argue against it on the grounds of "net neutrality". The net neutrality debate is highly relevant as we consider OTTs because traffic management gives networks and OTT providers the ability to make commercial deals based on traffic prioritization and quality of service. This is arguably one way in which OTT providers can contribute proportionately to the costs of networks and bandwidth. However, there is a fear that such an approach will favour the big players by offering them better deals, and stifle innovation by new entrants and smaller companies.

In this chapter, we have seen that net neutrality rules are in place in a number of jurisdictions. For examples in Europe (weak approach), in Brazil (strong approach) and the flip-flop between approaches in the USA. The repealing of the Obama era Open Internet order arguably would encourage much investments in the USA. Either way, each jurisdiction/country or even a region must take a clear and *informed* view on Net neutrality and traffic management. The Digital Economy policy makers, regulators and network operators need informed advice on this subject.

6.9.3 Clear Definition of OTT Required as Basis of Regulation & Taxation

OTT must be clearly defined: one cannot regulate or even tax what one cannot define. In this chapter, I have we hopefully made a cogent case for having action-oriented OTT definitions. Though the ITU states (in draft

323

form) that the question of definitions of OTT is one for each sovereign state as the ITU states, I disagree and strongly recommend it is one for regions, if not wider. We recommend countries and/or even regions start from Esselaar & Stork's OTT definition and the sub-classifications in this chapter. I encourage regional consensus common definition of OTTs. This chapter has presented an improved fine-tuned definition of OTTs from Esselaar & Stork (improved upon BEREC's). Their definition of OTTs is much more helpful to regulators and tax authorities than other definitions I know.

6.9.4 Countries/Regions must take a view on Competition Issues, Big Tech Regulation and Online Regulation

When policy makers and regulators are asked to "do something about OTTs", they need to think Competition Concerns, Big Tech Regulation and/or Online Content Regulation at the very least. In most cases, countries would not be able to do much about the Competition Concerns/Big Tech regulation unless you are the USA, China or one of the top-15 major economies and/or geopolitical regions of the world like the EU/EC. This is just the reality, most small economies would not be able to do much about these first two buckets of issues. However, all countries/regions – big and small - must understand and articulate the categories of OTT harms that need to be controlled (i.e. regulated) in their markets. It is unarguable that OTTs bring with them many benefits but many harms too. Countries/Regions would need to categorise the risks/harms and sub risks/sub-harms of OTTs and RAG[97] rate them. Categories could/would include: online harms not tolerated offline (such as cyber bullying), cyber threats, Critical National Infrastructure (CNI) attacks, Disinformation, Fake news, Elections risks, Terrorism, Social Harms, Pornorgraphy, Dark Web vs. Open Web, Illegal vs. Harmful Content, Hate Speech, Privacy/Data Protection (c.f. Data Breaches), etc. Countries would have to determine the most optimal ways to minimise the harms by regulations in their countries through local/regional statutes along with their rigorous implementations. Recall that Sir Tim Berners Lee - the founder of the world

---

[97] Red, Amber and Green

wide web – has opined on harms that the Internet value chain has brought with it including inequity and division.

6.9.5 Continue to Employ Best Practice Regulatory & Tax Principles

Even with OTTs, regulators and tax authorities must continue to employ traditional and best practice regulatory principles: regulate to pre-empt market failure, market failure analyses; relevant markets analyses, light touch vs. licensing, ex-ante vs ex-post mitigation, sectoral vs. horizontal regulation, analyses on consumer/citizens harms, etc. Such regulatory best practice on being good regulators like Ofcom UK are key (see Table 8). Most ICT regulators should know how to do this.

	Principle	Description	Application to OTTs
1	Annual plan	Principle 1 stipulates signalling a clear intent to all stakeholders in a Regulator's Annual Plan.	In many cases across the world, governments or tax authorities have just "sprung" OTT regulations (or mostly tax interventions) on unsuspecting subscribers without any warning, as was the cases in Benin, Zambia and Uganda.
2	Intervene if specific duty	Principle 2 stipulates intervening only where there is a clear duty to do so, or when working towards a clear public policy goal.	Beyond raising more tax revenues, it is difficult to discern clear regulatory duties which instigated OTT interventions across Africa. A typical duty of regulators is "to (i.e., shall) further interests of citizens & consumers in communications matters".
3	Bias against Intervention	Principle 3 stipulates a bias against intervention and that intervention needs to pass a high hurdle such as market intervention.	In Table 7 it is noted Senegal's regulator may impose any traffic management it deems necessary for competition; any such intervention needs to first prove market failure or 3-criteria test market justification.

Principle		Description	Application to OTTs
4	Accountability and Transparency	Principle 4 advises that even when interventions are necessary, they must be proportionate, consistent (with previous interventions), accountable and transparent in both deliberation and outcome.	There was a 2015 regulatory fine in Nigeria to MTN of more than $US 1 Billion in 2015 which led to MTN Nigeria (by its own admission) underinvesting in their own network in Nigeria. Such a quantum of fine was not proportionate, and this fine did not further the interest of Nigerian consumers and citizens. MNOs argue that regulation is not proportionate because less or minimal regulation is applied to OTTs and, consequently, OTTs derive an unfair commercial advantage. In best practice terms, regulation should be designed such that it is necessarily applied proportionately to parties that are in the same commercial position, and in the same part of the same market (i.e., same segment of the value chain). OTTs and MNOs are not in the same market; MNOs sell data access on a national level. OTTs sell mostly advertisements.
5	Least intrusive regulation possible	Principle 5 stipulates that a good regulator seeks the least intrusive regulatory mechanism. This can mean that some market players get lighter regulatory treatment than others. It recognises the commercial advantages of larger players, in terms of scale and scope economies, and the ability of larger players to share overhead costs.	In the mobile money sphere, lighter regimes may be applied to some market players, but the price of that lighter regime entails restrictions on the services they can offer, i.e., they will/may not be given the same level of privileges as a bank. Banks have greater privileges, but they are subjected to tighter prudential regulation. Therefore, even if OTTs were to be regulated vis-à-vis MNOs, some regulations may be asymmetric.

Principle	Description	Application to OTTs
6 Constant market research	Principle 6 advocates constantly researching the market and other markets in order to understand the impacts of regulatory (or other) decisions.	A regulatory impact assessment (RIA) is an assessment carried out by a regulator. In fact, it is a duty within the jurisdictions of most Communications Acts to conduct impact assessments. In Africa, new taxes on OTTs have not been preceded by any such impact assessments. Singapore has published an impact assessment indicating what it believes will be the impact of including VAT on digital services from international sources.
7 Consult and assess impact of regulation	Principle 7: The last principle requires a good regulator to consult widely with all relevant stakeholders before decisions are implemented.	In Africa, regulators that have, at times, imposed new taxes on OTTs have not consulted with the public prior to implementation. In contrast, regulators in Asia have conducted public consultations (e.g., Malaysia and Singapore).
Source	http://www.ofcom.org.uk/about/what-is-ofcom/statutory-duties-and-regulatory-principles/ (last accessed October 2019)	

Table 9: Ofcom Regulatory Principles
Tabulated and commented in Stork, Nwana, Esselaar & Koyabe (2020)

In addition, best practice tax regulatory principles should also be followed as many countries are minded to implement OTT taxes.

The GSMA has conducted extensive research into taxation of ICT services[98]. These studies suggest the following:

- Jurisdictions with simple and transparent tax regimes on ICT goods and services (e.g. Kenya and *Uruguay*) have higher ICT adoption rates.

---

[98]https://www.gsma.com/publicpolicy/wp-content/uploads/2014/02/Mobile-taxes-and-fees-A-toolkit-of-principles-and-evidence_fullreport-FINAL1.pdf (Last accessed November 2019)

- Conversely, sector-specific taxes on digital services are fairly distortive and have a negative impact on take up of digital services. Taxes on digital services are usually higher than other service sectors such as tourism.

- Higher taxes on digital services disproportionately affect groups sensitive to pricing and affordability of ICT services (i.e. low income groups). In other words, they are regressive.

- Transparent, simple, tax regimes are least distortive and disruptive.

- Each government will have to strike a balance between generating revenue from taxation, and guarding against the negative impact and risks of taxation on the take-up of digital services.

These are all eminently sensible.

Table 8 summarises the five best practice principles that contribute to an efficient tax system. All OTT or ICT taxes are strongly advised to abide by these principles.

6.9.6 Recognise and Collaborate with existing and relevant institutions to OTTs

Several aspects of OTTs in particular and the Internet Value Chain in general would already be subject to being controlled (or regulated) by several institutions and/or laws in your country. OTTs, Content and other Online services on the Internet value chain already have various institutions, laws and regulatory approaches in most jurisdictions. Any interventions must therefore be "joined up". OTTs truly challenges to Governments and regulators are truly collaborative – something they are not very good at.

Do not take my word for it, just look at Table 10. It is a table of typical laws, rules, regulations and their classic corresponding institutions – but this time mapped onto the Internet value chain. This is an important table which would typically be 'invisible' to Digital Economy Policy makers, regulators and network operators. However, it is yet another important 'tool' to both understand Digital Economy policy making/regulation as well as collaboration amongst policy makers, regulators and network operators.

Typical Laws, rules and regulations and corresponding institutions shaping the Internet Value Chain			
Internet Value Chain	Institutions	Laws	Other
Content Rights	⊚Broadcasting regulator ⊚Film and Publication Board ⊚Registration of copyright ⊚Courts ⊚Competition Commission	⊚Broadcasting Code ⊚Patent/copyright/trademark laws	Self-regulation based on company policies
Online services	⊚Courts ⊚Competition Commission ⊚Consumer protection agencies ⊚Data Protection Organisations ⊚Telecom & Media regulator [NEW], e.g. Ofcom UK	⊚Consumer protection law ⊚Hate speech laws ⊚Privacy laws ⊚Cybersecurity laws ⊚Patent/copyright/trademark laws ⊚Gambling legislation ⊚Online Content laws ⊚Digital Economy Acts ⊚Competition laws	Self-regulation based on company policies Co-regulation
Enabling technologies & services	⊚Courts ⊚Competition Commission	⊚Privacy laws ⊚Cybersecurity laws ⊚Financial sector regulation & laws	
Connectivity	⊚Telecommunication regulator ⊚Communications, science & technology agencies ⊚Courts ⊚Competition Commission ⊚Local authorities & municipalities	⊚Communication laws ⊚Competition laws ⊚Postal laws	Co-regulation
User interface	⊚Telecommunication regulator ⊚Consumer protection agencies	⊚Consumer protection laws ⊚Type approval from telecom regulation ⊚Competition laws ⊚Cybersecurity laws	

Table 10: Typical Laws, Rules and Regulations and corresponding institutions shaping the IVC

Source: Stork & Esselaar (2019a) – with some updates by H Nwana

Take 'Online Services' for example in Table 10. It depicts the many [largely offline] institutions and laws likely in place in your country shaping the Internet value chain. Any new Online regulations must build on these. For example, Online Services would typically be subject to consumer protection laws, hate speech laws, privacy laws, cybersecurity laws, patent/copyright/trademark laws and gambling legislation laws and competition laws. Thanks to the Digital competition concerns, Big Tech and Online content harms that come with the IVC, countries have also started enacting new laws such as UK's 2017 Digital Economy Act[99] and the evolving draft Online Safety Bill[100]. The UK Telecoms & Media regulator Ofcom has been given (and will be given) more duties and powers to deal with some of these new IVC online harms. Furthermore, the courts, consumer protection agencies and other Competition Agencies (like Competition Commissions) would adjudicate, rule and/or regulate based on these laws. Self-regulation and co-regulatory models are also most relevant. For example absent statutory regulation of online safety in your jurisdiction, the Big Tech content players like YouTube, Facebook, etc. carry out self-regulation. Co-regulation would also happen between telecom/media and competition regulators.

Take the "User Interface" segment on Table 10 too. The relevant laws would include consumer protection laws, type approval laws/regulations for equipment, competition laws (that could address Google/Apple Apps Store duopoly and IoS/Android operating systems harms) and cybersecurity laws (to protect User Interfaces).

The rest of Table 10 is hopefully self-explanatory.

Any new laws to address any digital harms would need to be clear on which IVC segment they would apply to, understand the scope of the current offline laws and regulators, as well as be clear on which of statutory regulation, coregulation, self-regulation or some combination would be best optimal. Table 10 is also clear on the fact that there would be much scope for collaboration between policy makers, regulators and network operators across the Internet value chain, and very little room for much silos and silo-mentality. Online/OTT harms are cross-sector by definition, and silo-single sector thinking is just inappropriate.

The key recommendation here is to recognise that OTT services and other online services on the Internet value chain already have various institutions,

---

99 Digital Economy Act 2017 - GOV.UK (www.gov.uk)

[99] Digital Economy Act 2017 - GOV.UK (www.gov.uk)
[100] Draft Online Safety Bill - Committees - UK Parliament (last accessed October 2021)

laws and control/regulatory approaches in most jurisdictions that they would be subject to. Any interventions must therefore be "joined up" with these.

6.9.7 Evidenced-Based OTT Interventions including stakeholder consultations should be mandatory

Any regulatory or tax intervention should be evidenced-based as possible in order to abide by best practice policy and regulation. We have shown real evidenced data from countries like Uganda, Benin, Nigeria, Ghana, etc. to make our argumentations (see more details in Stork, Nwana *et al.*, 2020). Interventions with regards to OTTs with respect to regulations and taxes should be similarly evidenced and rationally thought through. Where the data is not in place in your country, lessons should be from experiences (good and bad) from other countries.

Public bodies must provide members of the public, including those and others affected by their proposals a chance to comment on them. This consultation requirement can be fulfilled alongside other requirements to consult (e.g. the consultation on the proposals themselves), rather than in sequence.

6.9.8 Always Carry out Economic, Social & Regulatory Impact Analyses

An Impact Assessments (IAs) is a process undertaken by a Public Body (typically) such as an ICT/TMT Regulator in order to consider the total overall effect (positive and negative) of a proposed policy or regulatory action. A Regulatory Impact Assessment (RIA) is such as assessment carried out by a regulator. In fact, it is a duty in most jurisdictions prescribed within their Communications Acts to conduct such impact Assessments. The UK Communications Act of 2003 which founded Ofcom (the esteemed UK converged Communications Regulator) imposes a duty on Ofcom to carry out such RIAs, and Ofcom is almost likely to be litigated (and lose) without carrying out such RIAs.

The typical stages of impact assessment include:

- Assessment of benefits and costs;
- Dealing with uncertainty;
- Distributional effects: which part of society benefits and who loses?
- Impact on competition.

Governments should also carry out similar Economic Impact Analyses (EIAs) and Social Impact Analyses (SIAs) when introducing OTT taxes, in addition to abiding by best practice tax principles. It will usually fall to economists in a project team to articulate the potential benefits of enhanced competition as part of the impact assessment - this assessment may be qualitative or quantitative.

I note earlier the case of the 2018 Ugandan OTT not only being regressive but disproportionate. I note the monthly tax burden of 6000 UGX initially represented 75% of the monthly Average Revenue Per User (ARPU). Should this not have been well flagged before it was implemented that it was this disproportionate, as well as this regressive? This Ugandan OTT 2018 tax presents a classic case why it would have been useful to carry out such prior Impact Analyses before the OTT tax was imposed in the first place.

6.9.9 Implement OTT Light Touch Controls That Foster Innovation

> Regulate/control with a bias towards "light touch" and "sensible" controls to allow for innovation, creativity that come with OTTs – do not kill golden goose in your country.

OTTs not only promise but have already delivered hundreds of thousands (if not millions of thousands) of innovations, e.g. the Apps economy. Many emerging market countries are yet to see their own version of thousands of local or regional apps. For example, there is the story of Saya, a messaging platform developed by two students at the Meltwater incubator in Accra, Ghana in 2014. Saya has gone on to recruit many users in Turkey and Indonesia.[101] Light touch controls and regulations are essential to letting such innovations to thrive. So with OTTs, Governments and regulators must implement proportionate ex-ante and/or ex-post interventions if/as necessary – with a bias towards "light touch" and "sensible" controls that allow for innovation, creativity that come with OTTs.

Regulations and OTT interventions must not kill future golden gooses! This is truly key. Take sub-Saharan African countries for example where much of their economies are informal. There are hundreds of thousands of informal economy women groups, men groups, alumni groups, church groups, community groups, etc. currently run on Facebook, WhatsApp, etc. I personally know of a dozen of such groups who would never become fully fledged digital economy groups with a single whiff of them knowing that they would be subject to OTT or Digital Services Taxes (DST) taxes prematurely.

6.9.10 Collaboration amongst IVC Oversight Institutions

The Internet value chain leaves no room for lack of cooperation and coordination within countries, regions, across Ministries, Central Banks, Regulators and more. Meeting the SDGs signed up to by Governments needs cooperation. Cross border data flows forced on us by the Internet value chain requires collaboration between countries, preferably at regional levels. Clearly, tax authorities cannot make decisions on ICT taxes without collaboration with ICT Ministries and ICT regulators at the very least. ICT/TMT regulators working in their own "silos" disregarding other institutions in the country could work this way in the off-line domain; not so with the online IVC. ICT/TMT regulators need to collaborate with Central Banks on OTT Mobile Money regulations. Gambling Regulators

---

[101] See
http://www.infodev.org/sites/default/files/mobile_apps_at_the_base_of_the_pyramid_ghana_0.pdf

need to collaborate with ICT/TMT Regulators on Online gambling controls in your country. Ministries of ICT need to collaborate with ICT/TMT regulators and other Institutions such as the Courts, Competition Agencies, other Ministries, etc. to agree definitions of OTT services in your country. SDGs are inter-dependent amongst Ministries and needs cooperation across Government.

Collaborate, collaborate, collaborate some more.

6.10 Over and Out: Covid19 and Digitalisation

I think I have achieved all I set out to do with this book as I conclude this section.

Without Covid19 slowdown of international travels, I probably would never have penned this book. Arguably the biggest lesson Covid19 has taught economies is that digitization is paramount. It is no longer optional. Some estimates suggest that 65% of GDPs worldwide will have gone through some form of digitalisation[102] by 2022.

Who has been benefitting the most from Covid19? Yes you guessed right – Big Tech. Just research how their market valuations have grown. Unregulated Big Tech (thus far) are on the verge of dominating all sectors you can think of – just imagine how many sectors Amazon is in already, and can continue to go in, from food to grocery delivery, to media, to tourism, to logistics, to transport, to health care, etc. They can do so much more with their economies of scale and scope. As billions of us spend more time working living, being entertained, studying and working online, we are faced with so much Online harms. In Europe, countries like the UK, France and Germany have all introduced online safety laws that require Big Tech digital platforms to appoint local representatives and promptly remove

---

[102] IDC Reveals 2021 Worldwide Digital Transformation Predictions; 65% of Global GDP Digitalized by 2022, Driving Over $6.8 Trillion of Direct DX Investments from 2020 to 2023

illegal and harmful content or face fines. Criminality from Online platforms is estimated at ~US$1.5tn/year as they are used for trafficking counterfeit goods, narcotics, money laundering, selling weapons and much worse.

Digitalisation indeed has consequences. This has been the journey of this insignificant book. I truly hope this insignificant work has educated and informed you just that bit to speak (and hopefully live) the correct shibboleths to be admitted into the Digital Economy-informed-"club". And that it has also enhanced your scholarship.

Over and out.

Selected Bibliography

Baldwin, R., Cave, M. and Lodge, M. (2012) *Understanding Regulation: theory, strategy, and practice*, 2nd ed., Oxford: Oxford University Press

Berinsky AJ. (2017). Rumors and health care reform: experiments in political misinformation. *Br. J. Political Sci.* 47:241–62

Bode L, Vraga EK. (2015), In related news, that was wrong: the correction of misinformation through related stories functionality in social media. *J. Commun.* **65**:619–38

Esselaar, S. and Stork, C. (2019) Regulatory and tax treatment of OTTs in Africa, Report for Mozilla, https://blog.mozilla.org/netpolicy/files/2019/11/Regulatory-Treatment-of-OTTs-in-Africa-1.pdf

Esselaar, S. and Stork, C. (2019a) for A4AI . When the people talk: Understanding the impact of taxation in the ICT sector in Benin, https://1e8q3q16vyc81g8l3h3md6q5f5e-wpengine.netdna-ssl.com/wp-content/uploads/2019/03/A4AI_Benin-Tax-Report_Screen_AW.pdf.

Flynn D, Nyhan B, Reifler J. (2017), The nature and origins of misperceptions: understanding false and unsupported beliefs about politics. *Adv. Political Psychol.* 38:127–50

Ghappour, A (2012), Data Collection and the Regulatory State, *Connecticut Law Review*, **49** (5): 1733, "Data Collection and the Regulatory State" by Ahmed Ghappour (bu.edu) - https://scholarship.law.bu.edu/faculty_scholarship/255/

Hao, K (2021), "He got Facebook hooked on AI. Now he can't fix its misinformation addiction", *MIT Technology Review*, How Facebook Got Addicted to Spreading Misinformation | News | Communications of the ACM. Also from He got Facebook hooked on AI. Now he can't fix its misinformation addiction | MIT Technology Review

Jerit, J. & Zhao, Y. (2020), Political Misinformation, *Annual Review of Political Science*: **23**: 77-94, May. https://www.annualreviews.org/doi/10.1146/annurev-polisci-050718-032814

ITU (2019). Collaborative framework for OTTs, Recommendation ITU-T D.262, https://www.itu.int/itu-t/recommendations/rec.aspx?rec=13595

Kuklinski JH, Quirk PJ, Jerit J, Schwieder D, Rich RF. (2000), Misinformation and the currency of democratic citizenship. *J. Politics* 62:790–816

Manson, M. (2014), *Facebook Zero: Considering Life After the Demise of Organic Reach*, Social@Ogilvy Research, 5th March 2014, Microsoft Word - Facebook Zero Paper.docx (techenet.com).

Ramasoota, P. & Kitikamdhorn, A. (2021), "The Netflix effect" in Thailand: Industry and Regulatory Implications, *Telecommunications Policy* 45 (7), pp 1-17. https://doi.org/10.1016/j.telpol.2021.102156

Nwana, H. S. (2014), Telecommunications, Media & Technology (TMT) for Developing Economies: How TMT can Improve Developing Economies in Africa and Elsewhere for the 2020s, London: Gigalen Press, 550+ pages. http://www.amazon.co.uk/Telecommunications-Media-Technology-Developing-Economies/dp/099282110X, 550+ pages

Nwana, H. S. (2019*), Regulating Over the Top (OTT) Services*, Paper and Presentation to ITU-D Study Group on the Economic Impact of OTTs on national Telecommunications/ICT Markets. Internet Security Primer-research-190701 (itu.int) - https://www.itu.int/dms_pub/itu-d/oth/07/1a/D071A0000070001PDFE.pdf (last accessed August 2021)

Reidenberg, J. R (2001), "Yahoo and Democracy on the Internet", 42 *Jurimetrics* 42 *(261)* Available at: http://ir.lawnet.fordham.edu/faculty_scholarship/40

Stork, C., Nwana, H. S, Esselaar, S. & Koyabe, M (2020), *Over The Top (OTT) Applications and the Internet Value Chain: Recommendations to Regulators, Policy Makers and Tax Authorities*, Commonwealth Telecommunications Organisation Paper, May 2020 – a follow up to the 2018 CTO Report into OTTs. CTO-OTT-Final-Report-for-Publication-Web_Online-22-May-2020 - https://cto.int/wp-content/uploads/2020/05/CTO-OTT-REPORT-2020.pdf

Taylor, C (2018), *OTT services: economic impact and options for regulation:* a short report by Cenerva, https://cenerva.com/cenerva-publishes-otts-report

Worth, R (2016), "Terror on the Internet: the New Arena, The New Challenges", New York Times Book Review: 21, 'Terror on the Internet,' by Gabriel Weimann - The New York Times Book Review - The New York Times (nytimes.com) (NB: this requires a subscription)

Index

'google' as a verb, 170

"Rabbit-hole" effect, 190

21st Century Fox, 58

2G/3G USSD MPESA, 199

3Ds of Disruption, Distortion and Deterioration, 269

5G Covid-19 Quackery, 38

6th January 2021 insurrection, 44

9Game.com

an App store with thousands of malicious apps, 123

9pm watershed, 152

A 10 point Emerging OTT Framework & Checklist, 322

A Bifurcation of the Internet?, 159

A Brief Overview of the Sources of the User Interface Segment Positive Externalities, 118

A Brief Overview of the User Interface Segment Externalities and Concerns, 120

a lie gets halfway round the world before the truth can put its boots on, 38

A.T. Kearney, 3

Aadhaar ID system

Indian ID platform, 197

Abuse of dominance, 264

Abuse of dominance', 178

Abuse of dominant networks effects, 211

Abuse of multisided market platform power, 211

access network, 19

Accountability and Transparency, 326

Addiction, 238

Addictive Apps

definition of, 120

Afghanistan, 188, 271

age-appropriate design code, 140

Age-Appropriate Design Code, 136, 143

Age-Appropriate Design for Apps, 202

AI & Machine Algorithms

Facebook, 84

AI & Machine Learning Software getting it badly wrong, 274

AI and Big Data, vi, xiii, xiv, 23, 71, 82, 83, 85, 99, 241, 244, 297

AI bias

EdgeRank, 185

AI Blackbox Opacity, 277

AI Data Bias, 277

AI essentially put on steroids, 276

AI Gender and Racial Bias, 273

AI High Level Group (HLG) EC, 278

AI, Ethics, Privacy, Facebook & Misinformation, 183

AI-based digital assistants, 170

Airbnb, 9, 246, 285

Airtel, 11, 219, 316

Akamai, 10, 96

Alexei Navalny

Russian Opposition Leader, 94

Algorithms Concerns

AI & Big Data, 71

Alibaba, ix, 9, 61, 171, 195, 205, 246, 265, 285

Alt-right Extremism, 63

Amazon, ix, xiv, xv, xvi, xvii, xviii, xix, 7, 9, 11, 19, 31, 36, 59, 60, 61, 82, 83, 96, 101, 104, 105, 106, 107, 111, 126, 131, 132, 150, 151, 155, 157, 169, 170, 171, 177, 178, 193, 195, 201, 205, 206, 207, 208, 209, 210, 226, 242, 246, 263, 273, 274, 276, 277, 281, 285, 286, 314, 334

Amazon Data Breach, 281

Amazon Prime, 19, 104, 170, 177, 256

Amazon vs. European Commission (EC) – Conflicts of Interest, 104

American technological imperialism, 152

Amplification algorithms, 238

Android, 12, 101, 118, 122, 123, 124, 125, 129, 133, 134, 157, 210, 211, 212, 330

Android forks, 125

Angola, 317

Annual plan, 325

App Stores dominance, 122

Apple, 170, 201

Apple IoS, 122

Apple Macintosh, 119

Apple Music, 211

Apple Music vs. EC Case, 126

Apple Store, 158

Apple vs. U.S. App Developers, 127

Arab Spring, 79

Article 12 of the UN's Universal Declaration of Human Rights (UDHR) 1948, 245

Articles 12-14 of the 2000 EU Commerce Directive, 225

Artificial Intelligence, ix, 29, 60, 72, 151, 241, 242, 272, 273, 274, 278

Artificial Intelligence Act Bill EC, 278

asymmetric regulation, 149

Asymmetric regulation, 233, 257, 258

Thailand broadcast and film industry, 176

Atlantic Telecoms & Media Ltd, iii

Augusto Pretta, 57

Australia, 201, 264

Australia Emerging Big Tech Laws and Codes, 194

Australia's ACCC, 158

AVOD, 256

Azure, 11, 96, 170

Baidu, ix, 9, 31, 62, 83, 171, 195

Balance posts reshares vs. the impacts of hate speech/misinformation, 239

Balance safety vs. Freedom of Expression, 263

Balancing of citizens privacy and national security, 271

BATX, 172, 263

BBC, 6, 7, 8, 45, 48, 49, 50, 52, 53, 63, 64, 65, 67, 71, 80, 82, 86, 88, 94, 95, 131, 154, 157, 160, 180, 182, 186, 192, 217, 236, 240, 241, 259, 266, 273, 281, 301, 309

Behavioral Remedy, 207

Behavioural remedies, 265

Benin, 168

OTT Taxes, 316

BEREC, 247, 288, 297, 308, 309, 310, 312, 324

Best-practice principles for taxation, 321

Bias against Intervention, 325

Big 6, 213

Big data definition of, 243

Big Data, 241

Big Five (Big 5) Tech, 171

Big Four (Big 4) Tech, 171

Big Tech, 169, 178, 180, 192, 193, 200, 205, 213, 240, 263, 264, 265

definition of, 169

Big Tech 5, 213

Big Tech gatekeepers, 178

Big Tech Good Competition Outcomes and Typical Harms, 205

Big Tech Local Registrations, 266

Big Tech negative externalities are socialized with the rest of society, 178

Big Tech Policy & Regulation, 263

Big Tech regulation, vi, 23, 147, 177, 202, 240, 324

Big Tech Regulation, 324

Bill Gates, 178

Bing, 9, 12, 18, 30, 31, 62, 74, 101, 118

Bloomberg, 7, 52, 142

Body dysmorphia, 235

Body of European Regulators for Electronic Communications (BEREC), 247

botnets, 217, 235

Botnets, 62

Botnets & Democracy, 53

definition of, 53

Brazil's "Marco Civil" Law, 305

Breaking News Risk

definition of, 48

Broad Categories of Digital Economy Outcomes Sought, 201

Broadcast Value Chain, 16

broader social value, 91

Burundi, 317

Business to Business (B2B), 285

Business to Consumer (B2C), 285

Busting some OTT Myths, 302

Buy Box, 277

Amazon, 106

Buy competitors to kill off, 212

Buy-to-kill-off, 192

Bypass and SIM Bank Frauds, 115

ByteDance, 81

Cable (SDH) or Sea (IP) headends, 218

California dad killed his kids over QAnon, 46

call termination, 312

Cameroon, 188

Can Governments ignore such massive data breaches, 220

Capital One, 220, 221

Caricom Competition Commission

Caribbean, 267

CBS 60 Minutes program, 236

CDMA, 300

Cenerva Ltd, iii

CERT, ix, 271, 272

Charles Kettering, iv, 146

Child sexual abuse images, 65

Child sexual exploitation and abuse (CSEA), 238

Child Sexual Exploitation and Abuse (CSEA), 261

Children's Fundamentals, 235
Irish version of the UK's Online Children's Code, 143

China, 159, 266

China Big Tech Laws, 195

China is arguably creating a different kind of Internet, 159

China Mobile, 11

Chinese Big Tech (BATX), 171

Chinese State Administration for Market Regulation, 195

Chinese walls, 106, 207

Chris Anderson, 31

Christchurch (New Zealand) mosque shootings, 63, 88

Christoph Ungerer
Economist, 286

Christoph Ungerer (, 314

Christopher Wray
FBI Director, 88

CIRT, ix, 271, 272

Cisco, 88

citizen value, 37

civil liberties, 62

class action lawsuits, 157

Class-action lawsuit
definition of, 127

CNN, 7, 48, 64, 195, 220, 265, 290, 309

Coalition for a Digital Economy
skepticism about the UK Online Children Code, 143

Collaboration amongst IVC Oversight Institutions, 333

Colombia
OTT Taxes, 316

Combinatorial Auction/Combinatorial Clock Auction (CCA), 55

Comesa Competition Commission
19 African member States, 267

comparison sites, 132

competition concerns, 78

Competition Concerns, 71

conditional access, 17

conflict of interest, 178

conflicts of interest, xviii, 184, 188, 297

Conflicts of Interest, 210

Connectivity, vi, 4, 5, 6, 11, 14, 20, 21, 28, 33, 34, 57, 107, 109, 112, 114, 117, 144, 151, 155, 165, 196, 201, 252, 290, 300, 303, 306, 310, 313

Connectivity Platform

One of the three pillar Digital Economy platforms, 196

Connectivity segment and "bits pipes", 300

Connectivity Segment Negative Externalities, 165

conspiracy theory, 43, 44, 46

Conspiracy theory

The 'Birther' conspiracy theory, 46

Conspiratorial theories, 46

Conspriracy Theories

Amplified conspiracy theories, 54

Constant market research, 327

Consult and assess impact of regulation, 327

consumer surplus, 109, 159

Consumer to Business (C2B), 285

Consumer to Consumer (C2C), 285

Content Rights, vi, 4, 6, 7, 8, 14, 20, 21, 34, 38, 42, 43, 44, 57, 58, 59, 60, 70, 82, 104, 151, 152, 162, 233, 234, 242

cultural and competition perspective,, 59

regulations on European content quota, 59

Content Rights Segment Negative Externalities (, 162

Converged regulation, 150

Copyright Harms

Periscope and Meerkat, 55

Copyright Infringements, 70

Co-regulation, 330

Cote d'Ivoire, 317

Country code TLDs (ccTLDs), 154

Craigslist, 226

Criminal content

Online Safety Bill, UK, 262

Critical National Infrastructure (CNI) Attacks

UK House of Commons, 64

Cross-side network effects

Network effects, 211

CSIRT, ix, 271, 272

Cultural imperialism

Content rights, 152

Cyber-bullying

definition of, 51

Cybercrime, 63, 240, 269

definition of, 63, 114

Cybercrime Damages Reach USD 6 Trillion in 2021, 217

cybercrime marketplaces, 88

Cybercrimes categories, 269

cyberfrauds, 29

Cyber-Grooming, 65

Cyber-Paedophilia, 65

Cybersecurity, 240, 269

Cyberterrorism, 63

Dame Melanie Dawes

Ofcom CEO, 239

Dark and Deep web, 62

Dark Web

civil liberties, 62

Invisible Internet Project (I2P), 62

Tor, 62

data breaches, 27, 29, 63, 219, 220, 265, 281, 297

Data breaches, 280

Data Breaches

Equifax, 64

Jennifer Lawrence, 65

Data Privacy, 244

Data Protection, vi, ix, 23, 64, 104, 143, 150, 235, 244, 245, 261, 265, 280, 281, 282, 283, 284, 324

Data sovereignty, 280

Dating apps

Tinder, Grindr, etc, 71

DDOS Attack in Liberia-Cyber Sabotage, 217

Decreased trust in media sources and Government, 52

Deepfakes, 49

definition of, 49

Democratic Republic of Congo, 317

Denial of Service (DoS), 114

differential regulation, 150

digital advertising, 102

digital advertising market, 105

Digital Data Traffic Bypass, Illegal Operators and National Security, 218

Digital Economy Act of 2017, 260

UK, 266

Digital Economy Platforms, vi, 195, 231, 252

Digital Market Openess Index for Brazil (2018), 74

Digital Markets Act (DMA), 266

Digital Markets Taskforce

UK, 103

Digital Markets Unit (DMU)

UK, 194

Digital Services Act (DSA), 238, 266

Digital Services Act (DSA) Bill EU/EC Bill to regulate Big Tech, 193

Digital Services Coordinator, 263

Direct-to-home (DTH) satellites, 17

disinformation, 297

stop the steal, 44

what is, 43

Disinformation, 45, 238

Disney+Hotstar, 7

Dividing regions, 211

DOCSIS, ix, 11

Domain names

allocation of, 154

domestic terrorism, 63

Dr Martin Koyabe, 271

Dr Nozha Boujemaa, 276

DSO, ix, 16, 250, 255, 258

DTH, 17

DuckDuckGo

small search engine, 134

ducts, 19

Ebay, 155

EBay, 9, 246, 285

E-Bay, 226

EC, 201

EC Digital Services Act (DSA) Bill, 260

EC's Digital Services Act (DSA) Bill, 262

echo chambers, 187

EcoCash, 219

E-Commerce, 246, 285

E-Commerce Activities, 285

E-Commerce Laws

Issues covered by such laws, 285

EdgeRank

Facebook's core ranking algorithm, 85

Faecbook's News Feed algorithm, 183

Election integrity, 236

Election Risks, 53

The Muller Report, 53

Electronic Commerce, vi

Electronic Commerce Laws, 285

Enabling Technologies, xiv, 4, 6, 10, 20, 95, 96, 97, 99, 100, 105, 164, 197, 232, 242, 276

Enabling Technologies & Services Segment Negative Externalities, 164

Equifax

Data Breach, 281

Ethical AI principles, 278

Ethically balance
Personalisation vs. Supplier
Welfare, 277

EU Charter of Fundamental
Rights, 282

EU Court of Justice (CJEU).,
133

EU e-Commerce Directive,
225

European Board for Digital
Services (EBDS), 194

European Union, 168

Ex ante regulation, 265, 309

ex-ante regulations, 206

Exclusive deals, 211

Expedia, 9, 210, 246, 285

Externalities
Connectivity Segment, 107
Content Rights Segment, 42
Online Services Segment, 61
User Interface segment, 118

externality, xviii, 25, 26, 42,
65, 85, 91, 100, 122, 184, 188

Extremism, 66

UK Parliament, 66

FAAAM, 171

FAAMG, 171

FAANG, 171, 172

Facebook, ix, xviii, xx, 6, 7, 8,
9, 25, 27, 32, 33, 36, 37, 38,
61, 63, 64, 67, 77, 78, 82, 83,
84, 85, 87, 88, 90, 91, 92, 95,
96, 99, 100, 101, 102, 105,
111, 117, 120, 121, 139, 143,
150, 151, 155, 156, 157, 159,
167, 169, 170, 171, 178, 179,
180, 181, 182, 183, 184, 185,
186, 187, 188, 189, 190, 191,
192, 193, 201, 202, 205, 210,
216, 217, 220, 221, 224, 226,
227, 235, 236, 237, 238, 239,
241, 242, 243, 244, 247, 259,
260, 262, 263, 272, 273, 276,
277, 281, 288, 289, 291, 297,
301, 305, 311, 313, 314, 315,
319, 330, 333, 336, 337

brand pages, 83

Facebook acquisition of
WhatsApp, 289

Facebook bans 'loot-to-order'
antiquities trade, 88

Facebook Groups, 87

'Facebook Knows Instagram is
Toxic' for Teen Girls, xviii,
181

Facebook Messenger, 78

Facebook platform is
[allegedly] promoting
extremist groups, 187

Facebook's AI-powered
algorithms, 186

fake news, 190, 297

Fake News, 47, 237

definition of, 47

Factual news on Twitter takes 6x longer than fake news to be seen by 1500 people on Twitter, 54

Pope Francis endorses Donald Trump, 47

FANGAM, 171, 201, 205, 263, 264

FBI proclaims Capital Riots of the 6th of January 2021 as "domestic terrorism", 88

Federal Trade Commission, 192

First Amendment of the United States Constitution

Freedom of speech and expression, 94

First-price sealed bid auction, 44, 62, 115, 122

Fixed Submarine Cables, 111

Foreign Service Providers (FSPs)

OTTs, 316

Foundem

Lead complainant of Google Shopping vs. EC case, 132

France, 201, 264

Frances Haugen, 189, 239

Facebook whistle-blower, 189

Free speech, 48

GAFA, 171

GAFAM, 171

Gambling Regulators, 333

Gamified apps, 120

gatekeepers

Big Tech, 264

General Data Protection Regulations (GDPR), 282

GEOs, 11

German Network Enforcement Act, 262

Ghana, 317

Global Cybersecurity Index (GCI), 270

Good regulation

what is, 200

Google, ix, xiv, xv, xvi, xvii, 9, 10, 12, 18, 30, 31, 55, 61, 62, 74, 75, 76, 82, 83, 94, 95, 96, 97, 98, 99, 100, 101, 102, 103, 105, 111, 115, 118, 124, 125, 126, 128, 129, 130, 131, 132, 133, 134, 139, 143, 144, 150, 155, 157, 158, 169, 170, 171, 178, 189, 193, 194, 195, 201, 206, 210, 211, 212, 217, 224, 238, 242, 244, 247, 263, 265, 277, 288, 291, 297, 305, 313, 314, 330

Google Ads, 276, 277

Google AdSense, xvii, 133

Google Adsense and [Google Android] vs. EC, 133, 134

Google Android, 122

Google Android EC Case, 124

Google Apps and Apple Apps vs. South Korea, 128

Google Chrome, 125

Google Local, 210

Google Maps, xiv, 9, 61, 99, 210

Google paid-for advertising example, 97

Google Search, 242

Google SEO

Google's search engine optimisation, 97

Google Shopping, 265

Google Shopping/Google Search vs. EC, 129

Google Trips, 210

Google's Ads

formerly Google Adwords, 97

Google's revenue from search, 98

Governments make controversial Internet content decisions daily, 94

Gretchen Peters & Amr Al-Azm

Morning Consult, 90

GSMA, iii, iv, 2, 3, 4, 5, 6, 7, 8, 14, 19, 21, 27, 107, 108, 109, 320, 321, 327

Guinea, 317

Guinea - Central African country, 302

Hacking groups, 62

Haile Selassie

The Late Ethiopian Emperor, 87

Harmful (and sometimes Legal) Content, 49

Harmful (and sometimes) legal content

Molly Russell, 49

Harmful but legal Content

definition of, 49

Harmful content, 236

Harmful content, election integrity, privacy and data portabilit

Areas offered up by Meta (Facebook) for Online regulation, 202

Hate Speech, 48

Hausa, 234

Herfindahl-Hirschman Index (HHI), 75

Hollywoodization, 234

Hollywoodization/Americanisation, 257

Hotstar, 7

House of Commons, 64

Huawei, 160

ICANN, 154

ICT taxes, 302

ICT taxes - forbearance is key, 302

Identity (ID) Platform

One of the three pillar Digital Economy platforms, 197

Identity Theft, 64

Tiger Woods, Oprah Winfrey, Steven Spielberg, Will Smith, 64

Igbo

Nigeria, 234

Illegal Content

definition of, 49

Immoral and indecent' Entertainment, 70

Impact Assessments (IAs), 331

Implement OTT Light Touch Controls, 332

In-app purchases (IAPs), 127

Inbuilt AI Bias, 277

Independent Inquiry into Child Sexual Abuse

UK, 86

India, xii, xviii, 7, 21, 59, 80, 81, 82, 95, 122, 123, 124, 149, 150, 152, 157, 173, 188, 197, 201, 213, 232, 234, 253, 254, 282

India (Bollywood), 173

India bans TikTok, 80

Indian Premier League, 7

Individual liberty/privacy vs. public good, 159

Indonesia, 218, 317, 333

Information Commissioner's Office (ICO), 261

Information Commissioner's Office n(ICO)

the UK's independent data authority, 136

Instagram, xviii, xx, 6, 8, 36, 38, 50, 64, 81, 82, 85, 120, 135, 139, 140, 142, 143, 157, 158, 170, 179, 180, 181, 182, 183, 189, 190, 191, 192, 205, 224, 226, 227, 235, 236, 259, 262, 263, 289

Instagram and Teenage Girls, 180

Intellectual Property Rights (IPR) Infringements, 56

definition of, 56

interconnection, 204

International Interconnect & International Gateway Bypasses, 115

Internet Addiction

definition of, 69

Kaiser Family Foundation, 69

Pew Research 2020, 69

Internet Assigned Numbers Authority (IANA), 154

Internet Censorship and Surveillance, 71

Internet Corporation for Assigned Names and Numbers (ICANN), 20

Internet gateway or gatekeeping companies, 129

Internet Gateways (IGWs), 218

Internet Protocol (IP), vi, 20, 112, 300

Internet Protocol TCP/IP, 113

Internet Rights, 7

Internet Service Providers (ISPs), 225

Internet Society, vii

Internet Surveillance

China "exporting" Internet surveillance to other countries, 72

Internet terrorism, 63

Internet value chain

size and growth by segment, 6

Internet Value Chain, iv, 2

2010 Vodafone IVC, iv

History, 3

Internet value chain size and growth by segment, 6

Internet Value Chains, 3

Internet Watch Foundation (IWF, 65

Internet Watch Foundation (IWF)

Andrew Puddephatt, 65

Internet Zoning, 93

Intervene if specific duty, 325

Invisible Internet Project (I2P), 62

iOS, xvi, 12, 118, 122, 123, 127, 128, 129, 157

IP addresses, 154

Iphone, 12, 14, 25, 118, 119, 299

introducing the "Internet connection device", 119

iPod, 118

IPR Theft, 212

IPv4 vs. IPv6, 114

Iran, 282

Italian Competition Authority (AGCM), 103

Italian Inquiry into the Big Data Sector, 103

ITU, 153

ITU Global Cybersecurity Index (GCI) 5 Commitment Pillars, 268

Jacobson v Massachusetts

1905 USA Supreme Court decision, 89

January 6th 2021 Capitol Riots, 188

January 6th 2021 US Capitol riots, 92

Jeff Bezos, 178

Joaquin Candela
Facebook AI Leader, 185

John Giusti, 2

Jordan, 167

Joy Buolamwini, 274
Algorithmic Justice League, 273

Kazakhstan, 282

Kenya, 10, 21, 46, 72, 78, 150, 199, 253, 254, 318, 327

L6/7
Facebook engagement metric, 186

Larry Page/Sergey Brin, 178

Latin America, 282

Least intrusive regulation possible, 326

LEOs, 11

Liberia, 217, 318

Liberty
and privacy, 280

License fees, 313

LICRA vs. Yahoo

Internet Zoning, 93

Linear (broadcast) TV platforms, 257

LinkedIn, 8, 9, 32, 38, 289

Lonestar/MTN
Liberia, 217

long tail economics,, 8, 156

Long Tail Effect
Extremism and radicalization, 66

long tail theory, 233

Long Tail Theory, 29, 30, 32

Luxembourg, 281

Luxembourg's National Commission for Data Protection, 281

Machine Learning, 272

Machine Learning (ML)
definition of, 272

Made for Digital, 7

Made-for-digital, 8

User-Generated Content, 8

Malaysia, 168, 318

MapQuest, 210

Margrethe Vestager
EU Commissioner for Competition, 105, 106, 126, 127

Mark Zuckerberg, 6, 84, 85, 90, 157, 178, 179, 180, 182, 184, 187, 221, 237, 259, 272 announcing big changes to Facebook's ranking algorithm, 84

Mark Zuckerberg,, 179

Market concentration, 74

market failure, 295

market failures, 34

Market Power of the major Digital Platforms, 100

McKinsey and Co, 281, 286

Megan Brenan on American distrust of mass media, 79

Messages sent globally by platform, 301

Meta, 151, 158, 169, 170, 180, 190

Facebook's parent company, 6

Michelle Obama, 274

Microsoft, ix, 11, 32, 83, 95, 96, 111, 113, 122, 143, 169, 170, 171, 178, 212, 263, 273, 275, 289, 300, 314, 337

Microsoft acquisition of Skype, 289

Microsoft Teams, 289

Ministry of Digital Economy and Society Thailand, 176, 257

misinformation

what is, 43

Misinformation, 238

Political Misinformation, 45

Mix of statutory, co-regulatory and self-regulatory regimes, 258

Mobile financial services, 232

Mobile Money Hacks in Africa, 219

Mobile Operating Systems (OS) dominance, 122

Mobile Value Chain, 16

Molly Russell, 49, 50, 136, 180, 259

Morocco, 318

Mozambique, 318

MPESA, 10, 21

M-PESA, 254

MTN, 150, 219, 316, 326

Multi-sided markets, 100

Myanmar, 188

Myths vs. Facts in the OTT Debate, 303

National Broadcasting and Telecommunications Commission (NBTC) Thailand, 176

National Cybersecurity Strategy (NCS), 270

National Payment Corporation India, 253

National security

definition of, 80

National Security & Critical National Infrastructure (CNI) Threats, 116

National Security Concerns, 71, 80

Natural Enagagement Pattern on Facebook vs. Policy Line, 187

NBTC
Thailand, 257

net neutrality, 323

Net neutrality, 291, 304

Net Neutrality, 312, 323

net neutrality rules, 304

Netflix, ix, xvii, 6, 8, 9, 19, 36, 59, 60, 61, 82, 151, 168, 171, 172, 173, 174, 175, 176, 177, 200, 224, 233, 242, 255, 256, 257, 263, 289, 290, 297, 298, 309, 312, 337

Netflix - "the global Internet TV network"., 172

Netflix effect, 233

network effect, 82

network effects, 102, 211

Network Enforcement Act
Germany law to combat fake news, 237

Networks effects

with mega digital platforms, 100

New Zealand terrorist attack, 260

News Feed
Facebook, 84

Niger, 318

Nigeria, xviii, 18, 20, 21, 59, 109, 148, 150, 167, 173, 188, 196, 232, 234, 253, 255, 257, 318, 326, 331

Nigeria (Nollywood), 173

Nokia 3310 Phone, 13

Nollywood, 59

normal distribution, xiii, 87, 88, 89, 92

NTA Nigeria, 257

Numbers of Apps downloaded annually
RiskIQ, 119

Oculus
part of Meta, 6

OECD, x, 168, 278, 279

Ofcom
UK, 261

Ofcom Regulatory Principles, 327

Ofcom UK, 325

Offense harms, 54
definition of, 54

Offensive Language, 54

Offline ICT/TMT Outcomes, 203

Ofsted
UK Inspector of Schools, 86

Online and Big Tech Regulation, 177

Online Banking, 10

Online Child Sexual Exploitation, 65

Online content harms, vi, 23, 297, 330

Online free speech, privacy and anonymity, 161

Online Harms are literally numerous, 216

Online Regulation, 200, 202, 213, 234, 243, 259, 297, 324

Online Safety, 237

Online Safety Bill, 189

Online Safety Bill 2021
UK, 261

Online Service Providers, 8, 20

Online Services, vii, xiii, 4, 6, 9, 14, 20, 21, 23, 25, 28, 32, 33, 34, 38, 43, 61, 62, 65, 70, 72, 73, 74, 76, 77, 80, 83, 85, 96, 99, 100, 104, 144, 155, 156, 163, 169, 242, 246, 247, 261, 276, 285, 288, 296, 298, 301, 302, 306, 308, 309, 313, 314, 329

Online Services Segment Negative Externalities, 163

Online Terrorism, 63

Online troll
definition of, 67

Online/Internet regulation, 260

Open Internet, 161
Clearnet, 62

Open Internet Order, 305

Open Web, 62

Oprah Winfrey, 64, 273, 274

organic reach, 83

Organic reach, 83

OTT definition, 297

OTT Definition
BEREC, 308
Esselaar & Stork (2019), 310
ITU, 308

OTT definition and national sovereignty, 306

OTT is not equal to social media apps!, 302

OTT myths, 295

OTT Regulation, 294, 296

OTT regulatory developments in Africa, Latin America and Asia, 320

OTT services and being cross border, 314

OTTs, 303, 310, 328

levelling down, 290

OTTS

levelling up, 290

OTTS - calls "to do something" about them, 297

OTTs - the biggest "side effects" of the IVC, 296

OTTs "free-riding", 298

OTTs & "multitude of sins", 298

OTTs & Innovation, 300

OTTs and Net Neutrality, 295, 304

OTTs and Taxes, 296, 315

OTTs not being locally registered, 298

ouTube Music, 126

Over the Top (OTT) services, 247

Oversight Board

Facebook, 92

Over-the-Top (OTT) regulation, vi, 23

Package switching, 113

Packet Switched vs. Circuit Switched Networks, 113

Paid prioritisation of network traffic, 304

Paid-for Search items typically push down organic search results, 97

Pakistan, 135, 143, 158, 188, 282

Paul Goodman, 68

PayPal, 10, 21

Periscope, 55

Personal liberty vs. public good, 89

Piracy, 70

Play Store, 125

poles, 19

Political misinformation and hate speech

Facebook, 183

Pornography

definition of, 50

Positive Externalities

Source of, 34

Sources of, 35

Premium rights, 8

Premium Rights Content, 7

President Abraham Lincoln, 87

President Barack Obama, 46, 101, 291, 305

President Donald Trump, 156

President Donald Trump banned off digital platform, 157

President Joe Biden, 90

Privacy, 244, 280

definition of, 64

Privacy Harms, 64

producer surplus, 91, 109

Professor Hany Farid

on Facebook and Misinformation, 183

PSTN, 309

Public policy, 154

definition of, 89

Public Switched Telephone Network (PSTN), 311

QAnon

Conspiracy Theory, 44

QoS/QoE, 313

Quad Plays

using Big Data and AI, 60

Quality of Service/Experience (QoS/QoE), 153

Quidsi, 210

radicalisation, 66

RAN diversification projects, 117

Ransomware, 123

Reels

Instagram's short-video platform, 81

refusal to deal, 297

Refusal to Deal, 210

Regional Internet Registering (RIRs), 154

regulation

what is?, 34

Regulation, 226

definition of, 294

Regulation 101, 294

Regulatory Impact Analyses, 331

relevant markets, 325

Reliance Industries, 7

Reliance Jio

Cries of "foul play", 152

India, 152

Revenue Share Auctions, 49

roaming regulations, 312

Rogue Apps and App Stores, 123

Rohingya Muslim minority & Misinformation, 186

Rumors/Rumours

definition of, 46

Rumours, 46

Russian bot accounts

US 2016 elections, 191

Russian States, 282

SABC South Africa, 255

Same side network effects

Network effects, 211

Satellites carry less than 1% of the world's Internet traffic, 112

Saya, a messaging platform, 333

Section 230, xx, 90, 224, 226, 245

Section 230 of the 1996 US Federal Communications Act, 224

Self-regulation, 330

self-service kiosks, 120

Senator Elizabeth Warren, 135, 159

Senator Richard Blumenthal, 182

Senegal, 319

Serena Williams, 274, 275

set top box, 17

SIM box fraud

definition of, 115

Simultaneous Multi-Round Auction (SMRA), 47

Singapore, 319

Sir Tim Berner-Lee, 259

Sir Tim Berners-Lee, 179

Sky, 58

Sky/BSkyB, 58

Skype, 289, 298, 299

Skype out call, 309

Small Pacific States, 282

Snapchat, 235

Social & Community Media Harms

Paul Goodman, 68

Social and Community Media Harms, 68

Social Media Platforms and Elections, 78

Some Typical Big Tech Competition Harms, 209

South Africa, 167, 232, 319

South Korea, 264, 265

South Korea Law on Gatekeeping App Stores, 194

Spotify

Apple Music vs. EC case, 126

Star India, 7

Statutory content regulation the Facebook conundrum, 93

Steve Jobs, 14, 118, 119, 178, 299

stop the steal, 44, 156

Stop the Steal, 45

street cabinet, 19

Strong approach to net neutrality, 304

Structural Remedy, 207

Submarine Cable Map, 112

Sub-Saharan Africa (SSA), 253

Sustainable Development Goals (SDGs), 230

SVOD, 175, 256

Swahili, 234

Syria, 188

Taliban, 271

Tanzania, 320

taste and decency, 70

Taxing SMS and Voice in Guinea, 301

Telstra buys Digicel Pacific "to block China Australia, 161

Tencent, ix, 9, 77, 78, 101, 142, 151, 160, 171

Thailand, 167, 172, 233, 255, 319

The 'Birther' conspiracy theory, 46

The Access Act, 192
US Bill to regulate Big Tech, 192

The American Choice and Innovation *Act*
US Bill to regulate Big Tech, 193

The Australian Digital Platforms Inquiry by the Australian Competition & Consumer Commission (ACCC, 103

The Digital Advertising Big Three (Big 3), 171

The Digital Economy Problem Definition, 146

The Ending Platform Monopolies Act
US Bill to regulate Big Tech, 192

The EU, xx, 52, 105, 128, 129, 135, 152, 193, 194, 195, 201, 205, 212, 221, 224, 225, 226, 240, 245, 264, 265, 266, 267, 278, 282, 283, 287, 324

The EU Digital Markets Act (DMA) Bill
EU/EC Bill to regulate Big Tech, 193

The Facebook Conundrum, 87

The Furman Review
UK Digital Platforms Review, 101

the Future of Content, Broadcasting and Media Regulation, vi, 23

The good, the bad and the truly ugly!, 92

The Internet Society

The Internet Changes Everything, vii

The Long Tail Model, 30

The Long Tail theory, 156

The Merger Filing Fee Modernization Act

US Bill to regulate Big Tech, 192

The Mobile/Cellular Industry has literally changed the world, 108

the Muller Report, 53

The Netflix effect

Thailand, 168

The Online Age Identification Conundrum, 140

The rise and rise of OTTs, 295, 298, 299

The rise and rise of the OTTs, 289

The State Antitrust Enforcement Venue Act US Bill to regulate Big Tech, 192

The UK's Government Furman & Competition & Market Authority (CMA) Reviews, 101

The US Justice Department, 192

theory of harm, 206, 207, 208

Theory of harm, 125

Three Pillar Digital Economy Platforms, 196

Tiger Woods, Oprah Winfrey, Steven Spielberg, Will Smith, 64

TikTok, xx, 9, 70, 71, 80, 81, 82, 139, 140, 142, 143, 151, 157, 158, 195, 227, 234, 256, 262, 265

TikTok Mini-Case Study, 80

Time Warner Cable, 7, 8, 57

Tinder, 120

TMT Sector Value Chains, 14, 19

Traffic management, 304

Traffic Management, 323

Transcript of Steve Jobs iPhone2007 Presentation, 119

Trolling, 67

TVOD, 256

Twitter, xix, xx, 6, 8, 9, 36, 37, 38, 53, 54, 55, 71, 83, 120, 121, 156, 179, 190, 191, 217, 224, 226, 227, 238, 242, 276, 277, 289, 297

Twitter, Fake News and Bots, 190

Typical Key Areas of Offline TMT/ICT Regulation, 203

Typical Laws, Rules and Regulations and corresponding institutions shaping the IVC, 329

Uber, 9, 246, 285

Uganda, 219

OTT Taxes, 332

Social Media Tax, 315

Uganda OTT Taxes, 315

Uganda Rural Communications Development Fund (RCDF), 254

UK, 201

UK – Minister for Digital and the Creative Industries, 167

UK Children's Code, 235

UK Communications Act of 2003, 331

UK Digital Market Openness Index for the United Kingdom, 76

UK Digital markets Unit (DMU), 101

UK Emerging Big Tech Laws and Codes, 194

UK's Age-Appropriate Design for Apps, 135

UK's Children code, 87

UK's CMA, 158

UN 2030 Agenda for Sustainable Development, 230

UN General Assembly (UNGA, 250

UNCTAD, x, 286, 287

UNESCO, x, 278, 279

Union of Concerned Scientists (UCS

data on satellites, 111

Universal service funds (USFs), 250

Universal Service Funds (USFs), 253, 307, 313

Unlicensed does not mean unregulated!, 315

Unlicensed Operators, 116

Unwelcome Friend Requests, 67

US Communications Act, 305

USA, 201

USA Big Tech Bills, 192

USA Bills to Regulate Big Tech, 192

User Interface, 4, 5, 6, 11, 12, 13, 20, 21, 33, 118, 119, 120, 122, 123, 124, 144, 166, 170, 242, 289, 330

User Interface Segment Externalities, 166

user-generated content (UGC), 8

Verizon, 11, 290, 291, 305

Video on Demand (VoD), 19

Video on Demand (VOD) non-linear SVOD, 57

Violent & Disturbing or Graphic Content definition of, 56

Violent/Disturbing or Graphic Content, 56

Voice-Based Frauds, 116

Wall Street Journal (WSJ)

Instagram, xviii, 181

Walt Disney, 58

Weak approach to net
neutrality, 304

WeChat, 77, 80, 157, 171,
289

Weixin, 77, 171

What is "pornographic
material", 262

WhatsApp, 9, 33, 37, 61, 64,
77, 78, 82, 115, 151, 170, 171,
226, 247, 263, 281, 289, 290,
298, 299, 301, 302, 307, 308,
309, 312, 315, 333

Whatsapp Groups

number of, 37

Who's Protecting Our Kids

BBC Programme, 86

Wi-Fi, xi, 5, 11, 14, 20, 107,
109, 110, 111, 114, 149, 174,
204, 250, 299, 300

Wi-Fi's Positive Externalities
are typically Underestimated,
109

Wikipedia, 9, 13, 31, 43, 44,
45, 46, 48, 49, 56, 61, 62, 63,
64, 65, 71, 72, 73, 79, 80, 83,
88, 93, 94, 95, 97, 169, 170,
171, 197, 225, 237, 241, 247,
263, 288, 297

Wild West, 264

Wild West', 260

Windows Phone, xv, 125

World Economic Forum
(WEF), 278

World's Most Unbanked
Countries, 198

Xiaomi, 172

Yoruba

Nigeria, 234

YouTube, 139, 158, 170, 193,
256, 262, 309

Zambia, 320

OTT Taxes, 316

Zimbabwe, 219, 320

Zoning the Internet

definition of, 93

Zoom, 289, 300

ZTE, 160

About the Author

Prof. H Sama Nwana, CITP, FBCS, FIET, CEng, BSc (Hons), MSc (Dist), PhD, MA (Cambridge), MBA (Dist.) (London Business School)

Managing Partner, Cenerva Ltd UK (www.cenerva.com)

Prof H Sama Nwana is Managing Partner of Cenerva Ltd, a boutique training-led consultancy on all TMT regulatory across emerging markets based in London. He is a regular speaker across Africa, Americas, Europe and Asia – and has consulted/trained for the likes of ECA (Ethiopia), IFC East Africa, Facebook, Microsoft, ICASA (South Africa), the World Bank, NCC (Nigeria) and MTN, USAID, etc. Being African, he is passionate about connecting Africa's/ASEAN's millions of unconnected through a combination of entrepreneurial, commercial, regulatory and policy instruments.

Nwana was Group Director at Ofcom (the esteemed UK converged TMT regulator) and member of the Executive and Policy Board, as well as Chairman of its then-SCAP Board. Nwana oversaw the 2013 UK 4G auction, 3G Liberalisation as well as the implementation of the UK Digital Switchover Policy programme. He was Founding CEO/President of the Dynamic Spectrum Alliance (2014-16). He was MD/DG at Arqiva (2005-09) and prior was Director at Quadriga Worldwide Ltd (2001-2004). He was also a VC investor for a short time and a previous university academic too at the Universities of Calgary (Canada), Keele (UK) and Liverpool (UK). He was Senior Manager at BT plc.

He is Full Visiting Professor at the University of Strathclyde (UK) and other higher institutes. Nwana published an authoritative book entitled *Telecommunications, Media & Technology (TMT) for Emerging Economies: How `to make TMT Improve Developing Economies for the 2020s – published in April 2014.* He is a highly cited author with more than 100 peer-reviewed papers and books.

His company Cenerva Ltd acquired Interconnect Communications (ICC) Training/TRMC (Telecoms Regulatory Master Class) assets which are based in Bath UK – the Bath ICC TRMC- See www.icc-uk.com. Prof Nwana and Cenerva are trusted trainers of Regulators/Operators and Policy Makers across the globe.

Printed in Great Britain
by Amazon

77171272R10224